GROWING UP FIRSTBORN

GROWING UP FIRSTBORN

The Pressure and Privilege of Being Number One

DR. KEVIN LEMAN

Delacorte
Press

Published by
Delacorte Press
Bantam Doubleday Dell Publishing Group, Inc.
666 Fifth Avenue
New York, New York 10103

Library of Congress Cataloging in Publication Data

Leman, Kevin.
    Growing up firstborn: the pressure and privilege of being number one / Kevin Leman.
        p.   cm.
    Bibliography: p.
    ISBN 0-385-29769-6
    1. Children, First-born—Psychology. 2. Children, First-born—Family relationships. 3. Self-actualization (Psychology)
I. Title. II. Title: Growing up firstborn.
HQ777.2.L46   1989
306.87—dc20   89-7743
                                                        CIP

Design by Richard Oriolo

Manufactured in the United States of America
Published simultaneously in Canada

November 1989

10 9 8 7 6 5 4 3 2 1

BG

*To my wonderful
firstborn sister, Sally Leman Chall.
You have taught me so much about life that only
a big sister can teach a little brother.
I love you very much.*

CONTENTS

Part Four
Not Such a Bad Deal After All

PART ONE

The Firstborn Personality Type

1

It's Tough Being the Oldest!

There are many dangerous and virtually thankless jobs in this world.

I think of the city police officer who risks his life every day, simply because he believes that ordinary citizens have a right to be protected from criminals.

Or the fire fighter who rushes into a blazing building without regard for his own safety, intent on saving the life of someone else.

Then there's the coal-miner, who spends his days in a darkened world far below the earth's surface.

Such people have my admiration and my respect.

But I'll tell you something else. They have nothing on the person who has the toughest job in the family.

No, I'm not talking about Dad, although his job can be plenty tough at times. Nor am I talking about Mom, even though we know that she's really the glue that keeps the family together.

The toughest job in the family goes, hands down, to the first-born.

If you are a firstborn, you know from firsthand experience

what I'm talking about. You know very well that you have always lived your life in the limelight—you've always been the one who is supposed to set the perfect example for everyone else. You know what it's like to have that burning desire within you, that drive that compels you to conquer the world or die trying!

At the same time I can sense that there are a lot of people out there thinking "What's he talking about? Why, it can't be so tough to be the firstborn child!"

If that's your response, I can tell something about you right away. Namely, I can tell that you're not a firstborn, or you'd never talk that way!

Next objection?

"Well, Dr. Leman, I suppose the reason you say being a firstborn is so rough is because you're one yourself! Am I right about that?"

Sorry, but the answer is no. The truth is that I was the youngest in my family. That means I can vouch for the fact that the littlest star in the family constellation often has a few trials of his own. It's no fun being the smallest, because it means you spend a lot of your time wearing hand-me-downs that are either ragged, incredibly out of style, or still too big for you. Being the youngest also means that you get picked on from time to time and maybe called an unflattering nickname.

As for me, I was called "craterhead" because of deep scars left by a bout with chicken pox!

I also took my share of pounding at the hands of my older brother, Jack. I used to refer to him sarcastically as "God"—as in "Oh, I see God's home" or "Hey, God, you have a telephone call!" I remember that as a kid I walked around with perpetually sore shoulders. Jack didn't have a punching bag, but he did have those shoulders, and he seemed to punch them nearly every chance he got.

But I might as well confess that there are some pretty good things about being the youngest too. For one thing, big brother may pick on you, but he's not about to let anyone else push you around. If a bully is picking on you at school, usually all you have to do is sic your big brother on him, and your worries are over. Being the youngest means you get away with a lot of things too—like murder!

Mom and Dad are never as strict with the youngest—probably because they're so tired from making the older boys and girls toe the line.

So, for those of you who believe being the youngest is toughest I have to answer honestly "No way."

"But, Dr. Leman," someone says, "what about the child in the middle? I've always heard about the 'middle-child syndrome' and that the middle child is the one who has the toughest time of it."

Nah. You might be surprised to know that middle children grow up to be the best-adjusted and most monogamous adults.

Okay, I'll grant you that being stuck in the middle is no picnic. Being the middle child means you don't get as much attention as the oldest and youngest children. The oldest is important simply because he's the oldest. Mom and Dad would stand transfixed around his crib each night just watching him sleep. They could hardly believe that their union had produced this new life—and such a beautiful new life it was! This parenthood business was all so new and exciting! That's why the oldest is so special. As for the youngest, he's special because he's the baby, and he'll always be the baby, even if he's six four and weighs 245 pounds.

Being the middle child means living in a sort of anonymous haziness. But that's not all bad! If you're anonymous, you can get away with occasional laziness and indifference. You're not pushed as hard or expected to accomplish quite as much as the one who came before you. The drawback to that is that without being pushed you may never fulfill your potential. But it's still better than being pushed too hard and asked to perform beyond your capabilities. And that's what often happens to the first-born.

The firstborn is the kid who takes out the trash. All of his years at home, until he leaves for college, he'll be taking out the trash. When he comes home from college for Christmas, he's likely to find 300 pounds of trash waiting to be carted off. Perhaps I'm exaggerating, but any firstborn will tell you that I'm not exaggerating by much.

The oldest always seems to get stuck with the hardest chores, and he keeps them until he moves out to start a family of his own.

Who mows the lawn? The firstborn.

Who rakes the leaves in the fall? The firstborn.

Who serves as a built-in baby-sitter? The firstborn.

Who's expected to help Mom in the kitchen and help wash the dishes night after night? Again, the answer is the firstborn.

Obviously some of the chores I'm talking about have traditionally been divided along lines of gender—and I'm not going to get into a discussion about whether that's right or wrong—but the truth of the matter is that firstborns usually have the toughest road to travel.

Johnny may have been taking out the trash for 10 years now and figures it's about time Albert or Ruth took over the job, but it probably won't happen. Once the chore has been assigned, it's usually yours for life! That may be because parents don't want to expend the effort necessary to "train" someone else to do the job. But that's not fair. Little Buford may be the youngest, but he can pick up those dog plops in the backyard and toss them over the fence into the neighbor's yard as well as anyone else in the family.

Another problem for firstborns is that as a rule they have it much tougher than their younger brothers and sisters when it comes to discipline and the behavior that is expected of them.

For instance, firstborn Betsy sits at the dinner table and watches little Reginald push his peas away.

"Yuck," he says. "Gross!"

Mom sighs. "Okay, dear, you don't have to eat them if you don't want them."

Betsy doesn't say anything, but she remembers what would have happened to her if she had refused to eat her peas. She would have been sent away from the table and told to spend the rest of the evening in her room.

Firstborn Arnold sits in church and sees little Megan slouching down in the pew, drawing absentmindedly on the back of the bulletin and obviously not paying any attention to the sermon—and he remembers what it was always like for him:

"Sit up straight!" "Pay attention." "Quit slouching." And so on.

It's no wonder that firstborns grow up to be superorganized, superachieving, pillar-of-the-community type people.

Let me tell you a bit about my sister, Sally. Sally is a wonderful woman, and I love her dearly. She's had a tremendous influence on my life, and I mean it when I tell you that I don't know what I'd be or where I'd be if it hadn't been for her.

Sally is one marvelous and unique human being. I wouldn't consider her to be "typical" in any respect except for one. She's a typical firstborn in that she always wants to do things right and almost always does.

Not too long ago she and my brother, Jack, were visiting me at my home in Tucson. One day during their visit the three of us had to go downtown to a bank to sign some legal papers.

We were waiting in the lobby when I noticed all of a sudden that we were missing somebody. Where was sister Sally?

Oh, there she was, a few steps behind us. But what was she doing?

Upon closer investigation I discovered that she was straightening up the stacks of brochures on a table—brochures with titles such as *Everything You Wanted to Know About Deeds and Trusts* and *Do You Have a Will?*

"What are you doing?" I asked her. "Picking up a few brochures?"

"No, I was just . . ."

"Straightening up?" I asked her.

"Well, yes," she said, looking just a little bit sheepish.

I had to laugh. "Nobody but you would worry about straightening up the brochures in the bank's lobby."

It wasn't as if the brochures had been all over the floor. They just weren't stacked as neatly as they could have been, and that was driving Sally crazy! Nobody but a firstborn would have worried about straightening them up. But that's the way most firstborns have been trained to be.

In my office in Tucson I have two framed pictures that I have purposely hung off-center. This is enough to cause some firstborns to break into a cold sweat. They jump up wanting to straighten them and then can hardly believe it when I tell them they're hanging that way on purpose.

If you want something done properly, get a firstborn to do it! No wonder so many firstborns are doctors, lawyers, engineers— they sit on school boards, on city councils, and in the United States Congress in numbers far greater than their percentage of the population as a whole would dictate.

Now, if you are a firstborn, I can imagine that your chest is swelling with pride and you're thinking something like "Why, we firstborns are pretty good people. What could possibly be wrong with that?"

The answer is that there's absolutely nothing wrong with any of that. The problem starts when firstborns overorganize and seek to overachieve at their own expense—when they never feel that their efforts are good enough or they never feel free to be the people they really want to be. And, perhaps, were meant to be.

Every once in a while I run into someone who is extremely critical of this whole business of birth order, who doesn't believe your position in your family has anything to do with the way you behave. More often than not he'll be a firstborn, since firstborns tend to be very analytical and contemplative about things. They're not likely to accept anything without a thorough investigation. I recently ran into such a Skeptical Steven in Winnipeg, Canada, where I had gone to speak at a conference for families.

He started off by challenging me to figure out where he fit into his family. Sitting there at dinner, looking across the table at him, I could scarcely keep from laughing. If there ever was a stereotypical firstborn, he was it.

First of all, his clothing was carefully color-coordinated. His tie matched the color of his suit, and so did his socks. His shoes were polished to the point where they would have brought a smile to the face of any tough old sergeant. Furthermore, there wasn't a single hair out of place on his head, his mustache was carefully and neatly trimmed, and so were his fingernails.

He looked sharp, he looked dapper, and he definitely looked like a firstborn.

"You're the firstborn male in your family," I told him.

A flicker of surprise played on his face for just a moment, but then he regained his composure.

"Well," he said, nodding, "you're right about me." He shrugged his shoulders as if to say "Anyone can make a lucky guess."

About this time the waitress stopped by our table to refill our water glasses.

He looked at her and then at me. "What about her?"

"What about me, sir?" she asked.

"This man can tell where you were born into your family just by looking at you," Steven told her.

"No," I said with a laugh, "I can't do that. But if you'll answer a couple of questions for me, I think I can do it."

"Sure," she said. "Sounds like fun. Go ahead and ask!"

I asked two or three questions: what her father was like, what she wanted to do with her life, and so on. Her answers to those questions confirmed my suspicions.

"Lorraine," I told her, "you are obviously a firstborn female —but I'll bet you have an older brother."

She threw back her head and laughed. "That's amazing. How did you know?"

"It wasn't too hard."

"Listen," she said, "I've gotta run, but I'll be back later on. I want to hear more about this."

As she hurried off to see how the other diners were getting

along, I explained how I'd been able to pinpoint her exact location in her family constellation.

For one thing, she had described her father as "very disciplined, an engineer," but then she went on to say that he loved his children "very" much. She said he was friendly and outgoing but "very" firm. She spoke of the discipline and structure of his life in positive terms, which was another clue.

Firstborns are prone to using the word *very* and superlatives such as *best, favorite,* and so on. They also see organization and discipline as positive attributes. All of these combined to give Lorraine away.

And it wasn't just the way she answered the questions. It had just as much to do with the way she carried herself, the way she took our order, and the way she set our food on the table in front of us. In every move she made, she showed poise, organization, and efficiency. She was a firstborn all right, but in hearing her answers to my questions I was able to ascertain that she wasn't the only firstborn in her family.

It is possible in fact for there to be several firstborns in the same family, but more about that a bit later.

As I continued talking with my once-skeptical friend about birth order, I could see that his attitude was changing. Maybe there was something to this after all. Maybe firstborns *did* tend to act in certain ways that revealed them to be the "elder statesmen" of their families.

Before we were finished with our conversation, Lorraine stopped by to ask if we wanted any dessert. At least that was the reason she gave for stopping by, but she had another waitress with her, a tall, thin young woman of perhaps 20 whose name was Kathy.

"Can you do it for her?" Lorraine asked in her delightful Canadian accent. "Can you tell where she was born into her family?"

"Well, I—"

"Oh, I'm sorry," she interrupted me. "This is my friend Kathy."

Kathy stood quietly behind Lorraine, smiling demurely, as if she was a little bit embarrassed by this whole business. She rolled her eyes at me as if to say "I'm sorry about bothering you this way, and I want you to know that this certainly isn't *my* idea!"

Despite her obvious uneasiness I told her I would be happy to see if I could guess her position in her family if she would answer a few questions for me. I asked her the same questions I had asked Lorraine and quickly decided that Lorraine was a middle child. She was a master of negotiation and compromise, a woman who tended to be shy and secretive. She told me about her family and her feelings in the briefest possible way. She was friendly, but she didn't want to reveal too much. All of these are typical characteristics of the middle child.

When I told her this, she said I was absolutely right. She had two older sisters and a younger brother.

As soon as the women left our table Skeptical Steve threw up his hands and said, "I guess I was wrong about this birth order business. You've made a believer out of me!"

"Well, believe me," I told him, "I wouldn't be right all of the time." And I'm not. Where you were born into your family is one of the major forces shaping you into who you are today, but there are other forces at work in your life too, including your own determination and desires. It is impossible to pigeonhole everybody into airtight compartments, but at the same time it is true that most firstborns tend to display certain characteristics, as do most middleborns and lastborns.

Another thing I told Steve was that birth order is much more than a carnival trick akin to guessing someone's weight. It's a scientific theory with years of study and research behind it, and it's a beneficial tool when it comes to helping people understand themselves and improve their lives.

Of course Steve wasn't the only skeptic I've run into over the years. There have been hundreds of them, including dozens of men and women I've counseled in my private practice in Tucson. Sooner or later almost all of them have come around to believing in and understanding the role that birth order plays in all of our lives.

A typical conversation with a firstborn skeptic might go something like this:

FIRSTBORN: "You say that firstborns are supposed to be superorganized and driven, and I'm not. All you'd have to do is take a look at my desk, and you'd realize just how wrong you are."

DR. LEMAN: "Really? Well if it's that bad, how do you ever know where anything is?"

FIRSTBORN: "Oh, that's easy. It may not look like it, but I know exactly where to find anything I want."

DR. LEMAN: "So, in other words, you're telling me that there's a method to your madness."

FIRSTBORN: "Pardon me?"

DR. LEMAN: "I'm suggesting that you're not as disorganized as you would appear to be at first glance. If you know where everything is, that means you're fairly well organized, doesn't it?"

FIRSTBORN: "Well . . . yeah . . . I suppose so."

DR. LEMAN: "So what do you do at this desk anyway? What is your occupation?"

FIRSTBORN: "I'm an architect."

DR. LEMAN: "An architect! You might be interested to know that most of the architects I've known were either firstborn or only children. But aside from that, an architect has to be very careful about his work, doesn't he?"

FIRSTBORN: "You bet he does! There's no room for mistakes here or for being just a little bit off the mark."

DR. LEMAN: "Which is another striking characteristic of firstborns. Whatever they do, they do as well as they can. You don't hear firstborns saying things like 'Aw, that's good enough' or 'It's not perfect, but it'll do.' Firstborns are more likely to be overheard telling their friends 'Close counts only in horseshoes.' So far you're sounding more and more like a firstborn to me."

FIRSTBORN: "Well, I'm still not sure I'm ready to buy it, especially the bit about my sloppy desk really being organized. Seems to me that if I were really as organized and efficient as you say I am, I'd have a place for everything, you know, and keep everything in its place."

DR. LEMAN: "Well, believe it or not, people who have sloppy desks are sometimes more concerned with being perfect than people who appear on the surface to be neat and organized. The person who has the sloppy desk may be what I refer to as a 'discouraged perfectionist.' He wants everything in his life to be perfect, and because he knows it never can be, he tends to leave things half-done or not done at all. In other words he's afraid to attempt things that he knows he can't do perfectly."

FIRSTBORN: "Okay, well what about this? I have a younger sister—the third of three children in my family—and according to what you say, she's more like a firstborn than I am. She's always been the best at anything she's ever tried to do: student body president in high school, president of her sorority in college, editor of her college newspaper, president of the National Honor Society, and a law degree from a prestigious university. She's eight years younger than I am, and she's leaving me in her dust. I mean, from everything I know about birth order I thought lastborns were supposed to be happy-go-lucky types who take life as it comes. I thought they were supposed to have fun in life and not push themselves so hard."

DR. LEMAN: "That's true. But your sister may not be a lastborn at all. She may in fact be a firstborn, just like you."

FIRSTBORN: "What are you talking about? How could she possibly be a firstborn?"

DR. LEMAN: "Would I be correct in assuming that the child in between the two of you is a male?"

FIRSTBORN: "You would."

DR. LEMAN: "And how much younger than you is he?"

FIRSTBORN: "Three years."

DR. LEMAN: "All of this makes perfect sense to me. As a matter of fact, your baby sister is a firstborn on two accounts. First of all she's a firstborn because she's the only girl in the family. Now, that doesn't mean that she *had* to take on all the characteristics of a firstborn, but it means that it was a good possibility. The second reason she is a firstborn is that there is a five-year gap between the middle child and her. Whenever there is a gap of five years or more, the next-born child can be considered a firstborn."

FIRSTBORN: "Now I'm really confused. I was under the impression there could be only one firstborn in every family. Now you're telling me there can be several?"

DR. LEMAN: "That's right. Usually there will be just one firstborn or at the most two, due to sex differences, but if the children in a particular family are spaced far enough apart, it's possible that there could be four or even five children, all of whom take on the characteristics of firstborns. I doubt that you'll find very many families where there are several children all spaced five years or more apart, but it could happen."

FIRSTBORN: "Why does age make such a big difference?"

DR. LEMAN: "Primarily because it lessens the competition among siblings. Your brother is—what?—three years younger than you? That's close enough so that at least he probably had many of the same teachers you had. When he came to school, people remembered you and your accomplishments and he was under pressure to measure up. You see, the firstborn tends to look at his mother and father and want to be like them. They're the only role models he has, and that's one reason you find so many firstborn sons following in their father's footsteps, going into the same careers. But then little brother comes along and looks up, and he's not only got Mom and Dad to follow, but a big brother too. And he sees his brother doing a pretty good job of living up to Mom and Dad's expectations. Whoa—it looks like he'll have to find his own way to make everyone notice him. Let's say, for instance, that you were pretty good in sports . . ."

FIRSTBORN: "I was."

DR. LEMAN: "Okay, so that means your younger brother probably found it difficult to compete against you on the athletic level. Unless he happened to be born with a fair amount of natural athletic ability, he probably would have looked for another way to excel."

FIRSTBORN: "Yeah, he was really into music. Played guitar in a rock-and-roll band."

DR. LEMAN: "So I'd have to say that your brother is more of a lastborn than your sister is. It's typical of lastborns to seek out the limelight. They love to be the center of attention—and I'd guess that was one thing your brother got out of playing in a rock band. Lastborns, you see, often have a hard time getting attention. There's not much they can do that their older brothers and sisters haven't done before, and so from the moment they come into this world they're looking for a way to get their fair share of attention—and most of them can never get enough. For instance, remember the guy who was always the class clown when you were in school?"

FIRSTBORN: "Harry Wilson."

DR. LEMAN: "Well, old Harry was probably a lastborn. Class clowns almost always are, especially if they come from larger, overachieving families. If little Harry has two older brothers who are whizzes in sports and music and two older sisters who are top-notch artistically and scholastically, well, that doesn't leave a whole lot for him to claim as his own. Because of that, he's more likely to become the show-off or the rebel as a means of gaining attention."

FIRSTBORN: "My brother, Charlie, was always pretty funny. One time he took an alarm clock to church in his suit pocket. It went off right at noon. I suppose he wanted to let the preacher know it was time to wrap things up. I think he got the beating of his life over that one—but it was funny."

DR. LEMAN: "Typical behavior for a lastborn! I would be willing to wager that Charlie was always a pretty outgoing guy too—that he had lots of friends and was pretty good at getting them to go along with him on things. Because lastborns are generally so outgoing and personable, they make terrific salespeople. What does your brother do for a living?"

FIRSTBORN: "Well, I'll grant you that you've described his personality pretty well, but you've missed it on the career. He's not a salesman—he's an account executive for an ad agency."

DR. LEMAN: "But isn't *account executive* a fancy term for *salesman*? You have to sell your clients on your proposals, don't you? And besides, the entire purpose of advertising is to increase sales."

FIRSTBORN: "Hmmmmmm . . . yeah . . . I suppose so. But I still don't get it. According to what you're telling me, there are only so many personality types in the world—firstborns, middleborns, and lastborns."

DR. LEMAN: "And only children."

FIRSTBORN: "But only children are really an extreme variety of firstborns, right?"

DR. LEMAN: "Right."

FIRSTBORN: "So that means there are only three or four distinct personality types. I mean, even astrology allows for the twelve signs of the zodiac. As I look around me I see so many different types of people and personalities that it's hard for me to believe birth order plays such an important role in shaping the personality."

DR. LEMAN: "I need to say two things about that. First of all I never said that birth order was the only thing shaping the human personality. There are a tremendous number of variables entering into the equation that make you who you are. And even in birth order there are variables that enter in. For instance, consider the firstborn male who has younger brothers. He'll be the tough boss-of-bosses type, the kingpin. He'll be an achiever and probably do important things, but he won't understand women particularly well and might not make the best husband the world has ever seen. On the other hand a firstborn male who has younger sisters will probably be more sensitive. He'll still be an achiever, but he'll have a more compassionate, softer side that he will have learned through relating to his sisters. He's going to be more sensitive to women and their needs, and he'll do better in marriage. However, because he's always been older than his sisters and been the one to stand up for them and protect them, he'll probably tend to be a bit chauvinistic and believe that women need his help and protection. Then there's the firstborn male who has an older sister or sisters. He should have an even better understanding of the worth and abilities of women. Turn it around, and you can see that the firstborn female who has only sisters is going to view life in one way, skewed to a particularly feminine point of view, whereas the firstborn female with younger brothers will have a different outlook."

FIRSTBORN: "Hmmmmmmmmmmm."

DR. LEMAN: "Consider the only child. I can look at volumes of research and tell you generally how he is going to approach life

—but I can't be too specific, and I can't always be 100 percent right, because there are too many variables that enter into the situation. One important variable to consider is why he is an only child. I know that sounds a little strange, but it's an important consideration. Is it because his parents were physically unable to have other children? If so, they'll treat their one, precious child in a particular way, especially if they desperately wanted those other children they could not have. Or perhaps he's an only child because his parents took one look at little Junior's face when he was born and ran screaming from the delivery room, swearing that they'd never have another baby if this was the result. Or it could be that they planned for only one child, figuring that was the only way they could afford to give him the best of everything—the best toys, the best clothes, the best education. You see how all these things would alter the way they dealt with him, and this in turn would alter his approach to life."

FIRSTBORN: "Yes . . . I see what you're saying."

DR. LEMAN: "There's nothing at all magical about birth order. It's not set in concrete that if you're a firstborn you're going to act this way and if you're not you're going to act that way. It has to do with the way our parents relate to us, how we interact with our siblings, the sex of our siblings, the economic status of our families, where we live, and so on. All of these things go into the makeup of the family zoo."

FIRSTBORN: "This all sounds pretty good, but I'm still not sure I'm convinced. I'm going to have to think about this for a while."

DR. LEMAN: "Frankly I'd be surprised if you reacted any other way. As I told you before, the firstborn tends to be cautious and analytical. He's the sort of guy who wants to have all his facts straight before he makes up his mind. So take your time, think about it, and we'll talk again later."

* * *

Old firstborn may still not be convinced of the role that birth order plays in shaping our lives, but more and more people are beginning to pay close attention to the subject—including some of the most influential people in the United States.

I was in California for an appearance on an early morning television show and was sitting in the green room waiting to go on when I struck up a conversation with T. Boone Pickens, who was also scheduled to be on the show that day, just ahead of me. I found Boone, as he likes to be called, an engaging and fascinating person to talk to—just as you would expect, since he is one of the most influential people in American business today.

As we talked he became intrigued by the subject of birth order. He asked me question after question about it, and he took everything I told him and mulled it over and developed three or four more questions to ask.

We weren't able to talk for long before it was time for Boone to join the host on the set of the show. Then, 10 minutes later, it was my turn to go on. And something happened to me on that show that had never happened before in all of the 1,500 or so talk shows I've appeared on over the years.

Now, what usually happens is that a show will bring out one guest for a short interview, and then there will be a commercial break. The first guest is allowed to leave, and another guest is brought out. And because the people who usually appear on these shows are running from appointment to appointment, you'll never see them sitting down in the audience and waiting to see the rest of the show. It just doesn't happen.

So, quite naturally, as I was ushered onto the set the members of Boone's entourage stood up, as they were ready to escort him to his next appointment. But instead of leaving with them he waved them back down.

"Everybody take a seat," he told them. "I want to hear what he has to say about birth order."

Now, here's a man who's worth—what?—at least $3 *billion*? And he's interested in birth order. I think what had really piqued his interest was the knowledge that businesspeople

THE JOHNSONS AND THEIR
FIVE FIRSTBORNS

Suppose that a widow named Sally Barnes recently married a widower named Lou Johnson. She brought two children into the marriage—Tom, who is 12 and her firstborn son, and Larry, four, who also qualifies as a firstborn because of the age difference between him and his brother. Lou had four children of his own, making a total of five firstborns in one family!

It works like this:

Bill, 25, Lou's firstborn son

George, 23, Lou's middle child

Rhonda, 19, Lou's firstborn daughter

Tom, 12, Sally's firstborn son

Allison, 10, Lou's daughter and a firstborn because she's more than 5 years younger than Rhonda

Larry, 4, Sally's son and a firstborn due to being more than 5 years younger than Tom (or Allison, for that matter!)

would do very well to consider birth order when appointing people to key staff positions. I'm not saying that all decisions could be based solely on birth order, but it's another valuable piece of information that most corporations overlook. They'll ask you all sorts of psychological questions and put you through a battery of tests, but I've never heard of one yet that will ask you a single thing about your birth order. But finding out about birth order could potentially save any business millions of dollars every year. You could figure out which individuals would make the best salespeople, the best sales managers, which are the most organized, and so on.

If a man like T. Boone Pickens knows that an understanding of birth order can help him and improve his situation, certainly it is going to do the same for you and me!

On another occasion I was in Seattle appearing on a great show called *Seattle Today.*

When I came out, the host said, "Dr. Leman, I understand you can tell where people are in the family."

I never know for sure how to react, so I sort of hummed for a moment and then admitted, "Well, actually, yes I can."

He said, "I'm so glad to hear that, because you're going to get a chance to do just that, right after this commercial break."

Naturally I was sitting there thinking "Oh, great. He's probably picked out people who are complete deviations from the norm, and I won't get any of them right."

When the commercial was over, the host announced that he had picked four people from the studio audience and he wanted me to figure out their birth orders. He had them stand up and then asked, "Well, Dr. Leman, what do you think?"

I said, "Listen, I'm not Houdini. Do I at least get to talk to these people? Can I have thirty seconds with them?"

I was grateful that the host said okay, and after asking a few simple questions of each of them it was a piece of cake hitting on four out of four. One of the people was an only child, another was a firstborn, the third was a middle, and the fourth was a lastborn.

You should have seen the expression on the host's face. He was absolutely amazed that I was able to pick out all the birth orders correctly. He probably figured beforehand that there really wasn't much to this birth order stuff and that he'd have some fun with the subject. But once he saw that there really was something to it, the show turned into a probing and in-depth discussion of the subject.

On this particular show, based on the response of viewers who called in, I knew I was able to bring new insight and understanding to thousands of people, and I thoroughly enjoyed myself, because helping people is, after all, what an understanding of birth order is all about.

I have counseled thousands of clients in my private practice over the last 15-plus years. It is this, more than anything else, that has convinced me of the importance of birth order and of the leadership role that most firstborns play in our society.

If you're not convinced of this, play a little game with me. Ready?

Name one of the Mandrell sisters.

Time is up. Did you say Barbara? More than likely you did, and there's a good reason for that: she's the oldest.

Now name one of the Smothers Brothers.

Did you say Tommy? That's not surprising, because he's older.

But wait a minute, you say. Isn't Tommy the one who plays the dumb, constantly whiny, "in-the-way" little brother? Well, yes, that may be the role he plays, but the truth is that he's older than his brother and is usually the one people think of first.

One more try. Name one of the Wright brothers.

Did I hear you say Wilbur? He was older, by four years.

More than half (52 percent) of the U.S. presidents have been firstborns,[1] and if you want a dramatic example of the differences that exist between firstborns and lastborns, consider Jimmy and Billy Carter.

Jimmy, the firstborn, is the serious, studious, overachieving type of individual who worked his way to the presidency of the United States.

But over in Plains, Georgia, was his little brother, Billy (who, sadly, died far too young). Billy was famous for his beer drinking, for his rude off-the-cuff remarks, and for generally behaving as if he didn't have a serious bone in his body. And even though Jimmy may have been president, who was really standing in the spotlight? It was Billy. (And take it from this baby of the family, we lastborns certainly do know how to steal that spotlight. If we can't do it by being better than you are, we'll do it by being sillier—as Billy did.)

I occasionally conduct seminars for groups of corporate executives, and I recently decided to do a little surveying to see if my beliefs about firstborns would hold up. They did.

In a chief executive officers' organization 19 of the 20 attending were firstborns. In a meeting of a young presidents' organization, some 23 of the 26 dynamic young men and women attending told me they were firstborns.

Firstborns also appear in greater numbers than their siblings in *Who's Who in America* and *American Men and Women of Science* as well as among the ranks of Rhodes scholars and college professors.[2]

Is there a lesson to be learned from all of this?

I'd say so. If you're a firstborn, you'd better watch out, because you're likely to be a president someday. Perhaps of the United States, or of a business, or more likely of your neighborhood PTA. But any way you look at it, if you're a firstborn, you're born to lead!

Why are firstborns treated differently from later children? I believe it has a lot to do with the fact that firstborns are not allowed to be children for very long.

Let's say little Doris is three years old when her brother is born. All of a sudden her parents see her as such a big girl, especially because her brother is so tiny and so helpless.

When three more years go by, six-year-old Doris is seen as practically an adult, while her little brother is still looked on as a baby at three. Many parents seem to view their firstborn children as older than they really are. They expect them to grow up too fast, and they also expect them to set a good example for all of the children who follow them.

Firstborns are expected to be the smartest, the best-behaved, the best-looking, the most conscientious, the strongest, and so on. And a great many of them fail to measure up to their parents' exacting standards.

As a general rule firstborns grow up to be perfectionists or

THE TRAITS
OF THE FIRSTBORN

FIRSTBORN TRAIT	POSITIVE ASPECTS	NEGATIVE ASPECTS
Perfectionist	Does everything well	Overly critical and dissatisfied with his own performance
Driven	Ambitious, headed for success	Always under great pressure
Organized	Able to stay on top of everything	No room in his life for flexibility
Scholarly	Able to think problems through and solve them	Sometimes thinks too much; is overly serious
List-Maker	Gets things done; knows where he's going	Boxes himself in; becomes a slave to his list
Logical	Avoids pitfalls of compulsive behavior	Knows he's right, even when he isn't
Leader	Plays an important part in his family, community, etc.	Expected to do too much; always leaned on by others
Compliant	Known as a "good guy"	Known as an "easy mark"
Aggressive	Gets ahead in life; Others look up to him	Tends to be selfish and to disregard the feelings of others

near-perfectionists. Firstborns set goals; they are well organized; they are the sort of people who know where they're going, how they'll get there, and how long it's going to take to get there.

What's wrong with that? Absolutely nothing.

But the problem arises for those who become what I call "discouraged perfectionists." These are the people who could never measure up to the expectations that were set for them by their parents, and now, when they are adults, they can't measure up to their own expectations of themselves.

They may be grown and free from parental control, but they will never be free from the life-style their parents and their position in the family instilled into them.

It would be wise to take a moment right now to explain what I mean by the word *life-style.*

Every human being is following a particular life-style, or a subconscious plan for his life that was developed early in childhood. The things we do, the choices we make, and the way we perceive ourselves—all of these things are determined to a great extent by the life-style we are following. For example, little Louise may have discovered that the only way she could get attention was by being sick. Throughout her life she battles one sickness after another. She may not realize that the various illnesses are her subconscious effort to grab attention, but that's the life-style she's following.

The concept of life-style was developed by the pioneer psychiatrist Alfred Adler, who believed that understanding a person's goals is a key to understanding his behavior. He believed that all of us are following individual "life lines," or paths toward specific goals, whether or not we know what those goals are.[3]

The discouraged perfectionist would never believe that his underlying goal is to fail or at least to fall short of the standards he has set for himself, but in many instances that is exactly what he is doing. He sabotages himself at every turn!

Now, there is a tremendous difference between the perfectionist and the discouraged perfectionist.

The perfectionist is driven to do everything he does as well as it can possibly be done. He will give you every ounce of his ability, and as long as he knows he has done that, he will be satisfied with what he has accomplished.

The discouraged perfectionist, on the other hand, will never be satisfied with what he has done. No matter how good a job he has done, he always thinks that he could have done better, feels discouraged, and considers himself a failure.

The attitude of a discouraged perfectionist might be reflected in these words from the great genius Leonardo da Vinci:

"I have offended God and mankind because my work didn't reach the quality it should have."[4]

Surprising words from a man who gave us Mona Lisa and The Last Supper, among his many exquisite works of art, and who demonstrated his genius in an extraordinary number of other ways. But this is the typical attitude of the discouraged perfectionist.

And, by the way, Leonardo qualifies as a superfirstborn, because he was an only child. You could have guessed!

I like to picture the discouraged perfectionist as a high-jumper on a track team.

Here he comes, barreling down the track as fast as he can go, his legs pumping and his arms swinging wildly. Just before he reaches the high-jump bar he pushes himself up, up, and over the bar! But as soon as his successful effort is completed he jumps up and begins yelling "That bar wasn't high enough! Raise it another foot!"

If he gets over the bar at six feet, he wants it set at seven. If he should happen to get over it at seven, he'll want it put at eight— and so on, until he finally misses.

In this way the discouraged perfectionist is constantly stacking the deck against himself. He could be successful if he would allow himself to be, but he simply cannot allow it!

One of the amazing things about Leonardo, in fact, if he truly was a discouraged perfectionist, was the fact that he was able to accomplish so much. For very often the true discouraged perfectionist is unable to accomplish anything. He becomes so bound by his fear of failure that he is paralyzed and unable to do anything at all.

He already knows his effort won't be good enough, so he's afraid to get started. In school the student who comes in on the day his term paper is due and admits that he hasn't even started to write is probably considered to be lazy and indifferent. The truth may be that he is a discouraged perfectionist. He may have lost 10 pounds worrying about that paper and developed a painful ulcer, and he still hasn't written a thing.

In the office the woman who is constantly late with her reports or whose reports look like she just dashed them off during the last half hour may not really be disorganized and careless. It may be that she is a discouraged perfectionist.

Discouraged perfectionists come in all colors, sizes, shapes, and ages. They also come from various places within the family constellation, but by far the greatest percentage of them are firstborns.

I will never forget a young man I knew who was a brilliant student in college. He had never received a grade lower than an A and was about to be graduated summa cum laude. He had a tremendous future ahead of him. We all figured that he would be a success in anything he wanted to do.

And then he killed himself.

He left a note that said, in part, "I just couldn't measure up to the standards of this world; perhaps in the next world I can do better."

How extremely sad that such a fine young man felt so defeated and discouraged that he came to view self-destruction as the only way out. He was a discouraged perfectionist whose best simply wasn't good enough and who saw no hope of changing things.

But I want to show you that you can overcome the difficulties involved with being a firstborn, no matter what those difficulties might be or how deeply they affect you.

If you are caught up in the trap of discouraged perfectionism, you can be set free.

If you are resentful toward your parents because of the way they treated you when compared to the way they treated your younger brothers and sisters, you can overcome that resentment and establish a better relationship with them.

Why Aren't My Kids Alike?

In my counseling I am often asked by parents how and why children who grew up in the same family could be so different.

"After all," they say, "they all grew up in the same environment, so shouldn't they all act the same?"

The misconception here is thinking that children who grow up in the same family grow up in the same environment. They don't at all. The parents are the same, the house is the same, and the neighborhood and schools may be the same, but relationships within the family are entirely different.

The firstborn, for instance, is always looking out for the little ones, so he may perceive himself as the protector or even as the boss. My sister, Sally, remembers, for example, marching up the front steps of a house when she was a young girl, ringing the doorbell, and confronting a 38-year-old woman whose son was picking on her baby brother—namely, me. She made it clear that if the bully didn't stop picking on kids who were half his age, she was personally going to turn him inside out!

That's the way it is with firstborns. Mom and Dad may think they're in charge here, but the firstborn knows better, and so does his younger sibling.

That means, of course, that little sister has her own unique environment that brings its own set of problems. For instance, at least part of the time she may be torn between doing what her parents want her to do and doing what her older brother wants her to do.

Let's say that Mom has told her that she is not allowed to ride her bicycle to the corner store and that she will be grounded if she does. But then along comes big brother, who's feeling a bit mean today, and tells her that he wants her to ride to the corner store and buy him a candy bar. If she doesn't do it, he's going to "clobber" her. (If he's a decent big brother, he wouldn't really hit his sister, but I doubt that there's an older brother anywhere who hasn't threatened to do so at one time or another.) So poor Sis is caught in the middle in a "damned if I do, damned if I don't" situation—and that is the sort of environment in which she finds herself. She may also be the middle child, so she finds herself looking out for big brother's mean streak on the one hand and helping take care of little brother on the other.

And what about little brother? His environment is shaped not only by his relationship with his older siblings but also by the footprints they have left for him to follow. When he goes to school, he may find the teachers saying "I certainly hope you're going to be a good student, just like your older brother and sister." Or he may hear them murmuring "I hope this one isn't going to be a troublemaker like his brother."

Either way, the youngest one is being prejudged. A certain behavior is going to be expected of him, and it will be tough for him to prove that he is his own person.

So you see what I mean about children from the same family growing up in totally different environments.

Alfred Adler had these words to say about the effect that birth order can and often does have on our lives:

> The position in the family leaves an indelible stamp upon the style of life. Every difficulty of development is caused by rivalry and lack of cooperation in the family. If we look around at our social life and ask why rivalry and competition is its most obvious aspect—indeed, not only at our social life but at our whole world—then we must recognize that people are everywhere pursuing the goal of being conqueror, of overcoming and surpassing others. This goal is the result of training in

early childhood, of the rivalries and competitive striving of children who have not felt themselves an equal part of their whole family.[5]

Psychologist Karl Konig wrote several years later, "The family constellation shapes the social behavior of man. It determines the way he reacts to other people, how he is able to make friends or not, the way he finds companionship and community with others. Even the choice of a husband or wife is deeply influenced by the facts of the family-constellation."[6]

THE AXIOMS
OF THE FIRSTBORN

Everyone depends on me.
I can't get away with anything.
It's tough being the oldest.
I was never allowed to be a child.
If I don't do it, it won't get done.
If I don't do it, it won't get done right.
I never said I wanted to be a role model.
Boy! If I had acted the way you do . . . !
Mom never let me do that when I was your age.
Why do I have to do it? They never do anything
around here.

In the more than 25 years since Konig penned those words, numerous studies have validated them. Birth order is extremely important in your makeup, and your birth position has profoundly affected you, whether or not you realize it!

But remember what I said earlier. You do not have to be the oldest to be a firstborn. You can find firstborns just about any- where within the family zoo.

Any child who is more than five years younger than his im- mediately older brother or sister will take on the characteristics of a firstborn. I have seen it time and time again. That five-year time span apparently allows the younger child enough breathing room so that he is not stifled or threatened by the older child's achievements, and at the same time it is most likely true that his parents will treat him more the way they treated the older child. He will be expected to be more independent and will not be allowed to act like a baby.

It is quite possible that you could be the lastborn of eight children and, because of the time between you and the next older child, still qualify as a firstborn. Or if you're a mother who has spaced her children far apart, it is possible that you could have three or even four firstborns on your hands.

When you have come to see clearly how your birth order has affected your personality, you are taking a giant step toward understanding yourself better. It will help you see your strengths and weaknesses and realize why you make certain choices in life—whether they are good or bad choices. Once you understand yourself, you can begin to strengthen yourself, to improve on the areas where you're weak, and to make the strong parts of your personality even stronger. If you have a tendency to make the wrong choices, you can see what it is in your makeup that brings you to those choices—and you can change.

Now, don't misunderstand me. I am not saying that firstborns, as a class, have more than their fair share of troubles or that they need help above all other groups. But I am saying that firstborns have their own unique set of problems. Through- out this book I will seek to help you handle those unique prob- lems by showing you:

· How to take advantage of your birth order
· How to find out what you really want from life

· How to overcome strangling perfectionism and start feeling better about yourself
· How to overcome the hurts every firstborn suffers
· How to bounce back from failure
· How to make proper choices in your life
· Why it's important to stick to your guns
· How to develop meaningful relationships
· How to overcome parental abuse

Next up, the high cost of being the oldest.

2

The High Cost of Being the Oldest

Sometimes when I'm conducting a seminar I'll try a little experiment on birth order as an icebreaker. It's something you too might try in a large gathering and see if your results are the same as mine.

At some point I'll ask the participants to divide up according to birth order. All the firstborns move their chairs into this corner, the only children into this corner, the middle children into that one, and the lastborns over here. Then I ask them to arrange themselves in a circle.

While they're getting themselves arranged, I walk around and place a piece of paper on the center of the floor in each group. On the side of the paper facing the floor I have written this message:

"Congratulations! You are the leader of this group. Please introduce yourself to the others in your group and then have each person do the same. As you talk together, make a list of the personality characteristics that you all seem to share. Be prepared to report back to the rest of the seminar with your 'composite picture' of yourselves. Please start to work immediately."

Once I've left the paper on the floor, I don't do anything else. The groups sit there for a while, looking nervously at each other and then at me, wondering when I'm going to tell them what they're supposed to do. But of course I'm not going to tell them anything.

It's usually not too long before someone in either the firstborn or only children group takes the initiative and picks up the paper. Once in a great while someone in the group of middle children or even the lastborn group will pick up the paper first, but this happens about as often as it snows in my hometown of Tucson.

Usually the group of gregarious lastborns will be so involved in chitchat and getting to know each other that I can only assume they've completely forgotten the purpose of the seminar.

I'll wait for 20 minutes or so and then announce, "You have another five minutes to get your work completed."

At this point the groups who are working on their list will begin working faster, whereas the other groups will either look at me blankly, as if I'm totally out of my mind, or just ignore me and keep on with their small talk.

Naturally, when the time is up and I ask the different groups to make their reports, the firstborns and the only children are always well prepared, whereas the embarrassed lastborns and middle children try to explain, through their nervous laughter, that they didn't do anything because I never told them what they were supposed to be doing. They saw me put the piece of paper on the floor, sure, but they figured I was going to tell them what it was all about.

This little exercise illustrates that the firstborns are most generally the leaders, the ones who see what needs to be done and who then plunge ahead and do it. The firstborns are out there on the cutting edge, daring to take risks, while their younger brothers and sisters most often wait to be told what their role in all of this is supposed to be.

Taking the initiative is a natural tendency of firstborns, and it's a quality that often leads them into positions of leadership.

(No wonder that, as I said in the preceding chapter, firstborns are so common among the ranks of U.S. presidents and other groups of prominent people.) However, having this innate leadership ability is not what bothers the firstborn. And he's not *really* bothered by the fact that nobody else sees what has to be done until he points it out.

What drives him absolutely crazy is the fact that even after he points to the problem and articulates what needs to be done, almost everybody will still stand there looking at him with blank stares and shrugging their shoulders.

The attitude of the later-borns seems to be "Yup, you're right. Something ought to be done about this. I wonder who'll be the one to do it?"

The firstborn often makes promises to himself:

"I'm not going to be the one to do it this time. Yes, I can see that the trash must be taken out, but I'm not going to do it. Let someone else do it."

For three days he'll go around the house saying "I'm not going to take it out. It's not that big a deal, but it's a matter of principle." Pretty soon every wastebasket in the house is overflowing, and there are three big bags full of garbage sitting on the floor in the kitchen. And he fights it and fights it and fights it . . . and then he gives in.

"I can't stand it anymore! Okay, I give up—I'll take the trash out!"

Now, taking out the trash as an example of a personality type may strike you as rather silly, because obviously the issue is much greater than that. But for firstborns what begins early in life with little problems such as taking out the trash carries on through marriage and career, growing ever larger and ever more serious. Taking out the trash becomes taking on the world. As an American Airlines flight attendant once told me, "We are trained to take trash from people, smile, and say thank you."

When he is a child, the firstborn will most likely be the one to notice when the dog needs to be fed and when the hamster needs to have fresh water and a clean cage. He'll be more likely to keep his room neat and clean, and this can lead to some loud battles if he's sharing a room with a less organized younger sibling.

In a marriage the firstborn partner will be the one who tends to notice when the walls need painting, when the furniture should be replaced, and when the grass needs mowing. (He'll also be the one to notice when his partner should lose some weight, change a hairstyle, or stop talking too much—which is a prime reason a marriage between two firstborns can turn into a free-for-all, but more about that in Chapter 13.)

It is the firstborn female in particular who tends to carry a marriage. She is so dependable and so on top of everything that she teaches her husband to be irresponsible.

One such firstborn, a woman named Loretta, was so frustrated over this particular aspect of her life that she was about to walk away from her marriage of 15 years.

"The man is just impossible," she said. "I think he'd be content just to sit around and let the whole world fall apart."

"Is it that bad?"

"That bad? I believe this man could be sitting there with his shirt on fire, and he wouldn't make a move to put it out unless I told him to!"

"That's pretty bad," I had to agree.

Loretta admitted that her husband sometimes helped out around the house and with the children, but only when she pushed him and told him what needed to be done and why.

Loretta's life certainly didn't sound like a picnic. In addition to her full-time job as a receptionist, she was an officer in the PTA and served as a den mother for her son's Cub Scouts den.

"I'm the one who mows the lawn," she told me. "If I left it up to Bob, it wouldn't be too long before the National Geographic Society could film one of its TV specials in our front yard."

Loretta's life was a whirlwind of work and meetings, more work and more meetings, lawn-mowing, wall-painting, clothes-washing and clothes-mending, housecleaning, homework-helping, and on and on. If something broke around the house, she was the one who either tried to fix it herself or took the time to take it to the repair shop. What about Bob? He'd always say something like "Just leave it alone and I'll get to it." But Loretta knew he wouldn't get to it.

On one occasion she had gone without a clothes dryer for three weeks while he promised every day that he'd take a look at it just as soon as he had the time. So much for letting Bob take care of things. Meanwhile he seemed to be fairly relaxed and at peace, while his wife was tired and had constant headaches and frequent bouts with indigestion.

She didn't understand me at first when I asked her how many of the things she was involved in were absolutely necessary.

"Why . . . they're all necessary." She shook her head and looked at me with a deeply puzzled expression that seemed to say "Haven't you been listening to me?"

"Well, how about the Cub Scouts? Is that absolutely necessary?"

"I . . . uh . . ."

She didn't seem to be sure where I was headed, so I pressed on. "Being a den mother is wonderful, but don't you think it's a job better suited to a mother who doesn't have a full-time job?"

"I suppose so, but . . . well, somebody had to do it and . . ."

"How many boys are in your son's den?"

"Let's see, uh . . . right now there are fifteen."

"And don't you think that out of fourteen other mothers there's at least one other volunteer who could serve as the den mother?"

She thought for a minute and then slowly nodded. She had to agree that I was right.

"And what about the PTA? I know it's a good organization, but is it wise for you to get so involved right now, when there are so many other things going on in your life?"

"I see where you're going with all of this," she said. "But I want you to know that it's not my fault my life is the way it is. If I could just get Bob to grow up, to show some responsibility and some initiative, that would make me one of the happiest women in the world."

Fortunately Bob was anxious to save his marriage and so was willing to talk to me about the problem between him and his wife. His attitude was just what I suspected it would be.

"She drives me crazy!" he said. "She won't leave anything alone for a minute. She's always talking about what needs to be done here and what we ought to do there, and I suppose I've just learned over the years to tune her out."

When we talked about his wife's involvement in numerous outside activities, Bob shook his head and half-whispered, "And did you know that she mows the lawn every week? How do you think that makes me feel to have my wife out there mowing the lawn? All the neighbors must think I'm the laziest guy in the world—but she never gives me a chance, so I just let her do it."

I was finally able to get him to admit that all of the blame for this situation did not lie with Loretta. He did have a tendency to procrastinate, as attested to by his three-week delay in checking into the broken clothes dryer.

"But a lot of it," he said, "is a natural reaction against Loretta's constant pushing. Sometimes the more she pushes me, the more I want to drag my feet."

Sometimes, he said, Loretta didn't seem to give any regard to his feelings. For instance, if they were in a restaurant and the waiter came by to ask how their meal was, Loretta would quickly say "Oh, everything is fine," when in fact it might not have been fine with Bob. His steak might be too rare, he might have been given the wrong dish, but Loretta didn't give him a chance to express himself.

In this instance Bob and Loretta were able to work out their problems. Bob agreed that he would do a better job of showing initiative, and Loretta agreed that she would try to be more relaxed and make a real effort to separate what absolutely had to be done now from what could at least wait until later. It wasn't going to be easy, because it wasn't really in her nature, but she was going to make every effort to give the other guy a chance to volunteer first—whether it meant Bob's going out to mow the lawn or Jimmy Williams's mother's volunteering to go with the fifth-grade class on their field trip.

Bob even went so far as to draw up a list of the things around the house for which he was going to be responsible, and that included keeping the lawn mowed and trimmed. "Perhaps not every week," he said, "because it doesn't really need mowing every week. But at least every other week." The rest of Bob's duties were spelled out, too, and for her part Loretta agreed that she wasn't going to infringe on Bob's territory. Neither was she going to nag him if she thought he wasn't holding up his end of the bargain.

At the end of a four-week period they were due to report back so that I could check on their progress.

When I saw them next, I was delighted to find that their relationship had improved tremendously. Loretta admitted that it hadn't been easy at first to stand back and wait for Bob to fulfill his obligations. The first weekend, he had agreed to mow the lawn on Saturday, but he waited until Sunday afternoon instead. The suspense of waiting an extra day made her feel as if she was going to explode, but Loretta managed to keep quiet and eventually fought off the urge to get the old lawn mower revved up.

Loretta was fortunate, though, to have in Bob a husband who at least understood his wife's nature and who was willing to try to change his own behavior for her sake. What if Loretta hadn't been so lucky?

In that case she would have had some major remodeling to do with regard to her own personality, and the hardest thing probably would have been making an attempt to fight her own tendencies to do everything that needed to be done.

It is hard for the firstborn to keep his leadership abilities hidden. Other people just naturally seem to look to him to take charge. But it's often just as hard, or even harder, for the firstborn to ignore those feelings within himself that are constantly causing him to see what needs to be done and then compelling him to take the matter into his own hands and do it.

If you find yourself caught in the trap of "If I don't do it, it won't get done, or it won't be done right," you have to remember, first of all, that it's not always easy to change the behavior of others. It's easiest to start with yourself, and there are some definite steps every firstborn can take to change this aspect of his life.

Eight Steps to Overcoming Overresponsibility

1. PRACTICE SAYING NO.

The firstborn must learn to say no to others and to himself. If you're not used to saying no, spend some time practicing. You don't have to be angry or mean about it. You can be polite and friendly and still say no in a firm, strong way that leaves no doubts about your position.

The firstborn who is always called on to take charge will do himself a tremendous favor if he learns such simple sentences as:

"I'll have to say no to that, because I really don't have the time."

"I appreciate your asking me, but I'm going to say no this time."

"I'm sorry, but I can't possibly take on any more projects right now."

Even a simple "Thank you for asking, but my answer is no" will suffice. Remember that you don't really owe anyone an explanation. If someone won't take a simple no for an answer and presses you further, that's the time to be curt and say as firmly as you can, "I said no."

And say no to yourself too, such as "No, I don't have to clean out Joe's closet today. That's his job; he can do it."

2. LEARN TO LET THINGS GO UNDONE.

This is an extremely hard thing for many firstborn perfectionists to do. When they see something that needs to be done, they want to do it, and right now.

The frustrated firstborn may walk through her house and see a spot or two on the carpet. She thinks, "I really need to shampoo this carpet."

Then she sees where the dining room wall has been streaked and smudged by too many dirty little fingers and thinks, "I ought to paint these walls again."

As she walks into the garage, she is overwhelmed by the disorganized clutter that confronts her. "I'm going to have to get out here and give this garage a good cleaning."

On into the front yard, where she is reminded, "I've got to get out in the yard and do some work in my flower garden."

Everywhere she goes, everywhere she turns her eyes, she sees things that need to be done, and she knows that she's the one who will have to do them.

Does this sound at all like you? If so, you must make a conscious decision to see more of the positive and less of the negative. Remind yourself, "I am not going to see anything today that demands my immediate attention." I'm not saying that you will ignore any emergency that may arise, but you will make every effort not to dump a long list of projects on yourself.

3. WAIT 24 HOURS BEFORE VOLUNTEERING.

As we've discussed, firstborns have a natural tendency to take on more responsibility than could naturally be expected of them. In any situation where volunteers are sought, the firstborn is usually right at the front of things. As he sees his own hand waving wildly in the air, he thinks, "Why in the world am I doing this? I don't have time to take the Boy Scouts on a two-week nature hike!"

If this describes you, you must remember that you're the only one who can put a stop to this behavior.

If you're tempted to volunteer for some job or other, give yourself at least 24 hours to think it over. Don't commit yourself on the spot and then wish you'd kept your mouth shut. After you've thought about it for a while, if you still want to volunteer, go ahead. But you will save yourself much grief if you avoid making on-the-spot decisions.

And whatever you do, don't let yourself make decisions based on the assumption that "If I don't do it, nobody will." The fact that nobody else wants to volunteer doesn't mean you have to. If a volunteer can't be found, someone will be chosen for the job, and it probably won't be you.

4. LEARN TO EXPRESS YOURSELF.

There's no need for you to suffer in silence. If your family always depends on you to do everything, let them know that you're tired of it and you expect them to do their fair share from now on.

Make a list of the things you do for your spouse and your children and make an effort to cut back.

I knew one woman who spent more time in her yellow minivan than she did at home, running all the kids in the neighborhood to and fro. It wasn't really a taxi, but everybody seemed to think it was.

If your coworkers are content to let you do the majority of the work in the office, speak up and tell them that the situation isn't fair and you are no longer going to be doing their work for them. If you are handling four or five projects at once, while your coworkers have only one or two at a time, go to your boss and explain the situation. Ask for a more equitable distribution of the work load.

Remember, people will count on you to do everything once they know that you *will* do everything.

Your boss might even be saying something like "Oh, give that job to Martha. She's a real go-getter, and she loves to keep busy." He may never dream that you're feeling put upon and overloaded unless you tell him exactly how you feel. The same goes for your family. The best way for you to get others to pitch in and do their share of the work is to tell them how you feel about things.

5. TRY NOT TO WORRY ABOUT THE MINOR DETAILS.

Again, this is often easier said than done, but it *is* possible.

Firstborns tend to be precise and exacting. When a firstborn is taking a trip by car, he'll generally get out his map and plot the shortest, most direct route. If he's watering his lawn, he'll know exactly where the sprinklers should be set to get the job done in the most effective way. Firstborns are, in short, masters of detail.

And while that is a good quality, it's also a good way to drive yourself and others crazy. It could be that people always count on you to do what needs to be done because they know that you're the only one who can do the job to your exacting specifications.

If your son mows the lawn, but he knows that you're going to come out and redo it because he didn't do it exactly the way you want it done, then he'll be discouraged and won't want to do it anymore. If your daughter makes her bed, but you come in right behind her and tear it all apart and remake it, she'll decide she'll just let you do it from now on.

After all, why should they waste their time and effort doing something that you're only going to end up doing over?

I'm not talking about overlooking mistakes and letting a slipshod job go unchallenged. If your daughter has taken a couple of halfhearted swipes at her bed and it looks like someone is still sleeping in it, it must be redone—but you don't have to remake it. Show her a few times how you expect her to make her bed,

WHO DOES WHAT
AROUND YOUR HOUSE

DUTY	YOU	SPOUSE	KIDS	SHARED
Mowing and watering the lawn	___	___	___	___
Doing the laundry	___	___	___	___
Fixing dinner	___	___	___	___
Shoveling snow*	___	___	___	___
Helping kids with homework	___	___	___	___
Keeping bathroom clean	___	___	___	___
Tucking kids into bed	___	___	___	___
Keeping cars in good shape	___	___	___	___
Taking kids to doctors' appointments	___	___	___	___
Straightening, dusting, etc.	___	___	___	___
Making the beds	___	___	___	___
Taking care of pets	___	___	___	___
Dog plop patrol	___	___	___	___

*Residents of Tucson may ignore this one.

Where only one spouse works, the other spouse may do most of these, but chances are that the firstborn does more than his share. The overburdened firstborn needs to resolve to quit taking so many of these duties on his own shoulders.

Give yourself 10 points for each thing you do.

If you score 90–100, either you're a single parent or you're not getting much help. You need to make some changes and ask others to help out more.

From 70 to 80, you still do too much. Whose fault is it?

A score between 40 to 60 is just about right.

From 0 to 30, are you sure you're a firstborn?

and then if she tries her best and comes reasonably close to what you want, let it go.

If your son mows the lawn in such a way that it looks like a patchwork quilt, you can't just let it go. But there is a big difference between pointing out a job that hasn't been done right by anyone's standards and nitpicking. If you are a nitpicker, you can be assured that nobody else will want to do anything for you.

I had one client who worried so much about the minor details that she measured the furniture in her home so that she knew exactly how and where everything was placed.

In other words she knew that this chair was 35 inches from the dresser, which was four inches away from the wall, and so on. Can you imagine what this woman's life was like? Especially her sex life! Not much room for spontaneity there. She was the sort of woman who ironed the bath towels. (Incidentally, on a recent visit with my sister, Sally, I caught her ironing the pages of a cookbook that had fallen into the sink and become wet. She was determined to get the wrinkles out of those pages!)

Admittedly this is an extreme example, but this is where you can eventually wind up if you don't learn how to quit worrying about the little things.

I counseled another client who complained to me that she could never have any time for herself because she had to take care of her children. When I suggested that she find a good baby-sitter and spend some time alone with her husband, she said, "Oh, believe me, I've tried. But I just can't find one that measures up." She was nitpicking prospective baby-sitters to the point where not one of them would do, and the supposed "problems" were all of her own making.

6. TRY TO BE MORE ACCEPTING OF OTHERS.

This goes hand in hand with learning not to worry about the minor details.

If you would mow the lawn once a week, but your husband thinks once every two weeks is plenty, you can learn to accept his standard.

If your daughter's room is always messy, and you find yourself constantly cleaning up after her, make a deal with her that she will clean her room twice a week and the rest of the time you won't nag her about it. Learn to accept her standards. (Up to a certain point, of course. If you call the Orkin man and he won't go into her room because his insurance carrier won't allow it, then it's time for action.)

If your colleague at work isn't doing his report the way you think it should be done, remember that it really isn't any of your business. You should feel free to give your advice when he asks for it, but there is no reason for you to feel that you must do his work for him.

You must remember, for your own sake, that you are not the world's police officer and that you cannot expect everyone else to measure up to your exacting standards.

Their failure to measure up will not harm you.

I used to enjoy watching TV westerns like *The Lone Ranger, The Rifleman,* and the like. And I was always amused by the fact that the good guy would take a bullet right in the chest and walk away saying "I'm okay—it's only a flesh wound." Or he'd be shot in the back of the head at point-blank range, but he'd be okay because the bullet "just creased my skull!"

Well, you have to remember, whenever someone lets you down or fails to live up to your standards, that "it's only a flesh wound." Life can and must go on!

7. TAKE TIME TO RELAX.

Learn to take time for yourself. Instead of asking yourself "What should I be doing today?" ask yourself "What would I like to do today?"

Perhaps you can find a quiet place and spend a day reading a book. Or maybe you'll find renewal in putting on your waders and going after some rainbow trout. Take time to do whatever you think will renew your spirits and recharge your batteries.

Firstborns are notorious for moving forward just as fast as they possibly can—and they are unusually susceptible to stress and burnout.

I have counseled many firstborns who felt guilty about doing anything nice for themselves. They felt that they always had to be doing, accomplishing, moving forward—and if they weren't, then they were being lazy and nonproductive.

This is total nonsense! One of the best things you can do, for yourself and for others, is to do something nice for yourself.

8. DON'T BOX YOURSELF IN.

Setting goals and keeping a list of the things you want to do can be positive and helpful.

But they turn into a negative when your life becomes totally controlled by your lists and goals. You must allow yourself flexibility and not "overbook" yourself. I have clients who keep their "to do" lists short by spreading the items out over several days of their personal calendars. I think this is a good idea, but I also recommend keeping one day a week open for catching up on things you weren't able to get done on the other days. Make sure your lists are working for you, instead of the other way around.

But I Never Wanted to Be a Role Model

Life as the oldest can certainly be a drag! It was hard growing up, because not only were you expected to be a shining example, someone your younger brothers and sisters could pattern their lives after, but you were also stuck with the stifling and sometimes terribly embarrassing problem of having to take one of them with you wherever you went:

"As long as you're going out, Mark, why don't you take your little brother with you?"

"But Mom . . . I have a date!"

"That's nice, dear . . . and I'm sure Jimmy will have a nice time."

So there you went, off to your first date with a very special girl—a girl it took you three months to get up enough nerve to ask out, a girl you never even dreamed would say yes—and you ended up having to drag your little brother along. That certainly didn't impress her very much, and to top that off you couldn't even put your arm around her, much less steal a kiss, because you had to be on your best behavior as a role model!

Or maybe you were off to a rousing game of softball with your friends:

"Judy, wherever you're going, I want you to take Lisa along with you."

"But Mom . . . we have an important game today."

"I'm sure your sister would love to watch. Just see to it that she has a good time."

So there you were at the big game, forced to keep an eye on six-year-old Lisa. You were trying to play your position, but you weren't doing a very good job, because you were worried about your sister sitting over in the stands. Oh, no! She's eating dirt!

"Lisa, stop that!" You were so busy yelling at her that you didn't see the ball coming your way, and it rolled right past you. And—look out!—Lisa almost got beaned by that foul ball! It's enough to make you scream, but firstborn role models never scream!

Many firstborns spend their entire lives worrying about the impact they are having on the lives of their younger brothers and sisters. Some get so fed up with trying to be perfect that they take a swan dive off the deep end into all sorts of harmful activity—drugs, alcohol, promiscuous sex. They feel that they've never really had a chance to live life for themselves, so they say "to heck with you" and take up permanent residence in the fast lane. Perhaps they believe that living a life of decadence will free them from the bitterness they feel because Mom and Dad always wanted them to be someone to look up to. But of course it doesn't work.

Others live their entire lives stifling themselves because they don't want to do anything that could cause anyone else to stumble. But here again the result is resentment and bitterness churning deeply within because "I've never been allowed to be just me." These "professional" role models often have a problem with guilt too, because they know they're really not the people they're pretending to be.

I remember Dana, for instance, a lovely and vivacious young woman who confided in counseling what she could not bring herself to confess to anyone else.

"I'm such a phony," she sobbed.

"What do you mean? How are you a phony?"

"In everything!"

She went on to tell me that she was so confused about her life that she didn't know which parts of it were truly her and which parts were merely extensions of her "job" as a role model. She was one of those rare firstborns who had measured up to her parents' expectations in every way—an A student, a beauty queen, an accomplished musician. Now she was married, with two beautiful children who never seemed to misbehave. Her husband seemed to adore her. She dressed impeccably, her hair looked perfect, and, in fact, she could have stepped right off the pages of the latest fashion catalog!

Her friends marveled at the wonderful meals she fixed and how she kept her home looking so nice. She taught a Bible class at her church, and everyone admired her obvious deep faith. Whenever one of the neighbors or one of the women from church had a problem, she ran to Dana, because Dana always knew exactly what to do.

But it was all phony. Or at least Dana thought it was.

"I can quote the Bible backwards and forwards," she cried, "and I'm not really sure how much of it I believe.

"Jerry and I have some terrible fights—our marriage isn't as good as we want people to think—but I'm afraid to let anyone else know.

"People come to me for all sorts of advice because they think I'm so together . . . but I can see what I'm really like."

Her guilt had become so severe that she was having trouble sleeping and described herself as "like a used car that looks fine on the lot—but there are all kinds of serious problems underneath." She felt that her charade had drained all the joy out of her life.

The more Dana talked about her problems, the more obvious it became that they weren't really any more serious than those we all face. The difference, for her, was that she was afraid to be real because she didn't want to let anyone down.

What Dana didn't realize, and many other firstborns don't realize, is that we are all role models in one way or another. If people choose to look up to you, there is nothing you can do to stop them. But you cannot let their expectations dictate how you are going to live your life.

There is some ancient advice that still rings true today:

"To thine own self be true."

But to be true to yourself, you have to know who you really are.

Dana was eventually able to discover that she had a pretty good marriage. She and Jerry had their problems, yes, but they were always able to work them out. And as far as the Bible went, yes, she really did have faith in God, and she believed all those things she had been teaching. Those revelations didn't come overnight. It was even necessary for her to take a sabbatical from teaching and spend time in study, meditation, and, yes, prayer while she went through the sometimes painful process of separating the phony from the real.

The biggest step for Dana came when she stopped trying to be perfect.

She didn't want to at first, but she finally agreed to do her grocery shopping for the week without putting on makeup or doing her hair. That may not sound like much, but it really represented a major breakthrough, because Dana never went anywhere without her hair perfectly coiffed and her makeup done just so. That was all part of the illusion she was attempting to maintain—the price she had to pay for being everybody's favorite role model.

She said later that at the grocery store it seemed as if all the people were looking at her. She felt "almost like I didn't have any clothes on," and she found herself constantly putting her hands to her face, almost trying to hide behind them.

But after a while it became apparent that people weren't staring at her. They may not have looked upon her as Mrs. Perfection, but neither were they looking at her and thinking "Would you get a load of that slob! How could anybody ever think of coming out to Safeway without eyeliner on!"

More and more Dana found herself gaining the confidence to be herself instead of what others expected or wanted her to be.

If you're one of those firstborns who are caught in the trap of being perpetual role models, I believe there are four definite steps you can take to gain your freedom.

Four Steps to Break the Role-Model Mold

1. FIND OUT WHO YOU ARE AND WHAT YOU REALLY WANT FROM LIFE.

Start out by taking some time for yourself. Jot down some thoughts about yourself. What do you like most about yourself and what do you like least about yourself? When are you the happiest? What are your long-range goals? Do you do things that you really don't want to do because other people expect you to do those things? Don't be afraid to put yourself under the microscope and don't shy away from being painfully honest. It could be that you've been so busy being what everybody else wanted you to be that you've never really given any thought to what you want out of life. Start giving it thought now!

2. DON'T WORRY TOO MUCH ABOUT WHAT OTHERS THINK OF YOU.

Firstborns often feel like they have to be the most intelligent person in the room, or the prettiest, or the smartest, or whatever other superlative they can think of. But you have to learn that the only people worth knowing are those who like you for who you are and who respect you for who you are. If people admire you only because they think you're the best-looking or the most successful, they're making a pretty shallow assessment of you.

3. LEARN TO LAUGH AT YOUR MISTAKES.

In other words, don't take yourself so seriously. How can you do this? By understanding that every human being makes mistakes and that you are, after all is said and done, only a human being! When you goof up, try to smile and take it good-naturedly, even if it's forced and unnatural at first. After a while you'll find that you don't worry nearly as much about achieving perfection (which is unattainable anyway) as you used to!

You may feel as if everyone is watching you and that you are letting them down when you goof up, but that really isn't so. By facing up to and having a sense of humor about your mistakes, you may even be setting others free from the bondage of thinking that they have to be perfect. And most of us are lucky in that our mistakes don't make the evening news—as when a congressman gets caught in a scandal or a movie star has a drug problem. Nor are our mistakes listed in a box score on the sports pages for all the world to see, which is a problem that many professional athletes have to face. When you think about your mistakes in that light, it makes them easier to take!

4. TAKE STOCK OF THE STRENGTHS BEING A ROLE MODEL HAS BROUGHT YOU.

Sure, being a role model is sometimes hard to swallow, but so are a lot of things that are good for you—such as spinach and broccoli.

In other words, having to set artificially high standards for yourself has been good insofar as it has pushed you to improve yourself and to develop your natural skills and abilities. If nobody had ever expected anything of you, you would undoubtedly have taken the path of least resistance and fulfilled their expectations. But you are a better person in many ways simply because you have been pushed to succeed.

It's unfortunate that you have always been expected to set an example for those who followed after you. But do yourself a favor and count the blessings this has meant for you along with the problems it has given you.

Do you see yourself as plain vanilla in a world clamoring for 31 flavors? If so, remember that vanilla is still the most popular flavor in the world!

3

How Do I Forgive My Parents?

Sandra sits with her hands in her lap, leaning forward and staring at the floor while I wait for her to continue.

Then she leans back, looks at the ceiling, and breathes a loud sigh.

"I guess it must sound like I'm a pretty bad person," she finally says. "I mean . . . my parents really are good people, and they've always wanted the best for me. It's just that . . . well, it's like they always kept me on a leash—a really short leash—and when they thought I was even thinking about taking a step on my own, they jerked that thing so hard . . ."

Sandra is 35 but looks older today because her face takes on a bitter, angry look when she talks about her parents.

"I suppose I love them," she says, "but I really don't like them very much." She admits that even though she lives in the same city, she does her best to avoid them, seeing them three times a year at most. As she relives her growing-up experiences, the lines around her eyes and mouth seem to deepen, and her voice takes on a harder edge. She is the jealous older sister who resents not only her parents but her three sisters as well. And she is angry at her sisters not really because of anything they have done but because her parents treated them so much better than her—with each one getting successively more freedom.

Sandra is a very pretty woman, but this is offset by the fact that she is at least 30 pounds overweight. She is a classic example of the overweight woman who has "such a pretty face." Like many other angry firstborns, she discovered early in her life that she could find some comfort and solace in food. When she was angry at her parents, she ate. When her sisters irritated her, she ate. And so she is not only troubled by painful memories, but she also blames her parents—fairly or not—for her appearance, which embarrasses her.

"You know," she says, "I was never able to get away with anything! Not one thing!"

And as she tells me the rest of her story, it becomes apparent that she's not exaggerating!

She couldn't go to any school dances, because her parents didn't want their daughter associating with boys. She was not allowed to join Girl Scouts, because her parents didn't want her going out of the house on a weeknight to attend meetings. She remembers that her father "blew a gasket" when she came home with a C in math and grounded her for three weeks.

"When I was twenty-two years old and engaged, my parents wouldn't let my fiancé and me take a hundred-mile trip to the mountains, because that would give us too much time to be alone together."

And then two days before her wedding Sandra's mother and father wouldn't let her and her fiancé go alone to their apartment to set up the gifts she had received at a bridal shower. Instead they insisted that two of her younger sisters accompany her, just to keep an eye on things.

"And they didn't lift a finger to help us, either. They were there strictly to act as our chaperons and not to do any work." She shakes her head. "I still get angry when I think about them just sitting there on the sofa, watching us, without so much as offering to help us with anything."

Sandra was troubled and hurt by the stranglehold her parents kept on her, by their display of obvious distrust. But what hurt her even more was seeing how differently they treated her younger sisters.

"I really can't say that they treated the next one after me a whole lot differently. Some better, but not much.

"But the last two—it's like they did a hundred-eighty-degree flip-flop, and they can do just about anything they want—especially the youngest one.

"She's twenty-five, and so she ought to be able to live her life the way she wants to as far as I'm concerned, but it still bothers me to see her go off on overnight camping trips with her boyfriend, and Mom and Dad stand there and smile and wave as they drive off together. Now, don't tell me things have changed that much in the years since I got married!"

But then Sandra remembers that it was always pretty much that way. She got grounded for Cs, while Diane was offered a new bike if she could get her grades up to a C average. Sandra wasn't permitted to attend Girl Scout meetings, while Diane went off on an overnight ski trip with a group from school when she was just 12.

"And another thing. My husband is a wonderful guy—he really is—but my parents have always just tolerated him. They treat Diane's boyfriend like he's a member of the royal family or something, and to be quite frank about it, the guy's a no-good jerk!"

You might think from all this that Sandra is a person who is bitter about life in general or who loves to complain and eat sour grapes. But you'd be far from right.

Most of the time Sandra is a pleasant, cheerful, and easygoing person. She's warmhearted and outgoing, and she's not overly critical or shrewish in her behavior.

However, whenever she talks about her parents or her childhood, she seems to go through an entire transformation. Everything about her seems to take on a harder, sharper edge.

Poor Sandra! My heart goes out to her.

Most firstborns have at least some of the feelings Sandra expresses. They may not be as severe or as deep, but they are there nonetheless.

Some firstborns I've known, especially men, have tried to bury the feelings six feet deep in the subconscious and then pretend they don't exist at all. But they were still there and would occasionally erupt into the open.

And it's nothing at all new.

Nearly 2,000 years ago Jesus Christ told a story that we all know as the parable of the prodigal son.[1] Just in case you haven't been reading your Bible regularly, or haven't been to Sunday school in a while, I'll refresh your memory.

It seems that a father had two sons. One, the oldest, was an all-around decent fellow who never gave his dad a speck of trouble. He was the sort of son any parent would be proud of.

As for the younger son, well, to say he was a disappointment to his father would be putting it mildly. You can just bet that if there'd been 7-Eleven convenience stores in those days, he probably would have been hanging around all the time, smoking cigarettes and playing video games.

Finally he went to his father and said something along the lines of "Listen, Dad, I know I'm going to inherit some money from you someday, but I'm tired of waiting around for you to die. So how about giving me my simoleons right now?"

To keep peace in the family, that's exactly what Dad did. And as soon as the boy had the money in his pockets, he headed off for parts unknown. He had enough money to last him a lifetime but decided to throw it away on loose women, wine, and whatever else was objectionable back in the first century. It wasn't long before the money was gone and he had hit rock bottom. He was homeless, jobless, and terribly hungry.

Finally the young man decided to do the only thing he could do: namely, swallow his pride and go on back home. He didn't figure he'd get a very warm reception, but anything had to be better than what he was going through right now.

Well, if you remember the story at all, you know that the

young man got much more than his anticipated lukewarm welcome home. The Bible says that when his father saw him coming, he ran to meet him. He didn't lecture him on his reckless living or even give in to his impulse to say "I told you so!" Instead he called all his friends and neighbors and gave the boy a huge welcome-back bash, as if he were some sort of returning hero.

The firstborn son quite naturally boycotted the party. After all, he'd been at home all these years, faithfully helping his father with the family business. He'd never lifted his voice to his father, never put the slightest scratch on the family chariot, and he'd never had so much as a birthday party. Dad had never even given him so much as a goat!

Well, the parable ends happily enough, because the father goes to his older son and explains that he is celebrating because he feels as if his younger son had died but has now come back to life. The Bible doesn't tell us what happened after that, but the reader is left to assume that the firstborn son changed his tune, went to the party, and tried to be a good sport about things.

The point of the parable, of course, is that God is a gracious Father and that He is always ready to welcome back those who have turned their backs on Him and, in effect, spurned Him. And, if there is a real villain in this story—at least the way it's often interpreted—it's the older son, because he had an angry and unforgiving spirit.

But I want to ask you something about that. Namely, was the firstborn's attitude justified?

At the risk of turning the theological world against me, I have to say this:

Of course it was!

Or, if it wasn't completely justified, it was at least to be expected. I readily admit to you that if I had been standing in his shoes, I would have felt the same sort of resentment and anger toward my irresponsible and selfish younger brother—and probably toward my father for being so willing to forgive him and thereby give me a slap in the face as thanks for all my years of loyal and loving service!

Now, before anybody gets upset with me and starts thinking that I'm being heretical, I want to ask you to be totally honest with yourself. If you are, I think you'll see that I'm right and that the firstborn was behaving as almost any human being would.

Well, I'm here to tell you that the world is full of firstborns who are full of anger and resentment and who have every reason for it. They don't want to be angry and bitter, but those feelings are not always easy to overcome—especially when it sometimes seems that every time you resolve to be a "bigger person" about things and not take them so personally, you get another blow to the psyche.

But before I talk about a few ways to deal with and overcome the ill feelings and personal problems caused by this common plague of all firstborns—being treated like second-class citizens and not being able to get away with anything—let me say a few words in behalf of parents. Namely, I want to tell you that your parents treated your younger siblings better than they treated you because there is no teacher who can take the place of experience.

What I mean is that you didn't come with a set of instructions. Your parents may have read all the baby books they could get their hands on, but once you actually came into the picture they realized that all that "wise" advice was about as useful as a snow shovel in the Sahara. You're not dealing with a blender or a microwave oven, but with a living, breathing, thinking, feeling human being—a creature of body, mind, and emotions.

And besides, a lot of the information parents read is confusing and conflicting. I remember one young mother who told me, with tears in her eyes, that the more she read about rearing children, the less capable she felt and the more she was sure she was bound to fail in this most important of jobs.

Parenting is for most people a painful process of trial and error, and the only way you learn is through your failures and

---

THINGS ALL FIRSTBORNS HEAR

I don't care what *he* did—you're the oldest!

Take your little brother (sister) with you.

Couldn't you keep your little brother (sister) out of trouble?

What kind of example is that?

Will you please act your age?

When are you going to grow up?

He's littler than you. You should know better!

---

successes. If you try something with Johnny and it doesn't work, you know better than to do the same thing with the next child.

So to all you firstborns who resent the way Mom and Dad treated you, especially when you see that your younger brothers and sisters are treated much, much better, I say: please give your folks a break and try to understand that they most likely didn't intend to treat you badly. It's just that they didn't know any better. They didn't let you get away with anything because they themselves didn't know the parameters of parenting!

But now we come down to the question at hand. If you are a firstborn and you are resentful toward your parents and your siblings, what can you do to free yourself from the resentment that churns within you?

How to Make Peace with Your Parents—and Yourself

In my years of experience I have discovered that there are several steps you can take, and most of them involve changing your attitudes. Some of them sound quite simple, but they work:

1. TELL YOUR PARENTS HOW YOU FEEL.

Not in a bitter, accusing way, but as gently and lovingly as you possibly can. Talking things out with them will help all of you, because chances are that they know they didn't always treat you right. They may feel as bad about things as you do, but it's hard for them to face up to it. It's also possible that they haven't the slightest idea you have those feelings of resentment, and they will want to do everything they can to make things right between you. It could be that they sense there is a problem between you and them but don't have the slightest idea what has caused it. If they reject you or seem unwilling even to think about the possibility that they may have made some mistakes, you'll at least have the satisfaction of knowing that you tried to make things right. And that's much better than keeping your mouth shut and exploding from suppressed anger.

If you can't tell them in person because it's just too painful, put it in writing. But avoid being vitriolic and harsh. Express yourself as well as you can, but don't do it with words that are going to put your parents on the defensive and build walls between you. Be firm. But be nice.

If you can't talk to your parents because they have passed on, find someone else to talk to—a clergyman or other counselor who can stand in your parents' place and, acting in their behalf, help to bring healing to the relationship.

If you can't tell your parents how you feel because they refuse to listen or don't seem to care, the same advice holds true. Find a counselor who does care and who can stand in for your parents. If they are not interested in healing the relationship, remember that the loss is theirs.

2. IT'S NOT YOUR FAULT THAT YOUR PARENTS DIDN'T TREAT YOU AS WELL AS YOU WOULD HAVE WANTED THEM TO.

Remind yourself of this over and over, until you actually come to believe it. There was nothing "different" about you that made your parents decide to dislike you or treat you unfairly while they loved your little sister to pieces. This may sound a bit silly or superficial, but I have counseled hundreds of firstborns who honestly felt that there was something about them—other than their firstborn status in the family—that caused their parents to resent them and pick on them. It simply isn't so, and if you can't believe that, stand in front of the mirror for as long as it takes and tell yourself over and over, "It's not my fault."

3. MAKE A CONSCIOUS DECISION TO FORGIVE YOUR PARENTS.

If you wait around hoping that one of these days you're going to wake up feeling better about things, chances are it will never happen. And even if it does, look at all the time you're wasting while you're waiting!

If you're holding on to bitterness and unforgivingness, it's wise for you to remember that the person you're really hurting is yourself. One young woman I counseled told me that if she lived to be a thousand years old, she would never be able to forgive her parents for the way they had treated her when she was a child. Her parents had tried several times to bridge the gap between them, but she wasn't having any of it. Having done everything they could do to soothe their daughter's feelings, her parents had finally decided to get on with their lives. They were hurt, sure, but they weren't going to let their daughter's anger ruin their lives—which seemed to me what she wanted.

The daughter, on the other hand, was completely miserable. There was no joy in her life, and all of her friends were being driven away by her incessant anger and bitterness. She wasn't hurting her parents, but she was doing a tremendous amount of damage to herself.

It was only when she was able to make a conscious effort to forgive that her life began to improve.

When she told me that she couldn't just change her feelings overnight, I explained to her that forgiveness was an act of the will, not of the emotions. Forgiveness, for the most part, is something you do and not something you feel.

With that in mind, Penny told herself, "I will forgive my mom and dad," and then she set about the process of showing, through her actions, that this was what she had done. Her first step was inviting her folks to dinner, which, needless to say, caught them completely off guard. During the evening she was as polite and courteous as she could be, even though she certainly didn't feel like it at first. But as the evening went on, she felt more at ease, and treating her parents as if they were her parents began to come more naturally to her. That was only the first step, but it was a great start. Penny has now reestablished her relationship with her parents, and her only regret is all the years she spent hating them. She learned that acting as if you've forgiven someone is a very big step toward actually forgiving him.

I've had other clients tell me that they will forgive, but not until they are asked to forgive. Well, I'm sorry, but that doesn't work either. If you harbor bad feelings toward anyone, but particularly toward your parents and your siblings, do yourself a huge favor and forgive them right now.

Unforgivingness and bitterness hurt you much more than they hurt the person you won't forgive.

Holding on to resentment can be harmful to your health in several ways. Not only can it cause you lasting emotional pain, but we know now that it can cause all sorts of physical problems too. Ulcers, high blood pressure, chronic headaches, and even diseases such as cancer may be caused by refusing to let go of bitterness and anger. When you learn to forgive others, you're really helping yourself.

4. KEEP BUSY.

I'm not suggesting here that you should take on more projects than you can possibly handle. Don't overwhelm yourself with enough work to keep you busy 25 hours a day; but you can help yourself by getting involved in enough outside projects so that you don't sit around and think about how miserably unhappy you are.

Now, I'm sure that somebody is bound to ask me at this point, "But if you simply try to stay so busy that you don't have time to think about things, are you really helping yourself?" Of course you must deal with the problem at its root, because anger and resentment are like weeds. If you merely chop their tops off, there's a very good chance that they will grow back. But if you have a nice, thick lawn, there won't be any room for weeds to grow. So what I'm suggesting is that if you keep yourself busy in constructive projects and keep your thoughts focused in constructive matters, you won't be giving the weeds any room to grow there.

It may be that you will still need to take some other steps before you are completely freed from that churning resentment, but you are going a long way toward weakening it.

Fill your mind and your time with the positive, and you will not have time for the negative. There are so many things you can do to help others: volunteer to work in a community hospital a few hours a week, become involved with Meals on Wheels, give some time to a nursing home, etc. When you give to others in this way, you will find that resentment and anger have been replaced by true happiness.

I'm sure you've heard the old computer programming equation "garbage in, garbage out." This means, of course, that your computer relies on you to put the proper information into it. If you program it with nonsense, it's going to give nonsense back to you. If you fill your mind with garbage such as jealousy and resentment, your life is going to show the fruit of that kind of thinking, and it's not going to be very pleasant.

5. GET OUT THERE AND GIVE IT A SHOT.

What "it" am I talking about? Just about anything where you could show yourself, and others too, that you're a capable, intelligent person.

For instance, I remember Lisa, a thirtyish firstborn wife and mother who was practically crippled by her lack of self-confidence and self-respect.

She had never worked in her life, primarily because of her lack of self-esteem, and she was aghast when I suggested that she find a job—at least a part-time job. Why, she could never see herself even looking for a job, much less finding one. But because she really did want to change, she finally agreed that she would give it her best shot.

To her surprise she found a job working two days a week as a receptionist in a dentist's office. The first day she almost decided to call in and tell them that she had changed her mind about taking the position—or, at the very least, that she had come down with the flu. But to her credit, she didn't.

Her husband was proud of her but didn't think she'd last more than a couple of weeks. To be honest, neither did I. But a month went by, and then another one, and she stuck with it. Her self-confidence grew greater when her boss told her he appreciated the job she was doing for him. On a couple of occasions she caught and corrected scheduling mistakes made by the other women in the office.

She could hardly believe it when her boss called her into his office one afternoon and asked her if she would consider going to work full-time. When she thanked him but told him that wasn't really what she wanted to do, he said he understood, and then he agreed to give her a raise anyway. It was only 50¢ an hour, but it was another piece of evidence that she was doing a good job. She knew he wouldn't hand out raises just for the sake of handing them out.

The success she achieved on the job helped to turn her life around. She became more confident and poised, and her relationships with family and friends began to improve.

But none of that would have happened if she hadn't at least been willing to try.

6. GET PROFESSIONAL COUNSELING.

If you've tried everything I've suggested and more, and you still can't get rid of those terrible feelings of resentment, find a competent therapist and seek help in that way. There's nothing wrong with asking for professional help, and it certainly doesn't mean that you have failed or fallen short of the mark.

I have counseled many thousands of men and women over the years, and I am grateful to be able to say that I have helped the vast majority of them work through their problems and turn their lives around. That doesn't mean that I'm any sort of miracle worker, but it does mean that I know what I'm doing because I have put my whole life into learning how to help people. If you asked me to build a bridge across a river, you'd be in big trouble, because I wouldn't know what I was doing. But if you're interested in overcoming resentment and anger, and your own attempts at dealing with these feelings have been unsuccessful, I'm the one to call! And I've been called, as I said, thousands of times—by attorneys, engineers, homemakers, pastors, professors, businesspeople, etc.—most of them highly successful and "together" people who simply needed help in a particular area of their lives.

Why do I go into so much detail here? Simply because it is often hard for firstborns to seek professional help. Seeking counseling is seen as a sign of weakness and failure, and firstborns are never supposed to fail. But a competent professional counselor can be of great benefit, and you should never shy away from seeking his help!

I'm sometimes asked if I can suggest a few ways to be sure you're picking the best counselor. It's important, of course, that you find someone you're comfortable with, someone you can trust.

Look for a counselor who wants to get rid of you. In other words, find one who wants to help you and see you make it on your own, rather than becoming dependent on him.

You should also seek out a counselor who has children of his own, who values marriage, and who is certified as qualified by state and national professional groups.

4

Sibling Rivalry (Abel Had It Coming)

It's certainly too bad that history's first firstborn didn't have someone to help him deal with his anger and resentment. If he had, things might have taken a drastically different turn.

I am referring, of course, to Cain, whose resentment against his younger brother grew and grew to the point where he eventually committed murder. You can read the whole sordid story in the Bible, in the fourth chapter of Genesis. Now, I want to tell you, if you think you have trouble with your younger brothers and sisters, just imagine how Cain felt.

Here he was, the only little boy in the whole world! I mean, talk about having all of Mom and Dad's attention! And then all of a sudden, here's Abel, and he's expected to share all of his stones and mammoth tusks and things. Now, when Abel came along, poor Cain was taken completely by surprise. Nobody ever told him this was going to happen, and he didn't have any friends who had to deal with little brothers.

Can you imagine how he must have felt? Up until that time he had everything in the world all to himself—every tree to climb, every river to swim, every forest to explore—and now, all of a sudden, he's not able to go anywhere without his little brother tagging along.

Poor Cain! He is the unofficial mascot of all firstborns who have ever thrown up their hands in frustration and anger over their dealings with a younger brother or sister.

The final straw for Cain undoubtedly came because, in addition to merely living, Abel couldn't seem to do anything wrong.

One day, when the two boys were out in the field, something within Cain snapped, and he did the unspeakable. He killed his younger brother. (I said "unspeakable" and not "unthinkable" because I'm sure just about every big brother or big sister who ever existed has given fratricide consideration at one time or another.)

Why did Cain wind up being a murderer? Primarily because he didn't know how to deal with his feelings—he didn't know how to come to terms with his own feelings of jealousy and inadequacy, which were prompted by Abel's perceived "perfection."

Cain would have been much better off—and so would Abel— if he had followed the steps useful for dealing with resentment and anger that we've already discussed.

Beyond that there were several other important facts he should have kept in mind:

1. You are responsible only for what you do and not for what anyone else does.
2. You must try to understand and deal with your feelings, figuring out why you feel the way you do.
3. You must learn to exercise what I call "cognitive self-discipline," which includes going against your feelings. (What do I mean by this? Well, if we all threw caution to the wind and followed our feelings, it would be a pretty frightening world, and I imagine that sooner or later most of us would wind up

in jail! Or, at the very least, most of our friends would stop talking to us. Your past relationships may have been so destructive that they've taken their toll, so your feelings tell you that nothing is going to work out right for you. If you listen to those feelings, you'll never give yourself a chance.)
4. You must learn to develop a sense of humor.

Let's take a look at these important facts one at a time:

You Are Responsible Only for What You Do

Cain asked the question a little bit late and in a sarcastic manner:

"Am I my brother's keeper?"[1]

And he meant, of course, that he didn't know or care where his brother was—that it wasn't up to him to keep track of such matters.

But in reality many firstborns hurt themselves because they really do feel responsible for what their younger brothers and sisters do, and they aren't. They are particularly adept at comparing themselves with their younger siblings and feeling frustrated and angry instead of proud when a younger member of the family surpasses them in some way.

What I am saying here is that you have been given certain abilities and strengths that you and you alone possess. The same is true for every other member of your family. If you expect yourself to be the smartest, the most athletic, the most artistic, and so on, you are expecting far too much from yourself. There is absolutely no reason for you to go around comparing yourself to others. You will be better in some ways and not as good in other ways, and that's the way life has been designed. It keeps things more interesting. You must remember that you are responsible only for being the best you can be, and that does not mean you are required to be better than others.

Always remember that diversity has been built into the system in a number of ways, including the skills possessed by various members of the family.

Try to Understand and Deal with Your Feelings

When I've mentioned this to some firstborns, they've shot right back with "Of course I understand why I feel this way. It's because my parents always expected too much of me," or "because my parents were never fair," or some other, similar answer.

And that actually may be the case. If it is, you are a step ahead, because you do understand why you feel the way you do. But you need to make sure you're being honest with yourself. Are you absolutely certain the problem lies with your parents? Could it be that you are blaming them when the real problem lies within yourself?

Let me say right here that it's become fashionable in our society to blame parents for just about everything their children do, and that's not fair. Parents are held responsible when their kids break the law, or run away from home, or flunk out of school. But I've known plenty of decent, loving people who tried their hardest to be the best parents they could be, and they were rewarded with kids who were always in trouble with the law or who dropped out of school and couldn't seem to make anything at all out of their lives.

I've had parents ask me "What did I do wrong?" and as far as I can see, they didn't do anything wrong at all. What I'm saying here is that there is not always an immediate and obvious causal effect. Parents, because they are so obvious and so close at hand, are easy to blame for all of our troubles, but we'd better make sure we're not just copping out and looking for a scapegoat.

On the other hand, I have counseled clients who didn't under-

A FIRSTBORN AND
DESTRUCTIVE "FEELINGS"

FEELING	ACTION REQUIRED
Resentment toward parents	Admit feelings either in person or through a letter. Seek to rectify situation and give and receive forgiveness.
Self-directed anger	Learn to forgive yourself. Realize that everyone makes mistakes.
Jealousy toward siblings	Discuss feelings with siblings. Realize that they may be jealous of you.
Fear of failure	Analyze each situation. What is the worst that could result from your failure?
Feelings of inadequacy	Use positive self-talk. Make a list of your strengths.
Self-doubts	Refuse to give in to negative thoughts. Practice laughing at yourself.

stand why they should be troubled with feelings of resentment and anger toward their parents when it is clear to me that the parents are at least partly to blame.

One young woman felt particularly strong anger toward her parents, which she didn't understand because "they did everything they could possibly do for me." And it was true, they spared no expense and no effort to see that their firstborn daughter excelled in every area of life. They gave her piano lessons beginning when she was just six. She was also involved in riding lessons and became a proficient horsewoman. She was a baton twirler in high school, a winner of numerous beauty pageants, and came within an A-minus of being her high school's valedictorian.

With her father's help she managed to win a scholarship to one of the country's finest schools, which also happened to be his alma mater, and with a degree in business, she was doing quite well for herself. She was quite naturally the envy of her two younger brothers, who came nowhere close to matching her accomplishments.

Yes, sir, it was obvious that her parents had done everything they could do to make her life better. Why, then, did she feel such anger churning within her?

As we talked, it became obvious to me that this young woman's parents had never taken her feelings into consideration. Here she was, nearly 30 years old, a success in the world of business, when she honestly had never wanted to go into business in the first place. She really didn't know what she wanted to do with her life, but that was because she had never been given a chance to think about it. Mom and Dad had made all of those decisions for her, to the point where she felt as if she didn't have any life of her own.

When I suggested this to her, she was quick to tell me I was mistaken. But the more we explored this line of thinking, the more an obvious pattern began to emerge.

Actually, no, she hadn't ever asked for those piano lessons— or the riding lessons either. And she'd never cared about those beauty pageants, but they seemed to mean a lot to her mother. And as far as her choice of a college or a major went, she just did what her father wanted her to do.

Once she understood why she felt the way she did, she was free to deal with it. Now, I don't want anybody to misunderstand what was happening here. The last thing I was trying to do was to drive a wedge between this young woman and her parents. The wedge was already there, and it was growing wider. She was full of anger and resentment toward them but couldn't understand why. She told me that sometimes she almost felt as if there were a deep secret locked inside of her, something she'd forgotten, but which had left its mark on her and left her feeling angry and hurt toward Mom and Dad—whom she also loved very much.

Coming to understand why she felt as she did was a big first step toward making a conscious effort to forgive them. She couldn't just wave her hands in the air and say "I forgive my mother and father" if she didn't have the slightest idea what she was forgiving them for.

It could have turned out that her anger was self-directed and that she really felt that she had let Mom and Dad down by not living up to their expectations. In that situation she would have had to extend forgiveness in two directions—to her parents for the unrealistic pressures they put on her and to herself for putting herself down and putting the same pressures on her own shoulders.

It is not always easy to see the motives of other people, especially when it comes to people who are so close to you and who love you, as your parents most surely do. But if you will take a long, hard, analytical look at reality, you will be able to see more clearly why you feel as you do—and once you understand, you can deal with the situation in the proper manner.

There is most definitely some need for forgiveness in the life of the angry firstborn, but the question at hand is where that forgiveness must be directed. And, of course, understanding people's motives helps you forgive them.

Practicing Cognitive Self-Discipline

To practice cognitive self-discipline means that you know your true self, including your abilities and strengths and your weaknesses. It is coming to understand the events and relationships with other people that have made you who and what you are. It is understanding the things you do that may keep you revolving in a cycle of doubt and rejection and learning how to go against your feelings so you can get off that depressing merry-go-round ride!

If you remember all the way back to the ancient 1960s, you will recall that one of the most prevalent slogans of those days was "If it feels good, do it." Well, I'm here to tell you that too many people have reversed that on themselves and practice "If it feels bad, do it." So they go around kicking themselves, telling themselves that they're no good and causing themselves all sorts of pain.

Actually neither one of those slogans is any good, because following your feelings can sometimes get you into trouble.

You can't just close your eyes to reality and count on instinct and intuition to guide you home, especially when you know you've landed yourself in trouble before by doing exactly that!

What do your feelings tell you? Are they whispering in your ear that you're going to fail, so why bother to try? Do they tell you that something is bound to go wrong because it always does? Are they taunting you and telling you that unless whatever you do is perfect it's no good at all?

If they are, you simply have to refuse to listen or believe what your feelings are telling you.

If you believe you are going to fail, chances are great that you will fail. If you believe nothing short of perfection is good enough, you'll wind up so frustrated that you fall far short of the excellent work you could do.

I talked earlier about the person I call the discouraged perfectionist. This is a person whose feelings about himself have him hog-tied and manacled to the point where he can't do much of anything, even though he may be loaded with talent. A particular problem of the discouraged perfectionist—the majority of whom are firstborns—is that he often puts off doing things because he knows he's not going to be perfect.

If he has to write a report, he'll agonize over every word because he's so afraid it's not going to be perfect and he knows that anything short of perfection is worthless. So he perspires over a blank sheet of paper for several hours, and then he finally says, "I'll start on this tomorrow, when I'm thinking more clearly."

But when tomorrow comes, it's the same old thing. He can't even think of the first sentence to put on his paper, because every sentence he comes up with is less than perfect. He's capable of doing an acceptable piece of work, but he's so bound up by his fear of being less than perfect that he winds up doing a slapdash job at the last minute.

What he needs to do is practice cognitive self-discipline, to realize, "This report isn't going to be perfect, but I have the ability to do a good job. Maybe the first sentence won't be the sentence to end all sentences, but I've got to get this report written, and the only way to do that is to sit down here and start writing."

The old proverb reminds us that the longest journey begins with a single step, and that's something to keep in mind. Large successes are built out of smaller ones, bit by bit by bit. If you are too busy looking at the big picture and wondering how everything is going to come out all right, you'll more than likely leave the little things undone or not do them as well as you could and should.

Develop a Sense of Humor About Yourself

Do you remember the first time anyone ever laughed at you? You were probably two or three, and you said or did something that caused other people to laugh in spite of themselves. They didn't want to hurt your feelings, but they just couldn't control it.

One friend of mine told me he will never forget the time when, as a five-year-old, he was reciting the 23rd Psalm in front of a church group. He did fine until he came to "He maketh me to lie down in green pastures." He knew what he wanted to say, but somehow it came rolling off his tongue as "He maketh me to lie down in green plaster."

Well, as you can imagine, the place erupted into gales of laughter. My friend remembers that he could feel his face turning red and his eyes filling with tears. He couldn't believe that these people would make fun of him over something like that. That was over 30 years ago, and he chuckles now as he tells the story, but he also says he'll always remember how hurt and angry he was at the time.

Another friend remembers how hurt she was when she tried to impress her family by making biscuits. She was only nine at the time and figured her family would be impressed and grateful for years to come. Only something went wrong. First of all, the biscuits didn't rise. Second of all, they had the consistency of cement. They looked more like hockey pucks than they did buttermilk biscuits.

Her mom and dad tried to be nice about it and even tried to eat one or two of them, but she could tell that they really thought it was funny and that they were struggling not to laugh. Her older brother wasn't so kind and openly told her that these were the "stupidest-looking things" he'd ever seen. Then he and his best friend took them across the street to a little lake and used them as skipping stones. How humiliating.

"Well," she laughs now as she tells the story, "they worked pretty well as skipping stones, I must admit." She also admits that it was quite a few years before she could think of that incident without feeling twinges of pain.

Now, I would be willing to bet that as I told you these stories you thought of similar instances in your own life. We've all goofed up, we've all been laughed at, and most of us have had difficulty dealing with it, especially when we were children.

But what about now that we're grown up? Is it still difficult for you to laugh at yourself a little?

It's impossible for me to overemphasize the importance of developing a sense of humor.

Think about old Cain. Can you ever picture him smiling, laughing, facing up to his own mistakes? Of course not. Cain was a deadly serious, obviously self-righteous individual who wanted to have everyone's admiration and respect. He couldn't stand being in his younger brother's shadow about anything for one minute. Imagine how differently things might have turned out if he'd had a sense of humor or at least the courage to smile at his brother.

There are a few firstborns who are noted for their sense of humor—Bill Cosby is one who comes quickly to mind—but more often than not, firstborns are not known as the sort of people who like to yuck it up, especially at their own expense.

But again, my point is that you can learn to laugh at yourself if you'll remember three important things:

1. Everybody goofs up from time to time, so you're not alone when you do.
2. Some people make fun of you because they're jealous or because they know it can make you angry.
3. Laughter is good for you—physically, mentally, emotionally, and spiritually.

The next time you feel angry because you've goofed something up or because someone is putting you down, laugh. You may have to force yourself. It may take every bit of energy and acting skill you have, but put a smile on your face and let it roll off your back. You may be dying inside, but you don't need to let anyone else know that. If you practice smiling and laughing at your own mistakes, believe it or not, pretty soon you're going to be able to do it without effort—and mean it.

Laughing at yourself doesn't mean you think less of yourself.

Actually it shows that you respect yourself enough to know that your mistakes are no worse than anyone else's and that you believe in yourself enough to know that you can overcome them.

Don't let anger control you. It's a terrible taskmaster, and it never makes your life any easier.

Just look at what it did to old Cain.

5

Perfectionism

In *The Birth Order Book*[1] I reprinted a personal ad that I had clipped out of a daily newspaper. I hate to repeat myself, but it's such a classic that it bears repeating. The ad went like this:

CHRISTIAN, blond, blue eyes, 5'2" 100 lbs. prof., cauc./female, no depend., wishes to meet Protestant Christian, prof. man in 30s with college degree who has compassion for animals and people, loves nature, exercise and phy. fitness (no team sports), music and dance, church and home life. Desire nonsmoker/nondrinker, slender, 5'7"–6', lots of head hair, no chest hair, intelligent, honest and trustworthy, sense of humor, excellent communicator of feelings, very sensitive, gentle, affectionate, androgynous attitude about roles, giving, encouraging and helpful to others, no temper or ego problems, secure within and financially, health-conscious, neat and clean, extremely considerate and dependable. I believe in old-fashioned morals and values. If you do too, and are interested in a possible Christian commitment, write to PO Box 82533. Please include recent color photo and address.

Do you suppose this woman ever found the prince she was advertising for? I don't. In fact, if men were manufactured by some company in, say, New Jersey, I imagine they would have trouble building one this woman would give her approval to.

I don't know anything about the person who paid for this advertisement, but I would be willing to wager that she is a firstborn. If there is a trap that firstborns tend to fall into more than any other, it's the trap of perfectionism. Show me a perfectionist—and more particularly the person I refer to as the discouraged perfectionist—and the odds are about 10 to 1 that you're also showing me a firstborn.

Are you a discouraged perfectionist? Here's a brief quiz to help you find out for yourself:

1. You have been asked to look into the cost of new playground equipment and make a verbal presentation of your findings at the next meeting of the neighborhood association. Would you be most likely to

   (a) immediately be afraid you'd never get the report done in time for the meeting?

   (b) start worrying about whether you'd talk to the right people and get the right cost figures?

   (c) be proud of yourself for being recognized as someone who could handle the assignment and immediately begin working on it?

2. If you stopped by your best friend's house for a cup of coffee, and she told you she was sorry, but she was just too busy to talk to you right now, would you

   (a) wonder what you had done to offend her?

   (b) become angry and figure that her behavior showed you what she *really* thought of you?

   (c) tell her you understand (and mean it) and ask her to call you when she had time?

3. If you were 15 minutes late for work, would you

   (a) figure that everyone saw you come in late and they were all probably talking about you?

(b) march yourself into the boss's office, confess your misdeed to him, and then work during your lunch hour to make up for the few minutes you missed?

(c) realize that everyone gets held up now and then and promise yourself that you'll try not to be late again?

4. If you were balancing your checkbook, and you were 15¢ off, would you

(a) keep working at it for hours, vowing that you won't stop until you find the missing 15¢?

(b) decide that 15¢ isn't really worth worrying about, but then lie awake all night wondering where you made the mistake?

(c) decide that 15¢ isn't worth worrying about and then quit worrying?

In all of the above questions, the (a) and (b) answers are pretty much the normal routine for the discouraged perfectionist. Only the (c) answers show a healthy sense of self-esteem and a properly relaxed attitude about life in general.

Question No. 1: Discouraged perfectionists are world-beaters when it comes to anticipating their own disasters and failures.

Question No. 2: Discouraged perfectionists are also very good at reading between the lines and figuring out what people really mean. They are forever being rejected and slighted.

Question No. 3: Another favorite pastime of the discouraged perfectionist is magnifying his mistakes and flaws.

Question No. 4: Finally, the discouraged perfectionist has a difficult time figuring out when to let go. He will spend hours agonizing over and wrestling with the smallest problems, because he wants everything to be done right.

How did you do? If you saw yourself in any of these situations, you have tendencies toward being a discouraged perfectionist. But don't let it drive you crazy. There is hope! You can learn to deal with life's little inconsistencies and imperfections and keep smiling all the while.

In her book *Perfectionism—What's Bad About Being Too*

Good? Dr. Miriam Adderholdt-Elliott talks about some of the games perfectionists tend to play.[2] Not all perfectionists play all of these games, of course, but if you struggle with this attitude, you're bound to see yourself in some of these:

Mood Swinging: The perfectionist's mood always depends on his latest success or failure. If the boss liked your report, you're on top of the world. If he thought there was room for improvement, you're crushed and sitting at the bottom of a deep, dark pit.

The Numbers Game: This means that you gauge your worth by the quantity rather than the quality of your achievements. The result can be that you don't do anything as well as you could, but you keep on rushing from project to project, trying to get enough things done to feel good about yourself.

Telescopic Thinking: When you're looking at things you need to do, it's as if you're looking through a telescope, so they appear to be much larger than they really are. Conversely, when looking at what you've already done, you turn the scope around so that your accomplishments look positively tiny.

Focusing on the Future: You did well in something? So what? You don't have time to sit around and pat yourself on the back. You're already worrying about what comes next.

Pining over the Past: When you're not worrying about the future, you're brooding about past failures, wondering why you didn't do better and playing the "If only" game. "If only I had studied harder. . . ." "If only I had put a little more effort into that report. . . ." And so forth.

Putting Your Goals First: You might have time for recreation later, once your goals are met. You might be able to spend time with your family, but right now you have to keep pushing ahead on this project. Everybody has situations in which they have to put aside fun and friends to concentrate on the task at hand, but the perfectionist tends to do it constantly, going from task to task so that he rarely has time for himself or the others who are important in his life.

Getting It Right: "I'm going to keep doing this until I get it right!" In a school situation this might be translated into something like "Why are you taking geometry again this year? I thought you did pretty well in it last year." "Nah . . . I got a B, and I'm going to keep taking it until I get an A."

All-or-Nothing Thinking: The discouraged perfectionist is not satisfied unless he's the best at everything he does. She may be the captain of her bowling team, the soloist in the church choir, win the blue ribbon for the pie she took to the county fair, keep a neat home, and have eight wonderful children. But if Betty Lou Swanson defeats her in the election for president of the local PTA, she feels like a total and absolute failure.

How many of these games do you play? Give yourself 10 points for each, and let's tally your score:

70–80 Points: Look out! Your picture ought to be in the dictionary under "Discouraged Perfectionist."

50–60 Points: You're still giving yourself ulcers, but there's hope for you.

30–40 Points: You're doing pretty well for a firstborn, but you can do better.

10–20 Points: Everyone plays one or two of these games.

0 Points: Either you're from another planet, or you're not telling the truth!

Remember my sister, Sally? Well, I will never forget the time I had just bought a new boat. It wasn't a yacht or a cabin cruiser, but it was a nice boat just the same, and I planned to use it to do a lot of fishing on Chautauqua Lake in upstate New York, where our summer cottage is located.

I was as proud as can be as I backed the boat into the water and then secured it to the dock. I was the excited little brother who couldn't wait to show my big sister what I'd bought.

I didn't have to wait too long before she arrived at the dock for a look at my new toy.

I didn't say a word but just beamed at her and waited for her comments on my beautiful new acquisition.

But as she looked into the boat, the first word out of her mouth was "Footprints."

"Footprints?" What was she talking about? I looked down into the boat and, yes, sure enough, there were footprints on the maroon rug. In getting the boat into the water I had apparently gotten some mud on my big tennis shoes, and then I had stepped onto one of the seat cushions.

"Yes, Sally," I said, in my best impression of Mr. Rogers. "Those are footprints. Can you say, 'footprints'?" And then I bent down and swept them away with my hand.

We both had a good laugh about it, because we both knew that it was her tendency, as a perfectionist firstborn, to pick out the flaw in any situation.

What about you? Are you afraid to step out of the house without your makeup done to perfection? Do you stand in front of the mirror knotting and reknotting your tie until you get it just right? Are you your own worst critic and harshest judge?

Do you get down on yourself when you fail and tell yourself you'll never amount to anything? If so, it might surprise you to know that some of the most influential people in history were considered failures at some point in their lives.

Dr. Adderholdt-Elliott mentions five famous people who didn't get straight A's[3]:

Charles Darwin, who did not do well in school as a child and failed a university medical course

Albert Einstein, who performed badly in almost all of his high school courses and flunked his college entrance exams

Sir Winston Churchill, who was at the bottom of his class in one school and failed the entrance exam to another

Pablo Picasso, who was barely able to read or write at the age

of 10 when his father yanked him out of school; a tutor who
was hired to instruct him gave up and quit in disgust

Paul Ehrlich, the winner of the 1908 Nobel Prize for medicine, who was a poor student who hated exams and could not
give oral presentations or write compositions

What does all of this mean to you and me? It means that we
are in some mighty good company when we miss the mark every
now and again. It also means that one or two failures don't
bring the end of the world, nor do they signify that we aren't
capable of going on to do great things.

What if Louis Pasteur had decided, because he wasn't the top
student in his chemistry class, that he just wasn't cut out for this
science business and opted for another career?

And, perhaps the most frightening of all, what if Beethoven's
teacher, who called him a "hopeless dunce,"[4] had been able to
convince him of his own worthlessness, to the point where the
great musical genius never composed a note? What a terrible
loss that would have been!

Every human being who has ever tried to do anything at all
has failed at one time or another. I don't care how intelligent, or
how talented, or how fortunate you are; the only way to avoid
failure is to sit in a corner and do nothing.

And once failure comes your way, it's up to you what you
make of it. You can count it as an enemy and let it defeat you
and hold you back, or you can see it as a teacher.

"Yes, I see now where I went wrong this time, but now that I
have a better understanding of the situation, I won't make the
same mistake next time."

Failure can be the best teacher in the world, but only if you do
your best to look at it in a detached, objective way. To throw up
your hands and say "I knew this was going to happen! It always
happens to me!" doesn't do you one bit of good. But to look
closely at the factors that caused the failure to come about—
that is the way you will learn and improve.

Another thing: You are under no obligation to believe or even
listen to those who condemn you. The firstborn has been so busy

for most of his life living up to everyone else's standards that he's probably never stopped to figure out exactly what he really wants out of life. He's been living up to his parents' expectations, his teachers' expectations, and so on—and pretty soon he's trying to live up to everyone's expectations. And that means that he tends to believe what anyone else says about him.

"He said I'm a terrible writer. It must be true, so I suppose I'll have to give it up."

"She said I'm the world's worst actress. Too bad, because I've always loved the theater, but, well . . . no sense hanging around and making a fool of myself."

"She said I'll never learn to play the piano, and I'm sure she's right. I'm just not cut out for a career in music."

Who says you have to listen to the naysayers? You're not living your life to please them. Besides that, who knows what their motives really are?

Are you making unreasonable demands on yourself? You may remember that I talked earlier about lowering the high-jump bar of life. What about it? Are you trying to clear the bar at seven feet before you've gone over it at four? If so, there are several concrete things you can do to help yourself:

1. See your setbacks as learning experiences.
2. Learn to strive for excellence instead of perfection.
3. Take a realistic look at yourself.
4. Learn to live in the real world.
5. Face up to your fears.
6. Take responsibility for your actions.

Let's take these six steps one at a time.

See Your Setbacks as Learning Experiences

It was Bill Veeck, the late owner of the Chicago White Sox, who first made the statement "Winning isn't the most important thing—winning is the only thing."[5] His words have been picked up, repeated, and paraphrased again and again, most notably by the late great football coach Vince Lombardi.

I'm sure you've heard them before. But my question to you is this: Do you believe that winning is the only thing?

"Who, me? Oh, come on, Dr. Leman. Who do you think I am? I know that winning isn't everything!"

Well . . . okay . . . I'm sure you know it, at least on the surface. But do you really know it, deep down inside, where it counts?

How do you really feel when the neighbor slaughters you in a game of Trivial Pursuit? What was your reaction when the guy from the office humiliated you in a game of racquetball?

And here's a tough question for all you married men out there. How do you handle it when your wife gets the better of you—whether it's Monopoly, tennis, bowling, or Trivial Pursuit? (I have to say that if you're like most men, it is hard for you to accept defeat in anything at the hands of your wife. Whatever the reason, we husbands have to work at being gracious and smiling when our wives clobber us in some game or other!)

Now, if we were all to be totally open and honest with one another, we'd have to admit that none of us cares very much to lose. (Anyone who likes to lose is really in need of some therapy!) And it's also quite natural that it's harder to lose to some people than it is to lose to others. If the guy across the street is a braggart and a show-off, it's going to be tough when he outdoes you on the golf course. But if he's a gracious, good-natured fellow, defeat is going to go down a lot easier—although it will still be disappointing.

But if your disappointment doesn't disappear after a few minutes, or if losing makes your blood boil to the point where you want to put your fist through the nearest wall, you need to work on changing your attitude.

I'm not talking merely about games, but about losing in every area of life: when you think you should get the promotion and it goes to someone else, when you've worked day and night for two weeks on a report and the boss decides it's not good enough to show the client, or when you've been cooking all day for an important dinner party and nothing turns out the way you wanted it to be.

These are situations most of us have faced at one time or another, and they can cause anyone anger and frustration. But if you're a perfectionist firstborn, they can drive you completely up and over the nearest wall!

How do you deal with these situations?

First of all, it's helpful to look back over the times you have lost or failed and see what you can learn from them. It could be that you fell short because you took on more than you could reasonably expect yourself to handle. Or it could be that you honestly didn't try hard enough or were held back by your own fears. Perhaps you didn't prepare properly to tackle the task at hand. If, after an honest assessment of the situation, you can identify one of these as cause of your failure, you will at least have a better idea of how to approach the situation the next time it comes along.

However, your review of the situation could show that the fault was not yours at all. Did your boss really give you enough time to prepare adequately? Did he give you the wrong information, but now, instead of facing up to his own failure, he's insisting on blaming you? Could it be that your skills lie in one area but your boss is asking you to perform in another?

If any of the above are true, it won't make the failure any less real or frustrating, but it should be helpful to know that there is no innate problem that renders you incapable of attaining success.

Every human being has particular strengths and particular weaknesses, and you are not doing yourself any favors if you are concentrating on your weaknesses and overlooking your strengths.

In their book *When Smart People Fail* Carole Hyatt and Linda Gottlieb talk about the fact that failure has many lessons to teach us. Failure can teach us compassion and humility, it can help us reconsider and reorder our priorities, and in some instances tasting failure shows us that failing isn't really so bad after all. When that happens, it makes us bolder, less afraid of failing again. If you're not afraid of failing, you're not afraid of taking risks, and nobody has ever done anything great without sticking his neck out a bit.

Hyatt and Gottlieb also say that those who fail need to remind themselves that they have the power to

- "figure out what went wrong and to correct it."
- "reinterpret what happened to you and put in the most enabling scenario possible."
- "declare yourself the judge of what you do."[6]

They also use these poignant words about what it means to fail—words I quoted in my book *Measuring Up*[7], but which I think are appropriate for inclusion here:

Failure is a judgment about an event.
It is a word used to define a stage.
It is not a condemnation of character.
It is not a permanent condition.
It is not a fatal flaw.
It is not a contagious social disease.
It is a judgment about an event.[8]

Most firstborns need to learn to go easy on themselves when they fail. Billy Joel had a hit song a few years ago called "You're Only Human." The song was written with teenagers in mind, with lyrics designed to help them cope with the pressures of modern American life. But every firstborn ought to listen carefully to these words:

You're only human, you're allowed to make
your share of mistakes.
You better believe there will be times in your life

When you'll be feeling like a stumbling fool.

So take it from me you'll learn more from your accidents

Than anything that you could ever learn at school.[9]

Good words and true words from Billy Joel. You can learn a great deal from your failures if only you'll let them teach you.

Billy Joel had another hit record with an excellent message, and that was "Just the Way You Are," in which he advises his lady not to change herself in an effort to please him because he thinks she's just terrific as she is. Are you among those who feel they're not good enough the way they are and so are always busy trying to be somebody else? You'd be surprised if you could see yourself through the eyes of others and find out how highly they think of you.

Learn to Strive for Excellence Instead of Perfection

Here's a good way to drive yourself totally bonkers: Don't settle for anything less than perfection in whatever you do.

If you sing in the choir, make sure that your voice is the clearest, purest, and loudest and that you have all the important solos.

If you're painting a picture, make sure it's at least on a par with anything Rembrandt ever did.

Bowling is your game? Never settle for anything less than a 300 game. Golf? How does shooting an 18 sound?

I know what you're thinking. "Oh, come off it! You're being ridiculous. All the solos? Rembrandt? A 300 game is a once-in-a-lifetime feat for the best of bowlers. And shooting 18 holes-in-one in a row? Nobody could ever do that."

But you see, that's perfection, and that's the sort of life many firstborns are expecting themselves to lead.

Now, I've seen a lot of excellent rounds of golf, but I've never seen one that was perfect. I've seen some beautiful paintings, but you can almost always find at least a tiny flaw if you look hard enough. And I know some people who are delightful, intelligent, artistic, and sensitive, but I've never known any who were perfect. In fact, in all of human history there's been only one man who was perfect. So why are you torturing yourself?

I have said it before, and I'll say it again: life is not a gymnastics meet. There are not five judges sitting out there waiting to hold up scorecards after everything you do. You do not have to run through life racking up a perfect "10" score in everything.

Neither are your mistakes written up in the daily newspaper, the way they would be if you were a professional baseball player or the president of the United States. The only one who is judging you is you.

What does it mean to strive for excellence instead of perfection? Is there really a difference, and if so, what is it? Well, I believe there are at least eight differences between pursuing excellence, which is within reach, and chasing after perfection, which is definitely out of reach:

1. The person who is chasing perfection reaches for impossible goals, while the pursuer of excellence enjoys meeting high standards that are within his reach.
2. The perfectionist bases his value of himself on his accomplishments. The person who pursues excellence values himself simply because of who he is.
3. The perfectionist is easily crushed by disappointment and is prone to throwing up his hands in surrender. The person who is seeking excellence may also be disappointed and hurt, but he does not let his setbacks keep him from moving toward his goal.
4. The perfectionist sees failure as his enemy and lets it devastate him, while the pursuer of excellence seeks to learn from past mistakes so that he will be able to do better in the future.
5. The perfectionist is the type of person who tends to remember his mistakes and dwell on them. He thinks everyone else

remembers them, too. The person who is seeking excellence will do his best to correct his mistakes and learn from them, and then he will forget they ever occurred.

6. The perfectionist wants to be number one in everything and is happy only at the top. The pursuer of excellence is happy with himself as long as he knows he has tried as hard as he can.

7. The perfectionist hates criticism and will go out of his way to avoid it. The person seeking excellence may not always enjoy hearing criticism, but he will welcome it in the sense that it will help him improve himself.

8. The perfectionist believes that winning is extremely important and has to win to maintain a healthy self-esteem. On the other hand, the pursuer of excellence can finish second and maintain his healthy self-image.

The perfectionist often has the feeling that if he can't be perfect, he won't even try. The pursuer of excellence is a risk-taker, who says, "Well, I may not do this well, but I'm going to give it a shot." The pursuer of excellence is the person who is constantly getting better, constantly growing, and always enjoying life. The perfectionist is missing out on a great deal that life has to offer!

Take a Realistic Look at Yourself

Have you ever seen the TV show *The Dating Game?*

I don't know what you think about it, but it always made me shudder. It was one of those shows I'd come across when I was flipping channels looking for something educational, and I'd have to stand there for a couple of minutes and watch it. It was like coming across a bad accident on the freeway. You don't want to look, but you have a morbid curiosity, and you just can't help rubbernecking. Let's just let it pass by saying that it's not the most elegant moment on television.

But have you ever seen this scene?

"Bachelor number three, rate yourself from one to ten."

"Oh, I'm probably a nine . . . maybe a nine-and-a-half . . . yeah, or a nine-and-three-quarters. . . ." On and on he goes about how good-looking and appealing he is, and he's some puny little guy who looks like a rooster with acne!

And, of course, the "bachelorettes" invariably describe themselves as eights, nines, and tens, which a lot of the time makes you think they bought their mirrors from a carnival funhouse!

Wouldn't it be great to be so self-assured and confident?

On the other end of the spectrum, a few years ago there was a movie made called *Revenge of the Nerds.* It wasn't the funniest film ever made, didn't have much of a plot, and certainly wasn't a favorite of any critic. But it was enormously successful, earning millions of dollars at the box office.

Why was the film so successful? Primarily, I believe, because it banked, and correctly, on the notion that millions of Americans would welcome a chance to see the "nerds" win out over the "beautiful people." And this, of course, is true because we would equate ourselves with the nerds. Seeing them win one would be like seeing ourselves win one.

So which is it? Are we all "tens" or are we all "nerds"? The truth of the matter is that most people are somewhere in between. We are simply "average." We aren't all Christie Brinkleys and Tom Sellecks, but neither are we Alfred E. Newmans and Olive Oyls.

Self-image is a particular problem for firstborns because they are always being asked to be the best. The firstborn who knows she is not as attractive as her younger sister will exaggerate her own flaws and imperfections. The oldest boy who knows his younger brother is better than he is at football will come to see himself as a no-talent klutz.

I believe that most of us are basically unsure of ourselves and lacking in self-esteem, even if we do go around telling other people that we are "nines" and "tens." And the problem is compounded by the advertising messages that bombard us day after day. I'm still waiting for the day when a woman with zits on her face is selling some product on TV!

We are told there is no way we can be whole persons without using this brand of mouthwash, that brand of toothpaste, and the other kind of shampoo.

As I'm writing this, a certain automobile manufacturer has been running commercials showing a group of people—I suppose they're supposed to be design engineers—sitting around talking about all of the work that goes into a certain type of car.

During the course of their conversation one of the men says, "Well, you are what you drive." All of the rest of the men and women nod their heads in agreement. The message is, of course, that unless you're driving one of their company's cars, people are probably talking about you behind your back, laughing and pointing and slapping themselves on the back for being so superior to you.

Nonsense!

You're not what you drive, what you wear, what fabric softener you use, or any other such nonsense.

I've always gotten a perverse sort of kick out of the old commercial where the beautiful young woman is hoping against hope that the new guy in the office will notice her. And of course, we know right off the bat that if the man is alive and breathing, he's got to notice her. She has a beautiful smile, a perfect figure, and soft, silky hair.

When the young woman comes over to put some papers on his desk, the man looks at her approvingly, and we can't help feeling that romance is in the air. But then, all of a sudden, his smile turns into a frown. And why? Because this gorgeous creature has—ugh!—DANDRUFF!

That's right, dandruff! And no man in his right mind would want to be seen with a beautiful woman who has *dandruff.*

Can you picture this man and woman out on a date? They walk into a fancy restaurant, and all eyes turn their way. Immediately people begin whispering to each other, saying things like "What in the world is he doing with her? I mean, just look at all that dandruff!"

Yes, it is so ridiculous it's laughable. But millions of people, even though they may laugh at the absurdity of the commercial, still believe, deep down, in the message it's putting forth. We are all susceptible to the notion that our self-worth hinges on the products we use, but the firstborn, who wants so very much to be the best in everything he does, particularly falls victim to such preaching. And there are many other commercials that get this sinister message across in a much more subtle and believable way. And we spend our lives believing it.

I remember reading a few years ago about a restaurant in Florida that went out of business because its prices were too low. That's right—too low. I don't know exactly what the place was charging, but it was somewhere around $1.99 for a full dinner. The owner of the restaurant was quoted as saying he just wanted to give people a break and that he could give them a quality dinner for a low price and still make enough of a profit to keep his restaurant going. But nobody wanted to eat there, because they didn't want to be perceived as cheap! Besides that, we've been taught by advertisers that more expensive is better.

"Sure it costs more. But I'm worth it!"

It ain't necessarily so.

Let me make it clear that I'm not against advertising—just advertising that plays on people's fears, insecurities, and the belief that they're worth nothing if they're not perfect.

Many of us come to believe that we are worth something only when we are noticed, when we can be in control of the situation, or when we can look down on others because the products we're using are more expensive or more effective. The truth is that you don't have to be doing anything in particular, buying any special product or acting in a certain way, to have worth as a human being. You have worth because of who you are—a human being created in the image of God!

And that's the main thing you need to know about yourself.

God created you, He loves you, and as the old poster says, "He don't make no junk."

Do you tell yourself that you never do anything right or that nothing ever goes for you the way it should? That other people are better than you at just about anything? If so, it's time you stopped telling yourself lies. And that's what they are—lies.

When you tell yourself lies like these, you're picking apart your self-esteem and holding yourself back. And you may begin living your life in accordance with the lies you tell yourself.

Have you ever, for instance, tried hard to fit in with a group because you thought it would enhance your image, although deep down inside you knew you had no interest in the group at all? Have you pretended to be happy and cheerful because you thought that's what people wanted you to be, even when you really felt like crying?

We've all done that sort of thing at one time or another, but some people live their lives that way. They can never be simply what they want to be, because they're so busy being what everyone else wants them to be.

Ask a firstborn what he wants to do with his life, and he'll tell you, in no uncertain terms. But ask him why he made that choice, and suddenly he won't be so sure of himself. It may be because his father wanted him to be a lawyer. Or perhaps his mother always wanted him to be a doctor. The firstborn who is doing what he wants to do with his life, living the way he wants to live, and making his own decisions is relatively rare.

Oh, Mom and Dad may be long gone. It could be that they died 20 or 30 years ago, but the noble firstborn is still living his life for them, carrying on the dream. It's noble. But it's also sad. Especially if the dreams Mom and Dad dreamed for him were never the sort of dreams he would have chosen for himself.

Taking a realistic look at yourself involves discovering who you really are—finding the skills and strengths God gave you instead of the skills and strengths other people want you to have.

What are your skills and strengths? To find out, get out a pen and paper and take stock of yourself. Ask yourself the following questions.

1. What do I really enjoy doing?
2. When do other people compliment me?
3. What subjects did I do well in in school?
4. What comes easy for me?
5. What is hard for me?
6. If I could change my life in any way, what would I do differently?

Ask yourself any similar questions you can think of and be as honest with yourself as you can be. If you are, you'll learn some things about yourself.

And once you have, the next thing to do is to act on them. Learn to speak up for yourself and say what's on your mind. Not in a brutal "I don't care what you think" way, but as calmly and forcefully as possible.

I'm not talking about giving in to a mid-life crisis here. That's something that many firstborns do, and we'll talk more about that in the next chapter. I will say, briefly, that the reason firstborns are so susceptible to "freaking out" in middle age is the fact that they spend so many years being what everyone else wants them to be. They reach 40 or 45 and suddenly think, "Hey, I've never done anything for myself." So you'll see a middle-aged dentist close his successful practice and run off to Wyoming to become a cowboy.

That can be sad and pathetic. But what has happened is an act of open rebellion. The dentist probably has no real desire to be a cowboy. It's just that he's rebelling against the way his life has always been and wants to do the wildest thing he can think of.

This is not the sort of behavior I'm suggesting. What I am suggesting is that you learn to be as honest as you can with yourself in all things, great and small, on a day-to-day basis.

If you continue to hide behind a mask and pretend to feel one way when you really don't, you're going to continue to suffer rejection. For instance, in my book *Measuring Up*, I told the story of a woman named Juanita, who was devastated because her coworkers always let her birthday go by without giving her so much as a card. Meanwhile the birthdays of all the other women in her office were met with flowers, luncheons, and general celebrations.

Juanita felt unappreciated and unloved. What she didn't realize was that she had always told the others in her office that she didn't celebrate birthdays and didn't want them to do anything for her. In fact, when she had first come to work in the office, she had seemed so opposed to celebrating her birthday that the others thought they were doing her a favor by letting it pass without notice.

How were they to know that all of her protestations weren't supposed to be taken seriously? Juanita thought it was unseemly to seem to want to be the center of attention while, at the same time, she needed desperately to be reminded that she was cared for by her coworkers.

In his book *How to Raise Your Self-Esteem,* Dr. Nathaniel Branden suggests that you can learn to be honest with yourself by using a technique of "sentence completion."[10]

For example, he suggests completing the sentence "I like myself least when I . . ." Add everything you can think of. Be as honest about it as you can possibly be and don't worry about hurting your feelings!

After you've done that, turn the question around and write, "I like myself most when I . . ." Again list everything you can think of. And then resolve that you are going to act in the ways that make you like yourself.

You do not have to be what anyone else expects or wants you to be. You have to be only who and what you really are!

Learn to Live in the
Real World

Just as you must learn to have a realistic view of yourself, you must also have a proper view of the world around you.

Before I say more, let me tell you that there is nothing at all wrong with fantasizing or daydreaming, as long as it doesn't control your life. On the contrary, a healthy imagination is good for you. But some people get themselves in trouble because they don't know where the fantasy leaves off and the reality begins.

There are several "unreal" worlds to which firstborns often escape, and I want to touch briefly on each of these:

1. Comparison World. This is a world in which they constantly compare themselves to others, who are always stronger, better-looking, more successful, richer, and so on.
2. Past World. This is always a most pleasant place to live, especially if you're always looking at it through those ever-popular rose-colored glasses!
3. I-Won't-Choose,-Don't-Ask-Me World. This is an interesting place, where people refuse to make choices that would benefit them.
4. I-Won't-Take-Yes-for-an-Answer World. This isn't a nice place to visit, and you certainly wouldn't want to live there! This is a world for people who insist on setting themselves up for failure.

Let's take a quick tour.

1. COMPARISON WORLD

When I was in high school, almost all of the boys wanted to be like Elvis Presley, while the girls—whether they admitted it or not—dreamed of being Marilyn Monroe.

It's a sad but interesting fact that both of these people we admired so much are long dead, and both of them died during what should have been the primes of their lives. They had it all —fame, fortune, and adulation—but it wasn't enough to make them happy.

I'll never forget that summer day, back in 1977, when I heard on my car radio that Elvis Presley had died. I was so shocked I had to pull over to the side of the road.

Now, you have to understand that I'm somewhat of a nut about fifties and sixties rock and roll. I have an old-fashioned Wurlitzer jukebox in my bedroom, and I keep that thing loaded with some of the best music ever recorded—Chuck Berry, Fats Domino, and, of course, Elvis. I'm the sort of person who likes to get an early start in the morning, and when I'm home I like to get the day started right, with some good-time rock and roll! (My wife, Sande, is not what you would call a morning person, and I suppose she'll never understand why anyone would want to start off the day with "Sweet Little Sixteen" or "Don't Be Cruel," but it's something my firstborn wife has learned to deal with over the years!)

So you see, when I heard that Elvis had died, it was as if a great part of my childhood, my young-manhood, had died, too. The king of rock and roll dead? Why? How? Could it really be true?

But later on I read about the way Elvis had died—how he had grown so heavy, at 258 pounds, that it took several men to carry his body out of his Graceland mansion. He had spent the last few years of his life locked away from the world, a virtual recluse from his millions of fans. When he went on tour, he couldn't remember the words of the songs that had made him rich. He was stumbling through a terrible "Twilight Zone" of existence, when he should have been living life to the fullest measure.

How many millions of us admired Elvis Presley? How many of us wanted to be like him? But looking back from this vantage point, how many of us, now, would exchange our lives for his?

Not very many, I daresay. Elvis Presley had it all, but "all" wasn't enough.

But maybe you don't compare yourself to Elvis Presley, or Michael Jackson, or any other superstar. Maybe you don't want to be Kathleen Turner or Meryl Streep. It could be that you're comparing yourself unfavorably with the woman across the street.

My, how that woman has got it together! Four beautiful children and a successful husband who seems to adore her! She dresses exquisitely, manages to keep herself slim and trim, and still finds time to be involved in the PTA and sing in the church choir. Why couldn't you be more like her?

And then there's the guy next door. Vice president of a bank and drives a brand-new BMW. Not only that, but he's the perennial champion of the neighborhood tennis tournament. If only you could be like him!

But you don't see the woman across the street when she cries in her bed late at night because she is so unfulfilled and feels trapped in a loveless marriage.

And you don't see the guy next door when he's popping Valium and chugging down gin and tonic to help ease his mind after another day of heart-stopping pressure on the job.

The firstborn who plays comparison games is always striving to better himself. He no sooner gets to one plateau than he sets his sights on another. He is rarely able to stop and savor the sweet smell of success, because he sees someone—just ahead— who is more successful than he is, and he wants to catch up.

You're not doing yourself any favors by comparing yourself with others. Chances are there are millions of people who are better off in some ways than you are. They may be richer, better-looking, more successful, or more intelligent. There are also those millions who couldn't even begin to compete with you in those areas. But your job is to be the best you can be, to use the skills God has given you, and not to worry going around comparing yourself to others.

I said before that life is not a gymnastics meet, and neither is it a horse race.

If you want to daydream for a bit about being Michael Douglas or Jessica Lange, go ahead. It won't hurt. But don't compare your life with the one you think they're living. You are much better off living the life God gave you.

You never know, either, what success might do to you.

This was brought home to me when I was in New York to appear on *The Morning Show* with Regis Philbin and Kathie Lee Gifford. Also appearing on the show were Donald O'Connor and a well-known TV actress who, for obvious reasons, shall remain nameless. Sitting in the green room prior to the start of the program, I struck up a conversation with O'Connor. What a delightful gentleman! I had a hard time believing that this show business giant could be such a regular guy as we sat talking and drinking coffee out of our Styrofoam cups.

As for the actress, she didn't seem to want anything to do with the rest of us. She had demanded—and received—her own dressing room. She was surrounded by her entourage of gofers, and if I hadn't known better I would have suspected that we were in the presence of royalty! I came away from my appearance on that show with two very definite thoughts:

1. This world could use more people like Donald O'Connor.
2. Miss Actress might be better off with a little less success.

Yes, I always thought the life Elvis Presley was living must be a dream. Instead, it must have been a nightmare!

2. PAST WORLD

Living in the past is dangerous for two reasons: First, it can be full of exaggerated pleasant memories that shut out the reality of the present. Second, it can be full of exaggerated unpleasant memories that can keep you from pushing ahead and succeeding in the here and now.

Have you ever witnessed an automobile accident? Well, I

have, and let me tell you that what they say is true. You talk to four different people who saw the same accident, and you're going to get four totally different stories. That's because people's perceptions are different. They think they see things that weren't really there, and they miss out on things that actually happened.

A friend of mine teaches journalism at a university, and he occasionally asks a friend to come in and disrupt the class on some pretext or other in order to get the students to learn to notice what is going on. Once the "intruder" has left the class and order has been restored, the professor asks his students to take out pen and paper and describe what has just happened.

They are to give a brief description of what happened, who the man was, what he looked like, and so on.

He tells me that he is always amused by the responses he gets. Some students don't have the first clue about what the man looked like or what he wanted. Others have the event completely exaggerated and off the mark. There are always a few, he says, who give a pretty good description of things, but not too many.

What does that have to do with living in the past? Simply this: Whatever your picture of the past is, chances are that it's not altogether accurate.

Some people look back and believe the old days were better and that whatever happens now isn't as good as what happened yesterday.

It doesn't matter what it is—music, movies, books, government, fashion—it's just not as good as it used to be. Obviously having a distorted view of the past, in which it was so much better than life today, is not healthy.

I don't think there's anything wrong with nostalgia. I mentioned before that I have a jukebox full of fifties and sixties records, and I love the music of that era. But I also remember things like the day *Sputnik* went up, McCarthyism, and segregation. I know that every era has both good and bad aspects. So does every era in your personal life.

Now, it is true enough that there are some discouraged perfectionist firstborns who live in the past because they remember everything as having been dreamy and wonderful back then. But more often they tend to let the past hold them back because they stumbled and failed somewhere back then, and they don't want it to happen to them again.

"Who, me write this report? No, listen, I'm sorry, I tried to write a report back in '84, and I just couldn't do it. I'm sure I'd make a mess of it."

"What? Learn to use a computer? Hey, I tried once about ten years ago, and I couldn't get the hang of it. I just can't."

In this way past failure becomes a crutch—something to lean on so that you don't have to take any risks right now.

But you can't live your life that way, living in the past and letting it hold you back.

You've heard it said that if you're learning to ride a horse, and you fall off, the best thing to do is to get right back in the saddle. It's true. You have to learn from your mistakes and let them help you improve.

You can't forget about the past, because if you do, you're likely to make the same mistakes you made back then. But neither can you live in the past and let it keep you from enjoying the present or moving on to an even better future.

3. I-WON'T-CHOOSE,-DON'T-ASK-ME WORLD

I mentioned in the first chapter that the firstborn who is a discouraged perfectionist will often have trouble making his own decisions. That's because he's so used to living his life the way everyone else wants him to.

If you want to see a guy like that squirm, just take him to a restaurant that has a menu several pages long. Or take him to one of those multiplex theaters and ask him to decide which movie he wants to see.

"Oh, I don't know. What do you want to see?"

"It doesn't matter to me. You decide."

"But I don't know what to see. What sounds good to you?"

If you're dealing with a real live pleaser here, a person who seeks to please others in everything he does, you could be in for a long evening. You'll be standing outside the theater all evening playing the "You decide," "No you decide" game.

I know that we live in an imperfect world, and I believe this is because sin has corrupted things. The world is not what God intended it to be, and that means that innocent people sometimes suffer. Bad things may come your way for no apparent reason, and I've counseled hundreds of people who have had more than their share of misfortune.

I'm saying this because I hope you won't misunderstand what I'm about to say and think that I don't sympathize. But the truth is that many of the misfortunes that come our way are the direct result of our refusal to make the choice that would have benefited us.

Suppose you're driving down the road and your car starts making a funny noise. What are you going to do about it? You could just turn the radio up so you won't hear it anymore. Or you can get to a garage and have the mechanic take a look at it. Obviously the latter choice is the only sensible one. The discouraged perfectionist in you would choose to ignore the problem and allow it to worsen.

Billie's life is miserable because her husband is an alcoholic who can't hold a job and who is physically abusive. Poor, poor Billie. But she knew before she married him that David liked to drink. He even hit her once or twice before they were married, but she never dreamed being married to him would turn out like this. You see, Billie was faced with a choice to make, and she refused to make it. She should have seen it coming a mile away. David was a drinker and abusive, and she should have made the choice to tell him good-bye, but she didn't.

Incidentally, the seeds for Billie's life-style were planted early in her life by an abusive father who eventually walked out the door and abandoned his family when Billie was still in grade school.

And then there's Marshall, who sits and cries and wonders why Theresa could have left him. He would have done anything, if only he had known what she wanted. The truth, though, was that she had been trying to tell him for years what she wanted, but he was always too busy to listen. He never wanted to talk now because "it just isn't a very good time, so we'll talk about it later, okay?" Only he never found a good time to talk to her, and her impatience and exasperation over his inattention and unwillingness to change finally exploded in his face. He could have made the choice that would have saved his marriage, but he refused to do it.

Life is constantly throwing situations at you that you can change by making the proper choice. If you refuse to make it, then look out!

Nathaniel Branden lists several ways you can begin making proper choices:[11]

• Thinking, even when thinking about something may be difficult

• Making every effort to see things clearly, whether or not this comes naturally or easily

• Having respect for reality, whether or not it's painful, as opposed to a desire to avoid reality

• Being willing to take appropriate risks, even when you are afraid

• Dealing honestly with yourself

• Living in and being responsible to the present, rather than retreating into a fantasy world

• Being willing to see and correct your mistakes, rather than continuing in error

So, if you've been behaving like an ostrich, with your head buried in the sand, make the choice right now to change and face up to the decisions life is calling you to make!

4. I-WON'T-TAKE-YES-FOR-
AN-ANSWER WORLD

Some people live in a fantasy world of anticipated failure and rejection, so they put a negative spin on everything they do.

They even set themselves up for failure. Here's Derek the Discouraged, asking the beautiful Mary Lou for a date:

"Oh, excuse me for calling, Mary Lou. I mean, I know you have more important things to do than to talk with me. And I figured you'd already have a date for Saturday night, so . . . well, I know you wouldn't want to go out with me. Would you?"

Hey, what is Mary Lou going to say in response to an invitation like that? Is she going to admit that, no, she doesn't really have a date or that you're not wasting her time? And why should she say yes and be subjected to an evening of "Oh, poor me, I'm really surprised you'd go out with a bum like me"?

Derek needed to say, "Hi, Mary Lou, I was wondering if you'd like to go out for dinner and a movie Saturday night?" and let it go at that. There was no need for him to throw in all the negatives.

If Mary Lou wanted to say no, she could have done it without any prodding from him. But she just might have surprised him and said yes.

In other words, don't set yourself up for rejection. Keep a close watch on the things you say. Every time you hear yourself saying something negative about yourself, try to stop it. If you've caught yourself in time, try to recast the statement and put it in a more positive way. And then, each evening, spend some time going back over your day and seeing how many times you used words that put a negative shadow over what you wanted to do or say. Make a resolution to improve in this area and cut back on the number of times you use words such as *can't, won't,* and *wouldn't.* If you are constantly putting yourself down, whether consciously or unconsciously, people will come to believe you deserve it. After all, nobody knows you better than you do, and if you have a low opinion of yourself, why should anyone else disagree?

If you change your behavior, you'll still get a "no" answer once in a while, but you'll be getting a lot more "yes" answers than you used to.

A fifth way to lower the high-jump bar of life is:

Face Up to Your Fears

We are all afraid of something.

I don't care if you're a carbon copy of Rambo or fancy yourself to be tougher than Clint Eastwood; there are still things that cause your pulse to quicken and the hair on the back of your neck to stand up.

There are snakes, spiders, bugs of all types, flying, speaking in public—and I could probably go on for another 50 pages just listing all the things that scare people.

It could be that you're afraid of the dark, while someone else is terrified at the thought of speaking in front of a large group of people. You could spend hours agonizing over the threat of nuclear war, whereas someone else worries incessantly about the possibility of the stock market crashing.

Your fears are not the same as my fears, and my fears are not the same as someone else's—but they are just as real.

Some people deny that they are afraid, but they do it to their own detriment. You can't overcome your fears unless you face up to them and, in a sense, learn to accept them.

You can even begin to analyze your fears and see that being afraid does not mean there's anything wrong with you:

"I'm afraid because it's dark in here and I can't see. Not being able to see makes me feel insecure—and that's why I feel afraid."

Or "I feel afraid because I'm going to have to give a speech in front of the entire class. I'm not really accustomed to public speaking, so it's only normal that I would feel apprehensive."

Then take it a step further and ask yourself what would be the worst possible thing that could happen to you in a particular situation.

"Well, I know there aren't really any robbers or monsters with me in this darkened room. I guess I could stub my toe or bump my head on something—but that wouldn't kill me."

Or "I could forget my speech or say something stupid that would cause everyone to laugh at me. But I suppose that wouldn't be the end of the world."

If you can analyze your fears in this way, you have taken the first step toward conquering them.

"Yes, that's a snake, and I've always been afraid of snakes. But what could this snake do to me? I know it's not poisonous, and it's every bit as afraid of me as I am afraid of it," and so on. I know I've been speaking about fears that are relatively easy to overcome, but the principle is the same no matter what your fears are or how deep-seated they are.

Perhaps you can even begin to make light of your fears, such as starting off a speech with a joke about having to shout to make yourself heard above the knocking together of your knees!

Learn to admit that you are afraid, but show that you can laugh about it and go on with what you have to do in spite of it.

If you're telling yourself that it's wrong to be afraid and that you have no right to be fearful, then you're setting your high-jump bar too high. Fear is a natural part of human existence. Just don't let it paralyze you or make you feel bad about yourself. If you find that your fears really are getting the best of you, it's time to seek therapy. A lot of good can come from working out phobias with a doctor.

Take Responsibility for Your Actions

You take responsibility for your actions in two ways:

1. By realizing that you, and you alone, are responsible for what you do
2. By realizing that you are not responsible for what anyone else says or does

Firstborns have problems in both of these areas.

First of all, as we've discussed, firstborns tend to live their lives in ways that are designed to make other people happy. If Pater wants you to go to his exclusive Ivy League school, well, you certainly don't want to let him down. If Mater wants her daughter to be Miss Beauty Pageant Queen forever, well, you'd better keep those teeth bright and shiny, practice your smile, and keep plugging away with the voice lessons.

But it ultimately comes down to the fact that they aren't responsible for your life—YOU ARE—and you must take control of it.

I'm not advocating that you give everyone around you a kick in the pants and tell them to stay out of your life. We all want to see our relatives and friends happy, so we sometimes do things that we might not want to do in order to please them. But you can't let anyone control you.

You simply are not responsible for the happiness of other people. You can do your best to be sensitive to the needs and desires of others, but you have to remember that some people will not be happy no matter how much you do for them. They will always ask you for more, more, more, and when you give it to them they'll become even more demanding.

The reverse is true, too, in that nobody else is responsible for your happiness and well-being. You can love your husband, but you can't depend on him to make you happy. You can love your children, but if you're depending on them to make you happy, you're being unfair. You can't go through your life taking the blame for everything, and neither can you go through life assigning blame for everything. You must take control!

When it comes to feeling responsible for what other people say or do, firstborns are masters. Perhaps it's because they are taught so early in life that they are role models. Others are always watching them, patterning their lives after them, and so, by George, you had better well toe that old line for all it's worth!

If your husband has had a bad day at work and comes home in a bad mood, it's not your fault. You can sympathize, ask him if you can give him a back rub or something, but you must not let him pin the blame for his bad mood on your shoulders!

If he comes through the front door like a bear, growling and yelling at you about anything and everything, you can tell him that you're sorry he had a bad day and you'll do whatever you can to help him feel better, but that you're not about to let him turn you into a scapegoat because his sales are down or his boss yelled at him. Stand up, be tough, and don't yield!

If your next-door neighbor wants you to baby-sit for her while she runs out to the store, but you're tied up and can't do it, it's not your fault. If she becomes angry, that's too bad, but don't let it make you feel guilty.

Children are especially adept at making their parents feel guilty.

"I just know I'm going to flunk my math test tomorrow. I don't understand this stuff, and nobody will help me!"

"Oh, don't you worry, Schnooky, Mommy will help you. We'll work until midnight tonight if we have to, and I'll get you ready for that old test!"

Never mind that little Schnooky has had two weeks to prepare for the test and could have told you or the teacher several days ago if he was having trouble with the subject. Whose fault is it that he may flunk? It's certainly not yours. As a matter of fact, it's his fault! But when he says that there's nobody to help him, he makes you feel guilty, so you'll sit down there and spend hours working with him—time you really need to spend doing something else.

My advice would be to go ahead and let him flunk the test. Then next time he'll be quicker to ask questions when he's having difficulty understanding something.

You are not responsible for his bad grade, and neither are you responsible for the troubles of your coworkers. Having a compassionate heart is wonderful, but the truth is that there are people who are simply "emotional leeches," and if you let them, they will latch on to you for everything you're worth. They'll sap the strength out of you.

Suppose you have a coworker whose personal life is always in an uproar. Not only is he always unloading his emotional stories on you, but he's falling behind on the job and calling on you to help him get caught up. He has the sort of touch that makes you feel guilty and responsible for his problems, even though you really have nothing to do with them.

What are you going to do? Get tough and tell him that you just can't pick up the slack for him and do your own job too.

He may become angry, or he may increase the amount of time whining and complaining, but that's not your problem. You are not responsible, and you must not allow yourself to be taken advantage of in that way!

It might help to make a list of the things for which you are responsible and another list of things for which you are not responsible.

I AM RESPONSIBLE FOR:	I AM NOT RESPONSIBLE FOR:
The relationships I enter into	My spouse's bad mood
The way I spend my time	The rain that spoiled my children's plans for the day
The way I treat my body	The fact that my neighbor's regular baby-sitter is unavailable
What I put into my mind (books read, movies seen, etc.)	The unexpected traffic jam that made me late for an appointment
The way I treat other people	The way others treat me
My own happiness	Anyone else's happiness

Once again, I would never advocate that you live your life in total disregard of other people's wishes and desires. Nor would I suggest that you turn your back on people when they are in need. But there is a great deal of difference between offering a helping hand and feeling responsible for their problems.

Life is unfair and contains trouble in the way of accidents, diseases, and romantic problems that you have done nothing at all to bring about. But if you take responsibility for your life, you are improving your chances to be happy.

So lower that high-jump bar of life. Learn to see your failures as learning experiences, learn to strive for excellence instead of perfection, take a realistic look at yourself, learn to live in the real world, face up to your fears, and take responsibility for your actions.

It's time you quit sabotaging your own efforts. You'll never attain perfection, but neither will anyone else. Learn to settle for excellence, and your life will be transformed! You'll be clearing that high-jump bar in no time!

6

The Firstborn Enters Middle Age

Her name is Sharon, and she's a 36-year-old wife and mother of three children. She is petite and trim, an obvious firstborn in her tweed suit, black pumps, and tasteful earrings. She looks younger than she really is, except for the lines around her eyes—lines that reveal that she likes to smile.

But she's not smiling now.

She's torn between her mind and her heart, and right now her heart is winning.

"Am I being ridiculous, Dr. Leman?" she asks.

"What do you think?"

"Well, I think it *sounds* kind of crazy."

Sharon is right. It does sound crazy. She's ready to give up her husband of 15 years, who loves her very much, and her three children for an 18-year-old boy she's known for three months.

"I've always been in complete control of my life," she says. "I've always been happy—you know, not delirious, but I've never had any major complaints either. It's just that I didn't know how boring my life had become—until Rick came along."

Sharon's case may be a bit unusual in that it's not often you'll find a 36-year-old woman falling for a boy half her age. But it is fairly typical, in that the firstborn is much more susceptible than other members of the family constellation to suffering a mid-life crisis.

He's always been the strong one who set the example for everyone else. Then one morning, along about his fortieth birthday, he gets out of bed and thinks, "Life has passed me by. I've been so busy being what everyone else wanted me to be that I've never taken the time to find out what I really want out of life."

Sometimes the firstborn reacts by going out and trading in his sedate and functional station wagon for a souped-up sports car.

Other times he'll quit the job he's held for 20 years and decide to do something totally different.

And sometimes, just as Sharon did, he will decide that he's tired of being a faithful spouse and parent. Where is the excitement in that? He's tried so hard, and where has it got him? Nowhere. Then he'll look around and see someone who seems much more exciting than his wife. Why, maybe that's what he's missing! Someone younger, someone more exciting, someone who can really make him happy.

He doesn't realize, of course, that he would merely be exchanging one set of problems and disappointments for another.

In Sharon's case, she says, "It just happened to me before I even realized what was going on. When I first met Rick, I found him so easy to talk to. You know, he's much more mature than most people his age.

"And then . . . well, one thing led to another. And I don't think, now, that I would ever be happy without him in my life."

Sharon is fortunate in that her husband knows about her love affair, and yet he's willing to try to work things out. He's gone as far as quitting his job and taking another one in a town more than 200 miles away, taking his family along with him. He thought that if he could just get Sharon away from the young man, she would soon be over her infatuation and things would get back to normal.

But so far it hasn't worked. And now Sharon is thinking seriously about packing her bags and taking off to build a new life with her lover.

"Sure, I love my boys," she says. "But I love Rick even more."

How does a responsible, seemingly mature woman find herself in a situation like this?

"I'm just so tired," Sharon says, "of being the one everyone leans on. As long as I can remember, I've always been the pillar, the one who had to hold everything together.

"Oh, I don't think I ever minded all that much. I mean, I figured it was what I was supposed to do—and as long as it made everyone happy . . ."

What's Sharon's husband like? She freely admits that he's "a great guy. He's a terrific father, a good provider—and he's good-looking too." And yet all of that does not seem to be enough for a firstborn who is fed up with her role in life and wants to be what she has never been—and, in all likelihood, could never be.

What did Sharon decide to do? Unfortunately she has not yet made up her mind.

I told her that giving up her devoted husband and children and running off with an 18-year-old boy would be a mistake of colossal proportions. Under normal circumstances her firstborn nature would have convinced her that I was right. She would have been capable of reasoning with her head instead of her heart.

But when a firstborn goes into a state of rebellion, there's no telling what will happen—especially because he is rebelling against his very nature, which is to do the right and proper thing and to think of everyone else involved.

Throughout my years of counseling I've talked to a number of other "Sharons." Not all of them were involved in extramarital relationships. Some just felt tied down and held back by their families and their responsibilities and wanted something more out of life.

I remember Mark, who told me, "I'm not sure if I've ever done one thing that I really wanted to do.

"Even as far as my marriage goes, Sarah and I had been going together for a while, and she started talking about marriage. I wasn't really sure if I was ready for marriage, but I wanted to make her happy, so I married her. Now here I am 20 years later, 40 years old, with three teenagers in the house, working at a job I have absolutely no interest in . . . I'm trapped. I feel so hopeless. It's like the life is being sucked right out of me."

I'm sure that Mark's view of things was distorted. He had undoubtedly wanted the marriage every bit as much as Sarah had. And I'm sure he was every bit as excited as she was when the children came along. But playing the role of "dependable old Mark" for all those years had taken its toll.

Mark was one of those who took my advice and found that he could have more freedom without ending his marriage. He really did love Sarah and their children, and he didn't need to sacrifice them just so he could "find" himself.

Adele was one of those who didn't follow my advice and left her husband of 12 years, Steven, simply because he was "boring."

In the 10 years since she left him Adele has been married and divorced three times, and she's currently engaged again. But when she shows off her new diamond, there's very little joy and excitement in her eyes.

Ask her if she's happy about her impending marriage, and she'll shrug her shoulders. "Yeah . . . sure . . ." But the way she says it lets you know she has to think about it, and even then she's not too sure!

"You know," she tells me now, "I've come to realize that I'll never find anyone else like Steven. He's really a very special man."

That's too bad for Adele, because Steven's second wife, Roberta, also knows that he's a special man, and she's not about to let him get away.

Not only does Adele keep in touch with Steven, but she has

asked him for advice regarding problems in relationships with her various husbands and boyfriends.

"What do you think I should do about Ralph?"

"Do you like Tony? Do you think I should marry him?"

And so on. She asks his advice now because she admires the qualities in him that once seemed boring. "He's so stable and so levelheaded," she says.

She realizes now that when she left Steven behind, she was behaving selfishly. But very often the firstborn sees things in black and white. You are either "selfish" or "selfless." And when he goes from selfless to selfish, he does it in a big way.

The one who runs away from it all usually finds out, sooner or later, that he has traded one set of relationship problems for another, one package of job-related troubles for another, and that trading financial security for "freedom" was hardly a fair exchange.

I am seeing increasing numbers of firstborn women who are dissatisfied with their marriages and their families and who simply want out. (And no wonder, gentlemen, if she was looking for a knight in shining armor who would take her away from all of life's troubles and wound up instead with a balding, potbellied version of Oscar the Grouch, who keeps the neighbors awake with his snoring!) While it is true that there are many men who feel trapped in an unpleasant home life, my clients include a far higher percentage of women who find themselves in this situation. Perhaps this is because the husband often finds fulfillment in his work or other outside activities, while his wife is still tied more closely to the home.

Now, I know that I've been making it sound as if the firstborns are always to blame in these situations, but that's not the case at all. It takes two people to make a marriage work, and it is true that the firstborn is most often the one who has tried the hardest. He's given and tried and worked at it to the point where he can't give, try, or work anymore, and he doesn't see his partner making the same sort of effort, so he just walks away.

And there are also the times when he is surprised because his spouse walks away from him.

One time in Tucson an elder from one of the city's largest and most evangelical churches called me.

"Listen . . . ah . . . Dr. Leman, I wonder if I might come in and have a talk with you. It's, uh . . . it's . . . about my wife. Me and her, seems like we're having a problem . . . oh, what would you say . . . uh, communicating."

I could tell that he was embarrassed about the situation. He was in his mid-fifties, had been married for more than 30 years, and never for a moment believed he'd be talking to a counselor about his marriage. I told him I would be glad to talk to him and his wife and scheduled an appointment for the following week.

The first session was dreadful. I could see that he really wanted to get to the root of the problem, but she just sat there and said no more than was absolutely necessary to answer the questions I asked. I saw them together, and I saw them separately, and she just wasn't talking. And then finally, in an individual session, she got tired of playing games.

"Would it help if I told you the truth?" she asked.

"Well, we could try that for a while and see how it works," I said.

"Okay. There's someone else."

"What do you mean, there's someone else?" This was one of the least likely people on the face of the earth to be having an affair, so I didn't even understand what she was telling me!

"I'm having an affair!"

As soon as I picked myself up off the floor, I asked her to tell me how it had happened.

It seemed that her husband (a firstborn, naturally) was so busy being Mr. Super-Christian that he never had any time left for her. She hadn't set out to meet someone else, but her husband was so consumed by his obligations to the church that she felt left out and neglected. Nearly every night there was some sort of meeting. If there wasn't, he was off visiting with members of the church who were in his pastoral care, seeing to their spiritual well-being.

He was running himself ragged trying to be Mr. Everything-to-Everybody, and he just couldn't do it all. In the process he had let his priorities become fouled up, and now he was paying the price.

This is not to excuse his wife's behavior, because there is never a legitimate reason for becoming involved in an adulterous relationship. But it shows how his wife came to the point where she was easily enticed into such a relationship.

Once I understood exactly what the situation was, it was easier to work with them on restoring their relationship. Note that I said "easier" and not "easy." It certainly wasn't easy, but it did help all of us to know what we were really dealing with.

She wasn't really in love with the other person. She was just lonely and feeling unloved herself. She needed someone to pay attention to her.

Once her husband could see his role in this, accept his share of responsibility, and show his willingness to change, they were well on their way to a complete restoration of their marriage. Fortunately he really was a good guy and not the type to say "This is my job, woman, so you'd better get used to it!"

Let's see a show of hands. How many women out there are married to men who spend 70 to 80 hours a week on the job and then say "I'm only doing this for you"? (There are variations on this line, of course, such as "Well, you wanted that new car, didn't you?")

I'm telling you right now, Mr. Firstborn, if you want to avoid having a mid-life crisis or giving one to somebody else, you'd better get your priorities straight. And that means realizing that your spouse and children have to come first in your life.

Do you ever feel like Popeye the Sailor, who says, "I've stood all I can stands, and I can't stands no more"? Are you standing on the edge of a lulu of a mid-life crisis? If so, the first thing you must do is sort through your priorities and make sure you understand what things really are important to you.

Following that, there are several other steps you should take:

1. Learn to be spontaneous.
2. Be responsible for your own happiness.
3. Count your blessings.
4. Be willing to make adjustments in your life.
5. Discover the power of forgiveness.

Let me explain what I mean by each of these.

1. LEARN TO BE SPONTANEOUS.

Not too long ago one of my clients told me excitedly that she was following my advice and really learning to be spontaneous.

"Oh?" I replied. "How are you doing that?"

"Well, every Tuesday night I get together with three of the girls from work. We go out to dinner, and then we take in a movie. Or sometimes we go to the mall and do some shopping!"

"Oh, sounds like fun!"

"It is! We don't worry about dinner or helping the kids with the homework or anything. We let our husbands take care of all that."

I had to fight off my urge to chuckle, because this was so much like a firstborn, scheduling a time to be spontaneous and then doing the same thing every week. (It reminds me of my days as an assistant dean of students at the University of Arizona in Tucson. Walking through the Student Union building, I spotted a sign that read ORGANIZATIONAL MEETING OF THE ANARCHY CLUB, ROOM 302, STUDENT UNION, 4 P.M. TODAY.) Even the spontaneity could quickly become part of the routine. But all in all it was a very good start, especially for someone whose life had been given over totally to keeping schedules, meeting deadlines, and achieving goals.

Every firstborn needs to take some time for himself, to kick back his heels and do whatever he wants to do. If you feel compelled to schedule a certain time for your "spontaneity," go ahead and schedule.

Maybe you want to go off and see a movie once a week; maybe you want to take a day and go fishing, or join a bowling league, or do anything else that sounds like fun. But whatever you do, don't throw away a lifetime in the guise of being spontaneous. Don't throw away a 20-year marriage on a silly young thing who likes to laugh a lot or on a man who "really listens" to you. Don't give up your career and your pension because you read in a magazine that muskrat ranchers are striking it rich in Idaho!

You may feel that your life is dull and drab and that you need to change everything about it. You don't. All you need is a little time to do some things you really want to do. Take some time for yourself, and you'll soon have an entirely new outlook on life.

Even in the smallest of communities, where you might think there wouldn't be much to do, you can find a variety of activities that will enrich your life. You can become involved in a social or civic club, take those guitar lessons you've always wanted, join a bowling league, learn how to fly-fish, take singing lessons, teach an illiterate adult how to read, etc. Whatever it is, take a little time for yourself.

You see, a great number of firstborns are never allowed to have an adolescence. They can't do the flaky things most adolescents do, because they're the oldest and expected to be little grown-ups. Their younger brothers and sisters may be acting crazy and doing all sorts of weird things (in short, acting like typical adolescents), but not them.

Then, 20 years later, when they're in their mid-thirties—BANG!—all of a sudden it's time for adolescence. What I am saying, I suppose, is that all of us go through adolescence; some of us just go through it much later in life than others!

2. BE RESPONSIBLE FOR YOUR
OWN HAPPINESS.

Have you ever heard Kevin Leman's famous law regarding romantic relationships? No? Well, it goes like this:

If you have been through a divorce or the breakup of a serious romantic relationship, do not get involved in another relationship for at least four years.

Did I hear you say "What?!" I know, you don't think I'm serious, because four years sounds like an awfully long time. Well, the truth is, I'm following the lead of the highway department. On a dangerous curve they'll put up a sign that tells you the maximum safe speed is 25 miles per hour. They know when they put that sign up there that you're never going to go that slow, but they figure if they can at least get you down to 35 you'll be able to negotiate the curve.

Well, I'm telling you that four years is the best rule, knowing in advance that the most I can hope for is two. But four would be best. You need time to let the wounds heal and to be sure you are not entering into a relationship for the wrong reasons.

I have dealt with mountains of trouble that have been caused by people getting involved while they were "on the rebound."

Mary's relationship with Joe, which lasted four years and seemed destined to wind up at the altar, has suddenly fallen apart, and she's devastated. And then, six weeks later, she shows up and tells me that she's engaged to Merwin. There's something mighty strange about this. Just a little over a month ago Mary thought her life was over because this man she loved so much had broken off their relationship—and now she's every bit as much in love with a guy she just met!?

I don't believe it. I believe that Mary was angry and hurt over the breakup of a relationship that she thought was going to last a lifetime, and so she grabbed the next guy to come along. But I also believe that Mary thought she needed a man in her life to make her happy. She was counting on Joe to make her happy, and when he walked out the door she turned to someone else, and now she expects him to bring her happiness on a silver platter.

You cannot expect someone to make you happy. Happiness must come from within—because you're satisfied with yourself and with the life you're living. I have counseled people who have been married four or five times, but none of the marriages have had a chance to work because all of the partners were saddled with unfair expectations.

"Okay, I've married you; now make me happy." It just doesn't work that way. The glow of a new romance may make you happy for a while, but until you've realized that happiness can be found only within yourself you'll never find the lasting kind.

Perhaps you are not looking for happiness to come into your life in the form of another person. Perhaps you think happiness involves buying a bigger house, quitting your job, beginning a new job, having a baby, getting the kids grown and out of your hair, getting a raise, or any one of a thousand other things. Wrong again. Happiness comes only from learning to like and appreciate who you are and what you are doing with your life.

Happiness is a state of mind, and so is unhappiness. Neither one of them depends on anything concrete, including your present situation.

In his book *The Achilles Syndrome* Dr. Harold H. Bloomfield says, "Many of us live the first half of our adult lives postponing satisfaction and the last half with regrets. Fulfillment seems always to be just over the next hill."[1]

Dr. Bloomfield suggests that you can be happy even when life is throwing a multitude of problems your way, and I agree. He says, "Many people think anxiety, worry, and tension are unavoidable as long as they're struggling with a problem or a decision. This belief undermines their ability to solve problems and needlessly prolongs distress. To some people this idea may seem revolutionary, but problems don't have to make you unhappy!

Life will always have its share of difficulties, in the midst of which you can choose to be satisfied, loving, and healthy."[2]

He suggests that you learn to "choose satisfaction now" by learning to develop an "attitude of gratitude" and that instead of worrying about why you can't be happy you "focus your attention on appreciating the positive."[3]

You can find happiness if you put your mind to it!

3. COUNT YOUR BLESSINGS.

How often do you take the time to look around you and take stock of all the things you have to be grateful for?

Do you have your health? Do you have enough food to eat? Do you live in a country where you're free to live your life the way you see fit? Do you have a loving family? Does someone love you? Are you blessed with at least one good friend?

There are an awful lot of things that we ought to be grateful for, but we take most of them for granted.

You hear a lot of people complaining about the state of the world today, but the truth is these are pretty good times we live in.

Just think of the advancements in medicine that have been made over the past 50 years. Many diseases that a generation ago meant sure death, especially for children, are now easily cured or prevented. Those of us who were around in the early 1950s remember the panic caused by polio, as it struck down thousands of young men and women every summer, leaving many of them crippled and others confined to iron lungs. We remember not being allowed to visit the community swimming pool because you might come home with polio. We also remember the cups being passed around in movie theaters to raise money for research into the disease. Winning the war over polio is only one of the advancements that have been made in the world of medicine over the past 50 years.

Think too of the strides that have been made in communications and transportation. You can turn on your television and see, via satellite, events that are going on, right now, on the other side of the globe. If you want to talk to someone who lives in Europe, you can pick up the phone and give him a call. It used to take two weeks or more to travel across the United States, but now you can hop on an airliner and do it in five hours!

Do you remember when computers first came into the news? They were huge, monstrous things, and there was a sort of sneaking suspicion about them. Now millions of us have them in our homes, and we're using them for everything from playing games, to helping the kids with their homework, to balancing the family budget. At one time you would have spent at least $1 million for a computer, and now you can buy one for under $1,000. Do you carry around a pocket calculator? If so, how much did you pay for it—$10 or so? Remember how, 20 years ago, it would have cost $100?

And one final question. Do you have a color television set? I remember when the first people on our block bought one, back in the mid-fifties. It was thrilling, and we kept looking for ways to finagle invitations into their house just to watch something in color. All the people had green skin and orange hair, but hey, at least it was color! Of course the set cost a small fortune.

Now, don't think I go around wearing blinders. I know that there are bad situations in every age, and there always will be, as long as we live in this world. But we do have many, many things to be thankful for.

When you feel discouraged, frustrated, and on the verge of a personal crisis, take a few moments to sit down with pen and paper and list some of things for which you are grateful.

4. BE WILLING TO MAKE ADJUSTMENTS.

I talked earlier about learning to be spontaneous, and that is one way you can make adjustments in your life.

It could be, too, that you would feel better if you changed

other parts of your daily routine. Are you getting enough sleep or too much? Are you eating properly and getting enough exercise? Are you guilty of trying to do too much? If you are, can you cut back on your obligations? Any of these problems in your life, or a combination of them, can make you feel out of sorts, cranky, and depressed.

If you don't know what's wrong with you, but you just feel on edge and as if your world is about to cave in, it could be that your body is sending you an important message. You may feel distraught, angry, and like you need a fresh start in life when the truth may be that you simply need to develop healthier personal habits.

Another area worth searching out is your spiritual life. Are you finding time to spend with God? Are you involved in a church or synagogue? Human beings are spiritual creatures who need to be in a healthy relationship with God. If they aren't, they will simply not feel good. If that aspect of your life isn't right, make the necessary adjustment.

You may also have to adjust your relationship with your spouse. If you are a firstborn perfectionist, you may have spent much of your life trying to scrub all the spots off your mate, trying to make him perfect. Well, you'll never do it, and you won't be happy until you learn to accept his imperfections.

Does he drive you crazy by squeezing the toothpaste tube from the top instead of the bottom? Then buy two tubes—one he can squish up any way he wants and another you can keep perfect.

You know that I'm a lastborn, so I'm not always the most organized person in the world. Several years back I had a real problem with my checkbook. I'd write out a check but forget to keep a record of it in the ledger. Pretty soon I'd forget about it. I did that several times. And I'm not talking about a check for $5 or $10. It might have been $50 or $100 or even more. Then sometimes the bank would call and say, "Hey, Dr. Leman, you want to come down here and put some money in your account?"

You can imagine how this irritated my firstborn wife! And

rightly so! Finally she hit on the answer. She ordered checks with carbons underneath them, so even when I forgot to write the transaction down in the ledger, I still had a record of the check I'd written.

So don't let your imperfect spouse drive you crazy. You can adjust, and you'll both be better for it!

Before moving on I must say one other thing, and that is that marriage is a partnership. Too many men still believe that housework is a woman's job. That's where we got the old saying that "a woman's work is never done." Husband, if your wife seems grouchy and stressed out, ask yourself if any of it is your fault. How much do you help out around the house?

If you help out as much as you possibly can, that's great and I salute you. But if you're not too good about it, I strongly suggest that you make an adjustment.

Come on! Housework won't kill you!

Do you share the job of "parenting," or do you believe that's "the wife's job"?

I was in Chicago to appear on a radio show and had the family along with me. Without my knowledge they brought my kids on the show to talk to them about what it was like to have a psychologist for a father.

When I arrived at the studio and found that my kids were on the air, I wasn't the happiest person in the world. I didn't want anyone putting my children in the spotlight like that without at least talking it over with their mother and me first.

The interviewer kept pushing at Krissy, hoping she would give some insights into life with a father who wrote books and gave lectures on parenting and family relationships.

Finally Krissy looked up at the man with frustration written all over her face and said, "I don't think you understand. He's just my daddy!"

Well, I'm happy to be "just daddy" to my kids. I couldn't ask for a bigger honor or a more important responsibility.

5. DISCOVER THE POWER OF FORGIVENESS.

Another reason you might be feeling edgy and in need of a major change in your life is that you are full of anger. It may be anger directed at yourself or at someone else.

There's only one thing to do with anger, and that's to get rid of it. And there's only one way to get rid of it, and that's to forgive whoever it is who made you angry.

Patty was a young mother who moved back in with her parents after her marriage dissolved. They welcomed her with open arms and did everything they could to support her. But at the same time, they were always on her back.

She was 28 years old, with two children and a full-time job, and they were treating her like a teenager. She wanted to confront them, but she didn't know how, so she was letting the anger and frustration build up and fester.

I suggested that she write her parents a note and tell them how she felt. Not a harsh, angry note, but a letter that started out on a positive tone, telling them how grateful she was for their support and their willingness to take her family into their home during this time. She had always been able to lean on her parents, and she was truly grateful for this. Then she could explain to them how she felt about some of the problem areas.

She did as I suggested, and it worked. Her parents hadn't realized they had been causing their daughter anger and hurt on top of that caused by her divorce, and they eased up. The rest of the time she was home, until she and the kids found a place of their own, was smooth sailing.

Is there someone you need to confront, but you can't bring yourself to do it? If so, I suggest that you sit down and write a letter explaining how you feel. Don't be angry and vitriolic, but explain your feelings in the nicest possible way. You may get an apology and restore a relationship, but even if you don't, you have at least expressed yourself, and you should now feel free to let the situation go. Don't hang on to anger. If you do, it will destroy you and not the other person.

Perhaps you are angry at someone—a parent, for example—who is long dead, and so writing a letter wouldn't really do any good. Write it anyway, for the release it can give you.

In every situation, ask God to help you forgive and think about the forgiveness He has always given so freely to those who ask for it.

Now, sometimes it's easier to forgive someone else than to forgive yourself. That's especially true if you're a perfectionist.

You have to remember, though, that nobody is perfect. We all make mistakes, and the ones you've made are no bigger than anyone else's. Give yourself some room to be a human being and get off your back!

If you have to write yourself a letter, do that.

If you have to stand in front of the mirror and have a long talk with yourself in which you forgive yourself, do that.

If you harbor a harsh and unforgiving attitude toward yourself, it can and will destroy you, so make a conscious and sincere effort to forgive yourself, right now.

And then, if you need to ask someone else for forgiveness, go and do it.

Unforgivingness can destroy you, whether you need to forgive or be forgiven.

Whatever the situation, if you need to give or ask forgiveness, don't put it off! It's too important. There is a tremendous power in forgiveness, and it really can set you free!

If you're a firstborn who's had it with being superman, don't chuck it all and take off for the wilds of Alaska.

Remember the five steps to a healthier life-style:

1. Learn to be spontaneous.
2. Be responsible for your own happiness.
3. Count your blessings.

4. Be willing to make adjustments in your life.
5. Discover the power of forgiveness.

Dealing with Aging Parents

Another problem for firstborns entering middle age is that their parents are aging and may be in need of special care.

It's not easy watching your parents grow old, and it can be especially heart-wrenching if your mother or father should become incapacitated. You owe them so much, and your mind goes back to the days when you were small and helpless and they were always there for you.

I recently sat with a good friend who wept over his decision to put his mother in a nursing home. He didn't want to do it, and even though he knew he had made the only reasonable decision and the best decision for her, he still was overcome with guilt and sorrow. He and his wife had taken his mother into their home, but as hard as they tried, they could not give her the care she needed.

Caring for aging parents is not only heartbreaking; it can also be costly. And it is unfortunate that the lion's share of the burden usually falls on "ole dependable"—the firstborn.

It shouldn't be that way, and it doesn't have to be that way. If there are other children in the family, they should share in taking care of Mom and Dad, financially and emotionally.

What can you do?

1. Make sure your brothers and sisters understand the situation.
2. Get input from them regarding their wishes for Mom and Dad. If someone doesn't think you're handling the situation correctly, allow him the opportunity to do a better job.
3. Let them know, as clearly as you can, what you expect of them. There should be no room for an excuse such as "Well, if only I'd known . . ." If Mom needs more visits from her

children, tell the others about it. If she needs extra money for whatever reason, tell them about that too.

4. Remember to set aside some time for yourself. You need recreation, and you need to laugh. Go see a funny movie once in a while.

5. Remember that you are not alone. Nearly everyone goes through this at one time or another. Perhaps there is a support group you could join.

6. You can handle the situation better if you are prepared. Visit the local library and see what books are available regarding dealing with aging parents.

Next up—you and your firstborn child.

PART TWO

You and
Your Firstborn

7

Perfect Child, Imperfect World!

The ad might read something like this:

"Help wanted. Must have the wisdom of Solomon, the patience of Job, and the strength of Samson. Need to have your own striped shirt and whistle. Timid and squeamish need not apply."

What are we looking for? It ought to be obvious. A parent.

It's never been easy to be a parent, and the situation is definitely not improving as we head toward the 21st century.

Just consider the plight of the modern mother. In some instances she's expected to help bring home the bacon, and then she's still expected to fry it!

Her family expects her to cook like Julia Child, drive like A. J. Foyt, and have the sort of memory that is rumored to be the exclusive property of elephants. As for her organizational skills—well, every time she goes to the grocery store she saves $20 or $30 with all of the coupons she's saved, and she remembers the birthdays of everyone within a 30-mile radius.

As for old Dad, let's give him the wisdom of Robert Young on *Father Knows Best,* the patience and common sense of Michael

Landon's character from *Little House on the Prairie,* and the all-around good-guy qualities that the late Hugh Beaumont put into his portrayal of Ward Cleaver. He has to throw a football like John Elway, pitch a baseball like Joe Magrane, and when it comes to keeping things in working order around the house, have the combined skills of Mr. Goodwrench and Mr. Wizard.

And then there are the required parenting skills!

It is true that there are some areas of life where the best teacher is experience, and parenting is definitely one of these.

I've never met a set of parents who didn't start out thinking that they were going to avoid repeating all the mistakes *their* parents made.

"We're going to do this thing right, we're going to be the best parents in the world, and it's going to be wonderful!"

And I've never met a set of parents who didn't somewhere along the line throw up their hands and say, "Where did we go wrong?" or at least "What in the world do we do now?"

There is no job more difficult, more time-consuming, more painful (sometimes), or more rewarding (finally) than being a parent.

I have been asked what I believe is the biggest mistake most parents make. My answer is this:

The biggest mistake is to think that if you just love your children enough, they'll turn out all right.

Your children need your love—but they also need your discipline, your example, and your guidance in other ways.

Your firstborn will more than likely be a model of loyalty, obedience, and self-discipline. But the problem is that he may overdo it in some of these areas, including self-discipline. Parents must be extremely careful with their firstborns and avoid expecting too much from them, putting too much pressure on them, or being overly critical of them.

For example, my oldest daughter, Holly, is a model citizen. She believes rules are made to be followed and in the axiom "a place for everything and everything in its place." If Judge

Wapner ever decides to leave *People's Court,* I think Holly would be perfect for the job.

When Holly was a very tiny girl, before she was even talking, I remember the trips we would take to the beach. She'd play for a little while, but then pretty soon she'd come running up, holding her hands out, and going, "Unnnh! Unnnhhh!"

"What's wrong, honey? What is it?"

"Unnnnh! Unnnnhh!"

Well, pretty soon we figured out that her problem was that her hands were getting sandy. She couldn't stand having her hands dirty and wanted us to get the sand off. That's rather typical behavior for a firstborn perfectionist, and it pretty much tells you Holly's approach to life.

And then there's our middle daughter, Krissy.

I will never forget Krissy's first day of school. She was barely six years old, and as is always the case with seeing a child go off to school for the first time, Sande and I felt both proud and sad as we watched her board the bus that morning.

That afternoon, when the school bus made its stop in our neighborhood, Sande was panicked when Krissy was nowhere in sight. She was not on the bus, and the driver didn't remember seeing her.

We called the school, but she wasn't there. We didn't know what to do and were contemplating calling the police when the phone rang.

"Hi, Mom!" said the cheerful little voice on the other end.

"Krissy!" Sande shouted. "Where are you?"

"I'm at my best friend's house!"

"You're *where?* Whose house is that?"

There was a pause on the other end of the line, and then Krissy's voice was heard.

"What's your name again?" Sande heard her ask her "best friend."

Little Krissy didn't think anything about getting off the bus at a different stop and going home with another little girl she had just met. Would Holly do anything like that? Not in a hundred years!

And then there was the time when Sande and I were trying to be alone together in our room. I had just returned home from one of my frequent trips. We hadn't seen each other for a while, so we tried to steal a few minutes behind a locked door.

No deal!

After about 30 seconds Krissy and her little brother, Kevin, who was perhaps three at the time, began pounding on the door.

"Can we come in?" Krissy asked.

"Go away," I said. "Mommy and I just want to talk to each other for a while."

For two minutes there was silence. And then Krissy's voice called out, "We can't hear you talking!"

"Well, come on, Krissy. Just leave us alone for a little bit, okay?"

Again about two minutes of silence, and then this time, "Daddy! Can you slip our allowances under the door?"

By this time Sande and I were both laughing so hard we couldn't have walked over and opened the door if we had wanted to. Our giggling only made Krissy more determined than ever. When we didn't respond immediately to her by-now frantic pounding on the door, we heard her tell her little brother, "Kevy, they won't let us in. You better go get the hammer!"

For the sake of the door, we went over and let them in.

Now, there's not a doubt in my mind that Holly would have gone away and left us alone the first time we asked her. Firstborns and middle children are simply different animals!

Two Types of Firstborns

Now, I would never mean to imply that all firstborns are alike, but the truth is that unless you can keep things balanced, they tend to go off in either of two directions. They may join the ranks of:

1. The compliant
2. The powerful

The compliant types are the pleasers. These are the people who grow up to be overinvolved and who are forever trying to prove that they are good enough. They want to earn everything, including your friendship and admiration, and they have a hard time dealing with anything that is given to them or that they feel they didn't deserve.

The powerful ones, on the other hand, are the types who learn very early that being a firstborn carries with it a great deal of authority.

"I'm the oldest, I'm the biggest, and you'd better pay attention to me."

These are the ones my good friend James Dobson calls "strong-willed children." I prefer to call them "powerful little buzzards."

Whatever you call them, both of these behavior patterns are discernible in early childhood and can be dealt with.

THE COMPLIANT CHILD

Suppose you are watching little Megan, who is trying to draw a picture of a cat. She gets one almost finished but then quickly crumples up the paper and throws it away. The next picture gets the same sort of treatment, and on and on.

You notice, too, that her frustration is mounting with each picture she throws away.

Ask her what's wrong, and she says, "I just can't do it! It doesn't look right!" Little Megan is already showing signs of developing into a discouraged perfectionist—the compliant sort who will go to any length to prove herself capable and worthwhile.

How does a parent handle a situation like that? He needs to

sit down with the child and talk about the positive aspects of what she's doing.

"What do you mean, you can't do it right? That looks good to me!"

"Really?"

"Oh, yeah, that's a fine cat. And you know, cats are really hard to draw, too."

Something along those lines. I'm not suggesting that you lie to the child and tell her she's a modern-day Rembrandt when her cat is sort of lopsided and one ear is four times larger than the other. But do look for the positive and seek out ways you can honestly encourage and compliment the child.

Keep on the lookout for other ways in which your firstborn perfectionist is putting undue pressure on herself, and always seek to enter into the situation to build up and encourage.

You must be especially careful to avoid sending the message that your child's best efforts do not measure up. Suppose she has tried to make her bed for the very first time, and she calls you into her room because she wants to show you her "masterpiece."

Your first reaction, when you see it, is to wonder if there's somebody still sleeping in it. It's lumpy, and the sheet is hanging out from underneath the bedspread in several places. But it is, after all, her first effort.

What are you going to do? What sort of message are you going to send? You can't say "Oh, Megan, that's the most beautiful job of bed-making I've ever seen," because that would be a lie.

But if it's her best effort, and in this case you know that it is, you don't want to hurt her feelings.

Now, some parents might respond by saying that the bed looks terrific and sending the child out to play. Then, as soon as the daughter was out of sight, they'd remake the bed.

But then, a couple of hours later, when the child came back inside, she would see that her bed was not the way she left it. She may come and ask her mother or father what happened, or she may not say anything. But either way she knows that her effort wasn't good enough and that she has some distance to go to prove herself.

What the parent should have done is said something like this: "Honey, that's really great that you made your bed. You're helping me out, and I appreciate it." And then Mom or Dad should have left the bed alone.

There is a time for training and teaching, and perhaps that parent can set aside some time within the next couple of days to show the little girl how to make a bed. But not right now, not so that the child thinks, "I guess I didn't do a very good job."

The child has worked hard, and she needs to have a sense of satisfaction about the effort she has made.

Your next question to me might be "You mean if my child does a halfhearted and slipshod job, I'm just supposed to let it go?"

Of course not. But if the child has given his maximum effort, it should be good enough for you.

You ought to know your children well enough that you can tell when they're making a solid effort and when they're just goofing off. If your 13-year-old, for instance, knows how to make his bed, but he's just made a halfhearted gesture at it this morning, there's nothing wrong with telling him to get back in there and do it right. But again, if your child has made his best effort, even if he has fallen far short of the ideal, look for something positive to focus on so he will feel worthwhile and encouraged.

You may also need to encourage your child to stick up for his rights.

When Holly and Krissy were little, we would sometimes turn the tape recorder on when they were playing and record their conversations. What we have, a lot of the time, is Holly taking things away from her little sister and wanting to have whatever Krissy was playing with.

Most of the time, as I've said, Holly was doing her best to please Mom and Dad, to be the perfect little model citizen. But

when she thought Krissy was trying to invade her firstborn turf
—well, that was another story.

It's not the sort of thing that makes you think your little girl
will grow up to win the Nobel peace prize, but it's fairly common—and natural—behavior for children.

But not for the compliant, pleaser firstborn.

He's the type who will go out to play with his brand-new,
remote-controlled car and come home without it.

"Billy, where's your car?"

"Oh, I traded it to Bobby—for this." He holds up an old,
grass-stained baseball with the cover about to come off.

"You traded Bobby your brand-new Corvette, which cost
nearly $20, for that?!"

"Well, uh . . . Bobby really wanted it."

Of course Billy really wanted it, too, but he also wanted to
win Bobby's friendship. Billy's not dumb enough to think it was
a fair trade, but he couldn't bring himself to reject Bobby's offer.

Compliant children are easily taken advantage of:

"Hey, Billy, you don't really want that candy bar, do you?"

"Well . . . no . . . I guess not."

"Good, can I have it?"

"Okay."

They are also easily manipulated into doing things they don't
really want to do. These are the kids who live and die by peer
pressure.

"Hey, Judi, we're going to steal some bubble gum from the
drugstore, and we want you to take some, too."

"But I don't wanna steal anything."

"If you want to be part of our group, then you'd better do it."

"Well . . . okay."

And so goes the life of the compliant firstborn. That routine
starts out in early childhood, and it stays with him all through
life: he'll be the one the boss piles the extra work on; he'll have
friends who "borrow" money from him and never pay it back.
He'll be forever struggling to buy the respect and admiration of
his peers.

The time to stop this sort of behavior is now, when it is still relatively easy to unlearn. Little Billy must be urged to march over to Bobby's house and get his car back. Not because it makes you mad that he traded away an expensive toy for something that is practically worthless, but because you know he really liked that little Corvette, and you want him to have it back. He must be made to see that his feelings in this situation are important.

This is a difficult area, because most of us, as parents, are quite pleased when we see our children learning to think of others first, sharing their toys and generally obeying the Golden Rule. But I have often said that parenting is very much like walking a balance beam, and this is one of those dangerous areas where it's easy to tumble off that narrow beam. There is a world of difference between sharing with others because you know that is what you ought to do and refusing to stick up for yourself so that others can take complete advantage of you. As a parent you can usually get close enough to the situation to discover your child's motives.

To a great extent your child's sense of self-worth and self-respect depends on you. He needs to know that he has rights and that his needs and desires are just as important as anyone else's.

You can't let him believe that his desires take precedence over anyone else's, but he has to understand that he *does* matter. He must come to see that you respect his opinions, his efforts, and that he does have some say in family matters. You can do this in little ways every day and in somewhat bigger ways every so often.

"Billy, we thought we'd take the family out to eat tonight, and we were wondering if you'd like to pick the restaurant."

"Me?"

"Yeah, you. Come on, where would you like to go?"

"I don't know. I guess wherever everybody else wants to go."

"No, we want you to choose tonight. We don't really know where we want to go."

THE FIRSTBORN'S
BILL OF RIGHTS

You have the right to

1. Make your own choices in life
2. Have your own opinion
3. Go against the crowd
4. Be happy
5. Choose your own friends
6. Take control of your life
7. Be what you want to be
8. Take it easy once in a while
9. Pamper yourself occasionally
10. Express yourself
11. Pick up only after yourself

"Well, I'd kind of like to go to McDonald's . . . I mean, if that's all right with you."

"That sounds great! And after dinner we were thinking maybe we'd see a movie . . . or else play some miniature golf. Which sounds better to you?"

This sort of thing is a terrific way to help build up the self-worth of the compliant child.

THE POWERFUL CHILD

This is the second major grouping to which firstborn children belong.

I won't spend so much time just yet talking about the powerful child, because in the next chapter I'm going to be discussing the concept of "reality discipline" in some detail, and this is the very best way to deal with the powerful child.

But let me tell you that the powerful child is one who has learned very early in life how to get his own way, and the only way you can deal with him is to see that he doesn't get his way quite as often as he'd like.

The powerful child may be one who realizes very quickly that as the firstborn he is the biggest and strongest and that there is no one in the family to challenge his role as "king" over his brothers and sisters.

He's the one who, more often than not, causes Mom and Dad to get out their striped shirts and whistles and take on their second jobs as referees.

But he learns how to lord it over not only his brothers and sisters but over Mom and Dad as well, and he does this in a variety of ways. He's a fast learner, and he quickly finds out how to pull your chain and make you do a somersault!

When you think of a "powerful" child, you may think of one who gets his way by being a bully, who pushes everyone around and is the terror of the neighborhood. That could be the case, but it's just as often true that he may seem shy and self-effacing on the surface; that may even be the method he uses to get his way.

Here are some of the techniques used by powerful children:

Shyness. This child tends to cling to his mom and dad. He's too shy to speak for himself, so they have to do it for him. They are overly involved in his life because of this and always ready to run to the rescue. At first glance you might mistake the shy child for the compliant child, but actually the two are poles apart. The shy child comes closer to being a bully. He is like a king who counts on his servants to do all his work for him. Mom speaks up for him, Dad gives him extra attention, brothers and sisters do things for him that he's just "too shy" to do on his own. The shy child, in short, can be extremely manipulative. What can you do about it? Simply encourage the child to speak up and stand up for himself.

If you always let him get away with being shy, he'll never

learn how to stand up on his own two feet and say what he wants to say. If Mom is always rushing to the rescue and Dad is always saying "Well, Billy's just shy, so we'll leave him alone," they are acting as "enablers" and allowing him to retreat into his shell. There is no magical cure for shyness. The only way to overcome it is to put your child in situations where he has to speak up for himself. Letting him order his own meal in a restaurant is a good place to start.

"Come on, Sally, tell the waitress what you want."

Sally sits there biting on her finger and looking down at the floor.

"Come on, honey. The lady wants to know what you want, and you have to tell her."

I'm not suggesting that you turn it into an hour-long battle, but gently encourage the shy child to speak up for himself. Let him know that in order to get what he wants he has to speak for himself, and he'll begin to overcome his shyness.

Tears. Tears can be a child's favorite weapon, and the best thing you can do as a parent is learn to ignore them. Some children are terrific little actors who can cry on cue, and Mom and Dad must learn to tell the difference between these crocodile tears and real ones. And then don't give in!

Tantrums. This is closely related to tears, and sometimes it includes a great many of them. A child may throw a tantrum in a variety of ways—holding his breath, stomping his feet and screaming, lying down on the floor and refusing to get up, and on and on. It's amazing how innovative and creative children can be when it comes to doing what we used to call "pitching a fit." An interesting thing about tantrums is that children seem to learn from each other. If your little Johnny sees his next-door neighbor Judy getting her way by lying down on the floor and screaming and hollering, he's more than likely going to try the same thing the next time he's after something you don't want him to have. Tantrums can be handled by ignoring them, or you may remove the child from your presence and allow him to continue his tantrum in the privacy of his own room. However you decide to deal with it, there is one option that should never, ever be considered, and that is giving in.

Pity Parties. Having a "pity party" is one of the most effective power trips a young child can pull on his parents. To go around with a "woe is me" attitude is sure to bring his parents quickly to his side, offering to do whatever they can to help him out. Mom sees eight-year-old Edgar sitting at the dining room table with his head in his hands, his math book open in front of him. "What's wrong, honey?" "Oh, I just can't get all this homework done. Old Mrs. Johnson gave us tons of the stuff." Little Edgar hasn't asked for help, but he looks so forlorn and frustrated that Mom decides she'll sit down for a minute or two to see if she can help out. Almost before she knows what's hit her, she's doing the homework for him! I know that if your child is having a private pity party, it can really tug at your heartstrings. So give him a hug and an encouraging word—and offer any helpful advice you may have—but don't let him manipulate you with a pity party power trip.[1]

If your child learns that he can use one or more of these techniques to manipulate you, watch out, because you are in for some very tough sledding indeed. And I don't really need to remind you that the powerful child will spend the rest of his life using the same tricks and techniques to manipulate everyone with whom he comes in contact.

If you want to read about a powerful child, I suggest that you open your Bible and turn to the story of Samson and Delilah.[2] If Delilah wasn't an FBPC (that's firstborn powerful child), then she must have picked up the technique from an older sibling. Just look at the way she manipulated poor old Samson into telling her the secret of his strength. She'd probably used the same techniques many times before to get what she wanted from dear old Mom and Dad. No two ways about it, Delilah was a rat!

Are there any budding Delilahs in your family zoo? If so, it's time for you to nip them in the bud. Stop giving in. Start showing them that their power tricks simply will not work any longer. Remember, it's never too late to change.

Seven Rules
for Better Parenting

In *The Birth Order Book* I gave a list of seven rules designed for better parenting of firstborns.[3] They are very much worth repeating:

1. Don't reinforce your firstborn's already ingrained perfectionistic tendencies. Don't be an "improver" on everything he says and does. Go easy on reminding the child of what he "should" be like.
2. Realize firstborns have a particular need to know exactly what the rules are. Be patient and take time to lay things out for your firstborn, from "A to Z."
3. Recognize the firstborn's place in the family. As the oldest the firstborn should get some special privileges to go along with the additional responsibilities that always seem to come his way.
4. Take "two on one" time—both parents out with the oldest child alone. Firstborns respond better to adult company than any other birth order.
5. Stay away from making your firstborn your "instant baby-sitter." At least try to check with your firstborn to see if his or her schedule would allow for some baby-sitting later in the day or that evening.
6. As your firstborn grows older, be sure you don't pile on more responsibilities. Alleviate some responsibilities and give them to the younger children as they are capable of taking on these jobs. One firstborn told me at a seminar, "I'm the garbage person." By that he meant that he had to do everything at home while his brother and sister got off much easier.

7. Firstborns are extremely sensitive to criticism and being corrected. When your firstborn is reading to you, for example, and has trouble with a word, don't be so quick to jump in with a correction. Give the child time to sound out the word. Give help when *he* asks for it.

Four Special Problems and How to Deal with Them

Okay, I admit it. If I were going to give you the list of all the "special" problems that you'll encounter in the rearing of your children, I might as well title it "Four thousand eight hundred and ninety-two special problems and how to deal with them." I'm not trying to give you an exhaustive list, and I'm not trying to give you a little first-aid kit that you can pull out whenever you run into trouble with your firstborn.

But there are four common problems that can arise and that need expert handling and attention.

1. DETHRONEMENT

When your first child is born, he or she immediately becomes the "crown prince" or "crown princess" of the family. He has his parents' attention all to himself, he doesn't have to share his toys with anyone, and he's the apple of his granddad's eye.

And then, all of a sudden, Mom and Dad bring home a rather homely, wrinkled little bundle, which they tell him is his new brother.

What is firstborn to think?

"You know," he tells himself, "I think they're going to keep it!

"What's going on here? Wasn't I good enough for them? Why in the world did they have to bring home another kid?"

Now, the firstborn may not show his resentment right off. It could be, in fact, that he is genuinely happy to have a new brother or sister—at first. But pretty soon it's going to dawn on him what having a new child in the family will mean to him.

Namely, it means that he's no longer numero uno, the center of everyone's attention and the apple of all the older eyes in the family. It also means that he's going to be expected to share his toys and that he'll be told to "behave" himself or to "act his age" when that's really exactly what he's always been doing.

The firstborn isn't at all sure how to react to the usurper, and if he's young enough, he may decide that the best thing to do is to compete with the baby on its terms. In other words, he'll revert to his own infancy. He may become a fussy eater or develop bowel and bladder problems. He may begin to throw temper tantrums or revert to baby talk. After all, the baby does all these things, and they sure work for him!

The trauma of dethronement can be lessened by having a straightforward talk with your firstborn. Even if he's only three years old, he can be taken into your confidence.

"You know, Hector, your little brother will be coming home from the hospital soon. And as soon as he gets to be old enough, he'll be getting into everything, and it might be hard to keep him out of your toys. So why don't you go through your toys and put the things you really don't want him to play with up out of his reach?

"Oh, and while you're doing that you might see some things you don't play with anymore that you'd like to give the baby— or at least let him play with sometimes."

In this way you're telling him that you respect his things and that he is still important to you.

You can continue this sort of approach whenever your child shows signs of jealousy or resentment.

Point out to him the things that he can do that baby can't do.

"I saw you riding your tricycle, and it looked like you were really enjoying that. Your little brother can't ride a tricycle, because he's too small."

"Look at that—you've learned how to write your own name.

I'll bet you're proud. I wonder when Josh will learn how to write his name?"

It is also helpful to point out to him some of the special privileges he has because he's older.

"You get to stay up till eight thirty, but Josh has to go to bed earlier, because he's littler than you are."

Or "We're having your favorite for dinner tonight—barbecued chicken. But poor Josh can't have any. He has to eat his baby food because he doesn't have any teeth!"

You don't have to overdo it. You shouldn't make such a big deal out of it that the firstborn feels absolutely superior to his younger sibling. But, as I said before, whenever jealousy begins to rear its ugly head, it will not hurt to remind the firstborn of the special place he has in the family and of the privileges that place brings him.

It is especially good to spend time alone with him during the time he is adjusting to the arrival of another child into the family. As soon as the baby is old enough, hire a sitter for him and take your firstborn out for a special night of his own. In this way you'll be showing him that he's still extremely important in your life.

You may need to reassure him by telling him that you love him every bit as much as you did before his little brother arrived. Tell him that you have enough hugs and kisses to go around, and you're not about to run out.

Dethronement can be a major event in the life of a firstborn, and it can leave lasting scars. But it doesn't have to, and it won't if you learn how to handle it.

Dethronement also occurs when a parent remarries and brings other children into the family.

Little Johnny, for instance, has been the apple of his mother's eye for all these seven years, and now, suddenly, he has two little sisters with whom he must share the spotlight. It's not easy for him, nor is it easy for his mother or stepfather. This "blended family" can be the biggest hurdle a second marriage has to overcome.

I have a scientific name for the blended family. I call it "a mess."

How do you cope with a blended family? You'll need to handle dethronement in the ways we've discussed, and you will need lots and lots of patience!

You'll need to make sure all the kids get plenty of love and attention. You can also help the situation by refusing to play judge and jury. If the kids are fighting among themselves, be hesitant to get involved. Unless it's just not possible, put things on their shoulders and let them work out their own problems.

Don't let squabbling children disrupt the harmony between husband and wife! Love each other and resolve to let nothing—not even your stepkids—come between you, and you will be able to weather the storm.

2. LOSS OF THE OPPOSITE SEX ROLE MODEL

Many people just naturally assume that the most important parent-child combinations are mother-daughter and father-son. That's one of the reasons we see so many mother-daughter banquets, father-son fishing tournaments, and so on. Well, if it were up to me, we would be seeing a whole lot more father-daughter banquets and mother-son fishing tournaments.

I believe strongly, and it's backed up by years of research and personal experience, that the most important relationships are between a father and his daughter and a mother and her son.

I received an object lesson in this one day not too long ago when I had a bouquet of flowers delivered to Sande. It wasn't for any special occasion—just because I love her very much and wanted to let her know.

When the flowers came—and they were beautiful—she gave me a hug and said, "Oh, honey, how sweet!"

You know, she was touched, and she appreciated the gesture, but I'd be lying if I told you the flowers swept her off her feet.

But about 15 minutes later, young Kevin came marching up

to his mother with a huge smile on his face and one hand held behind his back.

"Mom, I've got something for you."

"What is it, hon?"

Kevin brought his hand from behind his back and revealed that he was clutching a bouquet of daffodils, direct from his mother's flower garden.

"I love you, Mom."

Well, you should have seen the look on Sande's face. She was thrilled, and I knew that my rather expensive bouquet couldn't begin to stand up to the one her firstborn son had brought her. I was no competition for Kevin, so all I could do was throw up my hands and admit my defeat!

You see, there is a very special bond between a mother and her son, especially her firstborn son. And the reverse is true, too, in that the firstborn daughter is going to be the jewel of her father's eye—no doubt about it!

Unfortunately, in my private practice I am seeing more and more single mothers who are trying to raise their daughters without the benefit of a man's presence in the family, and that is an awfully hard thing to do! A young girl needs to have a positive male image in her life.

If a single mother has a good relationship with her own father, her brother, uncle, or cousin, she ought to involve that man in her family frequently. Now, if her favorite brother lives in Albuquerque and she and the girls are in Dubuque, I would go so far as to suggest that she pick up her family and head for New Mexico. It's that important!

Unless there is a positive male influence in the family, the girls will often begin to strike out at one another and at their mother. And later on in life their relationships with men will typically not be good ones. I may be accused by feminist readers of being a male chauvinist, but I assure you that I have seen it happen time and again—and let me hurry to add that I think it's every bit as important for a boy to have positive female adult role models in his life.

And that brings up another point I want to make to single mothers of boys. Don't worry about trying to be a mother and a father to your sons. What they need most in their lives is a good relationship with their mother, and if you're giving them that, you're doing a good job of parenting.

Don't try to get into sports or worry about teaching your son to throw a curveball or a 30-yard touchdown pass. You can see to it that your son has a male authority figure in his life, in the form of a scoutmaster, church youth leader, Little League coach, or what have you, but the key figure in your young man's emotional life is his mother.

I've talked to many single women who were worried that their sons would have some sort of gender identification problems because of the absence of a father in the home. But my answer to this is something I learned a long, long time ago. Namely, if it ain't broke, don't try to fix it!

Now, I realize that the advice I've given is aimed at single women with children, and I don't want any of you single fathers to feel left out. The plain fact is, though, that there are far more single mothers than there are single fathers. But if you are a single father, the advice I've just given goes for you too. Don't try to be a mother to your daughter. Just concentrate on being the father she needs you to be. Remember that the most influential person in any child's life is his opposite-sex parent.

3. SUFFOCATION

What I mean by this is that the firstborn may often tend to dominate his younger brother or sister. His intention is to help, but his actions are actually harmful. This is something that you, as a parent, should keep on the lookout for.

For instance, I counseled one mother who was worried about her 24-month-old son, Chad. His vocabulary was not what it should be at that age; in fact he hardly ever spoke at all. She wondered if there might be "something wrong" with him.

As a matter of fact, yes, there was something wrong with him.

And that something was five years old and named Bernice! Little Chad never talked because he didn't have to talk. Bernice did all of his talking for him.

"Chad's thirsty." "Chad's hungry." "Chad wants a cookie." "Chad needs to go to the bathroom."

It was fortunate that the little guy had ever learned to walk. Bernice had been like a mother hen since the day he was born. If he wanted to go somewhere, she carried him on her back or else pulled him in her little red wagon.

She was cute, she was sweet, and she was a perfect little mother. But she was suffocating her little brother and stunting his growth.

This was the way Bernice had chosen to handle her dethronement—by becoming the perfect and indispensable little mother.

It's fairly easy to solve the problem, but you first have to be aware of the situation. It is sometimes hard to see that all the love and attention the firstborn is showering on the baby is not beneficial.

For Bernice and Chad's parents, the solution was simply to begin insisting that Chad do things for himself. If Bernice said Chad was thirsty, Mom would respond by saying "If he's thirsty, he can tell me himself."

"But Mom! He needs a drink of water!"

"I'm sorry, honey. Your brother is getting to be a big boy, and he's old enough to ask me for a drink if he wants one."

This sort of response was met with indignation by both of the children at first, and especially by Bernice, who put her arm around her little brother and shot Mom a look that seemed to say "How can you be so mean?"

This was not easy on Mom, and she didn't feel any better about it when Chad walked off without his drink. But she knew that for her son's sake she had to resist the temptation to call him back into the room and give him a glass of water.

It wasn't long before Chad had developed into his own person, and he had also developed a pretty good vocabulary. When he wanted something, he asked for it himself. He and his sister remained close, but she was no longer suffocating him.

4. WHEN FIRSTBORN IS PASSED BY

Your firstborn is supposed to be the "king of the siblings." But what happens when he isn't?

Suppose firstborn's little sister is better in school or little brother is better in athletics? What if the firstborn is the size of a jockey, while the little brother seems destined to be a lineman for the Chicago Bears? Finally, what happens if your firstborn has a handicap of some sort that holds him back?

To see a younger sibling race past him in some field of endeavor is a very bitter pill for the firstborn to swallow.

The only exception is when the siblings are not of the same sex. For one thing, girls do mature faster than boys as a general rule. If you have a 10-year-old boy and a nine-year-old girl, chances are that your daughter will be more mature. She's likely to be bigger than her brother, and she may be more serious about her schoolwork and other matters. It won't be that big a deal, though, because competition between siblings of the opposite sex is not nearly as intense as that between two boys or two girls. It is usually true, too, that boys and girls have different interests, so they will not be competing in the same areas.

For instance, firstborn Debbie is not likely to be upset that her younger brother can throw a football twice as far as she can. She probably doesn't care very much about football anyway. But if eight-year-old John throws that pigskin 20 yards farther than 11-year-old James can toss it, there's a problem. (Now, if Debbie is a younger sister, and she can throw the ball the distance of a football field, that may be a difficult situation for James to deal with!)

How do you handle it when a firstborn's same-sex sibling seems to pass him by? The answer is: very, very carefully and with a great deal of tender loving care.

An acquaintance of mine, who's in his late thirties, still winces when he remembers how people used to think that his little brother was the older one.

"So, how much older are you?" they'd ask the younger brother.

"I always got this terrible, burning feeling in the pit of my stomach," he remembers. "Especially when he told them that I was older. I could see that they found that hard to believe."

How can two children from the same family be so different in makeup? One may be short, skinny, and sickly, while the other is tall, big-boned, and athletic. Well, sometimes life just isn't fair. But you, as a good parent, need to do everything within reason to ease the sting.

A wise parent will see what strengths the firstborn has and seek to encourage him in those areas.

The firstborn who has been passed by will need much in the way of reassurance.

"Listen, I saw your face when that guy asked you if Billy was your older brother. I know it hurt your feelings, and I'm sorry. But you know, you're a very special kid, and I wouldn't trade you for anyone. I'm so glad you're the oldest of our children."

Don't overdo the negative and go on and on about how it's sad that he's not as big as his younger brother, because if you do that, you're only making him feel worse about himself. But when you see a particular problem arise, act quickly to reassure your firstborn that he is a very special child in your eyes. After all, it's what you think about him that matters most.

Suppose your firstborn is handicapped in some way—perhaps confined to a wheelchair. How do you comfort him when he sees his younger siblings doing things he knows he can never do?

First of all, you do the same thing you'd do with any firstborn who was bypassed, and that's administer large doses of encouragement.

Beyond that, you should always let the firstborn enjoy the privileges that go with being the oldest—a later bedtime, a bigger allowance, and so on. He may not be able to do all the things his younger brothers and sisters do, but because he is the oldest he also has some special privileges that are not (yet) granted to them.

Remember that one of the best things any parent can do is to identify with his children and express his feelings to them. If they know that Mom and Dad are proud of them and really do love them, they can weather just about any other storm that comes their way!

8

Help Your Firstborn: Stick to Your Guns

I was scheduled to be a guest on a radio show to talk about my book *Sex Begins in the Kitchen.*[1]

It was almost time for the show to start, and I was sitting in the green room—the room where all the guests remain prior to going on the air on a radio or TV show—waiting for the show's host to arrive. It was two minutes before airtime, and still no sign of him.

Suddenly the door burst open, and a tall young man bounced into the room carrying a copy of my book. I was sitting with my legs crossed, and he reached over and whacked the bottom of my foot with the book.

"Come on, Doc. You're on."

I thought, "What a great intro!"

As I followed him out the door and into the studio, he apologized for being late but explained that he had "just got in."

As we settled into our chairs in the studio, I noticed for the first time that his eyes were glassy and his pupils dilated. The man appeared to be stoned.

He gave the cover of the book an amused glance and said, *"Sex Begins in the Kitchen,* huh? Great book!"

And then he added in a rather contemptuous tone, "I'm so glad you're not one of those born-again Christians."

With that comment, the red light came on, and we were on the air. I was already writing the evening off as a total disaster. The host had probably been out all night partying, and he obviously hadn't read the book, or he wouldn't have made the comment about born-again Christians. As for me, I didn't know whether to immediately correct his wrong impression or just to flow with things for a while and see what happened. I figured that if I started sounding "too religious," the occasion might turn into a verbal battle between the show's host and me, and I didn't want that to happen—so I said nothing.

Surprisingly the show went along smoothly. The guy was in his element at the helm of a show, and the phone lines stayed lit up as we received calls from listeners.

Near the midway point of the show a call came in from a young woman who said that she was a 24-year-old virgin and that she planned to stay a virgin until her wedding day.

"What I want to know, Dr. Leman, is whether you think I'm doing the right thing."

The host shot me a devilish wink.

"Hey, Doc," he smirked. "Whaddaya think of this little filly saving herself for her husband?"

His tone said that he knew what my answer was going to be. He thought I was going to tell this young woman to quit being ridiculous, to get on with "life," and probably to give her virginity to the first man who wanted it.

And that's when I felt that little nudging from the Holy Spirit. It was as if God was saying to me, "Okay, Leman, you're on."

"Well, you know," I began, "we were talking before we came on the air about born-again Christians—and I am one of those people. And so I think this woman is right on in what she's doing."

I looked over at the host to see if he had swallowed his headset. So far he hadn't, so I went on.

"I think she's using good judgment. She's decreased her chances of getting cervical cancer and a number of other diseases. In my opinion she's increasing her chances for a long, happy marriage, and she's practicing good self-respect and good psychology as well."

I knew that my words were not what the host expected of me, and now I wasn't quite sure what to expect from him.

He sat still for a second or two, and then he began slowly nodding his head.

He looked directly into the microphone, as if he were looking into the face of a friend.

"You know, you guys know how I feel about these things—but I kind of like what this guy is saying. I think he's making a lot of sense."

Well, I don't know if anyone was more surprised to hear those words come out of his mouth than I was.

But I learned a valuable lesson that night, even though it was something I had been stressing for years. Namely, I learned the importance of sticking to your guns—especially when you know that what you're doing is right.

What does this have to do with parenting your firstborn son or daughter? Plenty.

Think about the poor firstborn for a minute. The follower of rules, the kid who tries so hard to toe the line he always has chalk marks on the front of his shoes. What is going to happen to him if Mom and Dad aren't consistent?

The firstborn is very much in need of consistency in his life. He needs absolutes. He needs to know that if he does this or that, the natural consequence will be this other.

I'll tell you another thing about your firstborn, and that is that he's a pretty smart cookie. He knows when his parents are inconsistent, and he'll push them to the limits before they know what hit them.

Earlier I mentioned reality discipline. This is one of my favorite concepts, because it really works. I know, because I've seen it work time and time again.

Reality discipline not only means that you are consistent and that you stick to your guns. It also means that your child is responsible for whatever consequences his actions bring his way.

Here's how I explained it in *Making Children Mind Without Losing Yours.*

"Action-oriented discipline is based on the reality that there are times—sometimes several per day—when you have to pull the rug out and let the little 'buzzards' tumble. I don't mean that literally, of course, but when I talk about pulling the rug out, I mean disciplining a child in such a way that he accepts responsibility and learns accountability for his actions."[2]

Marianne is a nine-year-old firstborn who was a very picky eater. Supper time ought to be a happy time for every family, but it certainly wasn't the case in hers. She turned it into a nightmare, and it got so bad that her mother dreaded seeing supper time roll around. Marianne just didn't seem to like anything. What could Mom do to change the situation?

The answer was a simple one. If Marianne didn't want to eat, she didn't have to eat. But if she got hungry later on, that was tough. Her tummy might rumble, and she might ask her mother if she please, please, could have something to eat—but she still wasn't to have anything.

Mom wasn't too sure about this, because it seemed kind of cruel, but she finally agreed to try it.

A few nights later Mom was fixing spaghetti for supper. Marianne had let it be known on many other occasions that she hated spaghetti, so Mom didn't even bother to put a place setting on the table for her.

When the girl came in from playing, just prior to supper time, she noticed right away that something wasn't quite right.

"What's going on here?" she asked in a rather suspicious tone of voice.

"Well, dear," Mom replied, as cheerfully and nonchalantly as she could, "we're having spaghetti tonight, and since I know how you don't like spaghetti, I figured it wasn't fair to make you eat it."

Marianne stood there for a moment trying to figure out if dear old Mom had really blown a gasket this time. But after sensing that this was no joke and that Mom was serious, she went over to the stove where the spaghetti was cooking.

Peering into the pot where the meatballs were cooking, she took a couple of deep whiffs.

They smelled mighty good.

"Well," she said, "I think I could eat *that* spaghetti." She said it in a way that gave her an out, as if this were some sort of extraspecial tasty spaghetti when it was really the sort that Mom always fixed.

"All right, dear. Why don't you go ahead and fix yourself a place at the table then?"

Marianne did exactly as her mother requested. She ate two large helpings of spaghetti and meatballs that night and even told her mother afterward how good it had been. It wasn't the end of all the pickiness with Marianne, but whenever the girl complained, Mom was quick to say, "You don't have to eat if you don't want to. But just remember that you won't get anything later."

It wasn't too long before Marianne quit complaining altogether, and mealtime became the happy time it ought to be.

And that's reality discipline.

Help! Mom's Drowning in the Sixth Grade!

Another mother came to me with the complaint that her son was just about to fail in school, and this despite the fact that she did everything she could possibly do to help him.

Now, this poor woman had been through the sixth grade about 20 years ago, and she didn't have any desire to go through it again, especially at 32 years of age—but that's basically what she was doing.

It may have been Johnny's homework, but it kept Mom busy every night. She didn't have time to watch any of her favorite shows or to read the daily newspaper or to sew or to do any of the other things she would have liked to do. As a single mother with a full-time job, by the time she got supper fixed, the dishes washed and put away, and then helped Johnny with his homework, the evening was gone and it was time for bed.

You might say that homework was the centerpiece of the family. It was what Mom and son seemed to spend most of their time together doing.

And yet for all the time she spent with him, his grades were getting worse, and he seemed to be working much below his capabilities.

I suggested to her that it was Johnny's responsibility to get good grades in school. He was supposed to earn those As, not Mom. Perhaps the problem was that he was leaning too heavily on good old Mom, expecting her to pull him through. But she wasn't there in class with him during the day, and that's when he fell apart. Johnny was a firstborn discouraged perfectionist who was conscientious about his schoolwork but simply did not trust himself and did not think he was capable of doing a good job on his own. (And those discouraged prophecies many times are self-fulfilling.)

It wasn't but a few days after talking to me that the moment of truth arrived.

Johnny called her at work, as he often did, and asked her what time she was going to be home.

"I don't know, dear, why?"

"Because I've got a math test tomorrow, and I just know I'm going to fail. I don't understand this stuff. I need you to come home early so you can help me study."

"Oh, honey, I'm sorry, but I can't do that. In fact, I was planning on playing tennis after work, and I'll be home a little later than usual." She wasn't lying. She was planning on playing tennis—for the first time in months—and had arranged for a baby-sitter to stop by and fix dinner for her son. But any other time she would have immediately scrapped her tennis plans, told her boss she needed to leave a few minutes early, and rushed home to bail Johnny out. But not this time.

"But what am I gonna do?" The boy sounded as if he were on the verge of panic.

"Well . . ." Mom thought for a moment. "The only thing I can suggest is that you study really hard and do the best you can."

"But Mom—"

"I'm sorry, honey. You'll do fine, I'm sure. Gotta go." And she hung up the phone.

You'd better believe it wasn't an easy thing to do. She wanted to rush right home and rescue her little boy, but she didn't. Instead she went off and played tennis—although rather poorly, because her mind was at home doing homework.

Do you know what happened? That's right, Johnny got an A on his test. He could hardly believe it himself. When he saw what he was capable of doing, he began to bring all of his grades up. Not only that, but homework was no longer a two-person job, nor did it consume the entire evening as it had for so long.

Now, it might not have turned out that way. Johnny could have flunked the test. But whatever the outcome, it was Johnny's responsibility and his job to face the consequences.

Reality discipline will pay off. Sometimes sooner, sometimes later, but it will eventually bring about the desired effect in the lives of your children. I can't guarantee that the results you're seeking will always come about immediately, as they did with Marianne and Johnny, but I cite those two kids as proof that the system works!

I know a little bit about marketing strategy, and the companies that are able to market themselves and their products successfully know this important truth:

Never Choose Short-Term Success at the Expense of Long-Term Goals!

That's a strategy that pays off in marketing and in dealing with children in general and firstborn children in particular.

What do I mean? If Johnny's mother had kept her eyes on short-term successes, she would have rushed home and helped her son get ready for his math test. But even if she had helped him get an A on this one, it wouldn't have been of any benefit to him when the next test rolled around. Instead we would have seen a repeat performance—a panicked Johnny, Mom speeding to the rescue, and the two of them struggling for hours to get over yet another hurdle.

The goal was not to pass a test. The goal was to improve Johnny's study habits, to show him that he was capable of learning on his own, and to change what had become an endless chain of homework nights.

Reality discipline involves keeping your eye on the big picture and coming to understand what your long-term goals for your children really are.

And that "reality" part has another meaning too. It means that you try to have a realistic view of your children's capabilities and that you don't put undue pressure on them.

This is one of four common mistakes parents make in dealing with their firstborn children. Those four mistakes are

1. Expecting too much from your firstborn
2. Using your firstborn as a shock absorber
3. Using your firstborn as a scapegoat.
4. Letting your firstborn watch you fight.

Let's take a closer look.

1. Expecting Too Much from Your Firstborn

Little Gertrude may be working at the top of her capacity to learn her "gozindas" (as in, two gozinda sixteen how many times?). So don't expect her to be conquering the advanced formulas of trigonometry and calculus.

If eight-year-old Cornelius just swam the width of the swimming pool for the first time, you shouldn't take him out the very next day and expect him to swim the English Channel!

Unfortunately, that's what some parents seem to do.

Reality discipline makes allowances for a child's capabilities, and it recognizes that everyone makes mistakes. (There's a tremendous difference between a mistake and purposeful disobedience.) It also recognizes that there are varying calibers of mistakes.

If four-year-old Henrietta spills her milk at supper time, that's a small mistake—even if it happens to be chocolate milk and it runs all over your brand-new and very expensive ivory carpeting. Four-year-olds are going to spill their milk occasionally; it's just one of those things that happens, and it doesn't require punishment.

By the same token, if 11-year-old Henry leaves his jacket in his locker at school, that's also a typical kind of kid's mistake. But if he does it six days in a row, after Mom repeatedly reminds him not to forget it, then his mistake has taken on much greater proportions and calls for corrective action.

But please, Mom and Dad, don't expect too much of your children. I don't care how many books you read about turning toddlers into geniuses or how many new theories spring up about how much little children can handle. The plain fact is that children are children, and they should be allowed to be what they are! Our modern children, and especially those guinea pig firstborns, are living under tremendous pressure, and much of it is applied by their parents.

That's why we have seven- and eight-year-old children who are stressed out, drawing black pictures in school, and talking about death.

I once got a call from a very proud woman who asked me if I did any work with "gifted" children.

"You see, my little Josephine is really gifted. In fact I think she might be a genius."

"Oh, really. And how do you know about this?" I asked her.

"Well . . . she can count backward from ten to one."

"Uh-huh. And. . . ."

"And, well, like I said, she can count backwards from ten to one!"

What I felt like saying, but didn't, was "Lady, give me a break!" or "Lady, give your child a break!"

I explained to her that it was not an unusual event for a three-year-old to be able to count backward from ten to one. The only problem was that I don't think the woman believed me, and somewhere along the line, when her little girl starts bringing home "average" grades, this mother is going to let her daughter know how "disappointed" she is, and the little girl will be hurt.

I said earlier that I believe the most serious mistake a parent can make is to believe that if he just loves his children enough, they'll turn out all right.

The *most common* mistake parents make is expecting too much from kids—and it's almost always the firstborn who gets hit with his parents' overexpectations.

2. Using Your Firstborn as a Shock Absorber

Not only are firstborns expected to be able to do practically everything, but they're also treated as if they're shock absorbers.

In other words their parents may lean on them and expect them to handle things they're not emotionally ready to handle.

"Well, son, let me tell you. Your mother and I aren't getting along so well, and I just don't know what we're going to do about it."

"Let me tell you, Harriet, this family is in sad shape financially. We're just not making enough money, and we might have to sell the house and go live in a tent."

"Harley, I'm sort of worried about myself. I just don't feel good, and I'm afraid I might have some deadly disease or something."

These are the sorts of things firstborns hear, and they're often coupled with words like "But now, don't tell your little brother and sister, because they're too young to worry about these things."

Well, what about the firstborn? He's lying in bed at night, unable to sleep, carrying a 10-ton load on his shoulders when he should be thinking about baseball or cartoons.

Sometimes Mom might be really angry at Dad, and she just needs someone to talk to. She turns to her firstborn, pouring all her feelings into his lap, and once again he's simply incapable of dealing with it. He never dreamed Mom could feel this way, and finding out that she does has dealt a powerful blow to his sense of security.

You should be able to bring your children into your confidence to a certain extent, but you must keep in mind that a child is not ready to handle the stresses, pressures, and uncertainties of life that we adults face every day. If you must talk to someone about a deep, distressing problem, talk to a trusted friend, a clergyman, or a professional therapist—but don't use your firstborn as a sounding board.

3. Using Your Firstborn as a Scapegoat

If you're old enough, you're bound to remember the old TV commercial from the 1960s. The man comes into the house after a hard day at work, and he's fuming.

"Billy!" he screams. "How many times have I told you to keep your bike out of the driveway?"

Little Billy looks as if his poor heart is breaking, and his remorseful father puts his hand to his head while we hear him thinking, "Sure you've got a headache, but don't take it out on Billy."

Now, in case you don't remember the commercial, I won't leave you in suspense. Dad quickly gulps down a couple of Excedrin, and in no time at all he's back to his normal, happy, good-humored self, and he and Billy are having a fine time together.

That was an effective commercial. It sold a lot of Excedrin. But it was also a pretty good little morality play. If you have a headache, don't take it out on your children. And especially if your headache comes to you in the form of a demanding, critical boss, an insensitive husband, or a gossipy friend, don't take it out on your firstborn. That, unfortunately, is what far too many men and women do.

The firstborn is often the target of anger that Mom actually feels for Dad or vice versa.

For instance, Herschell had a habit of going out with the boys after work and not bothering to call his wife, Margie, to tell her what his plans were. If she had dinner ready and on the table, and he didn't get home to eat it, so what? His attitude was that he worked hard all day, he deserved some time to "play," and she had no business turning it into a big deal.

This sort of thing happened just often enough to keep Margie

stirred up and angry. And her anger was more and more difficult to control. When she tried to express her feelings to Herschell, he simply wasn't interested. If she wanted to yell, that
was fine with him, but he wasn't going to pay any attention to
her, and he wasn't going to change his ways.

So what did Margie do? She began to notice things about her
eight-year-old firstborn, Jeremy, that reminded her of Herschell.

"You're just like your father!" she would say to him whenever
he did something to cause her the slightest inconvenience. She
seemed to snap at him about everything. Poor Jeremy kept on
his eggshell-walking shoes all the time, but they didn't seem to
help. No matter how hard he tried to stay on Mom's good side,
he couldn't seem to do it.

Then one night, after she had been particularly hard on him,
she walked past his bedroom door and heard him crying softly.

She opened the door just a crack and asked him what was
wrong.

"It's, it's, it's . . ." he couldn't seem to choke the words out.

"It's what, honey?" she asked a bit impatiently.

"It's just that . . . that you don't like me anymore, and I
don't know why."

Well, you can imagine that hearing those words helped to jar
Margie back to reality.

Did she have a right to be angry? You bet she did. But she
had no right to take it out on her firstborn.

She resolved at that moment to stop doing that, and her relationship with her son began to improve. Unfortunately, her relationship with Herschell didn't improve until she finally told him
she wanted a divorce. This drastic step jarred him to reality, and
he made an honest and mostly successful effort to change his
behavior.

I have also seen numerous incidents where one spouse would
accuse the firstborn of taking the side of the other spouse in
family squabbles.

"Sure, Betsy, go ahead and take your father's side! You always take your father's side! You and he against me—is that the way it's always going to be?"

The truth is that all Betsy wants is for Mom and Dad to get along. She's doing her best to be neutral and may even wonder how she got dragged into the war.

Here again she is being used as a scapegoat. The only thing she's done wrong is to get too close to the battle zone!

Remember, Mom and Dad, when you're mad at someone else, don't take it out on your kids! My firstborn daughter, Holly, has taught me much about life. For example, one night I was "getting on her case" for no good reason. Holly caught me by surprise when she looked up from the dinner table and said, "Dad, you know what you should do? Read your own book!" Talk about wise words from an eleven-year-old. Holly was right. I was using her as a scapegoat.

4. Letting Your Firstborn Watch You Fight

Many modern and sophisticated parents think nothing about having an all-out verbal battle in front of their children. They don't believe in "sheltering" their children from reality. And besides, fighting in front of the kids teaches them that we can have our disagreements, but we can also get over them and still be friends.

Well, let me say this about that: Bullcrumble!

This is a dose of reality that your children can do without.

It doesn't help them in any way. All it does is make them feel insecure and damage their self-esteem.

This sort of thing is especially hurtful for the firstborn, since he's usually the one who gets closest to the action and who understands better just what's going on here. In fact he will be the one who tries to shield the other children, putting his hands over his little sister's ears, for example.

If you must fight—and I suppose that sooner or later just about all married couples must—take the battle into your bedroom, behind closed doors, and keep your voices down.

Remember, Mom and Dad, your love and marriage is your child's main source of comfort and security in an all-too-insecure world.

So, stick to your guns and refuse to expect too much from your firstborn, stop using him as the family shock absorber or a scapegoat, and refuse to fight in front of him!

Those Trying Teen Times

Now, it's quite a bit easier to stick to those guns of yours when your children are smaller and your word is law. But what about when those cute little tykes turn into teenagers? All I can say is that it's more important than ever to chart a steady course through those stormy teen-age seas.

As always, this means using reality discipline. It also means giving your children much greater freedom to make right or wrong choices for themselves. By this time in their lives you have to trust that they have learned some things, that they've absorbed some of the values you've tried to teach them over the years.

Evelyn, for instance, wanted to go to a party, but she wasn't really sure it was the thing to do. She knew there'd probably be some drinking and pot-smoking, but if she didn't go, she'd feel like she was left out and missing something.

So she asked her mother what she should do.

"I don't know, honey," her mother told her. "You're seventeen, and you know what's right and wrong. So you just do what you think is best."

Mom felt pretty good, because she was sure that once Evie thought about it, she wouldn't want to go.

That's why her chin fell so far it almost hit the kitchen floor when her daughter told her the following day that she had decided to attend the party. What's more, she wanted Mom to drive her there.

The party was two days away, and Mom didn't take it all that well. She came close to putting her foot down and telling her daughter she couldn't go, but she understood the importance of allowing Evie to make her own choice in the matter.

When Friday night came, and they pulled up in front of the house where the party was being held, they were greeted by the sounds of loud, heavy metal music. There were cars parked everywhere, up and down the street, and in the front yard several young people were standing around drinking beer.

Mom was hoping that Evie would change her mind once she saw what was going on there, but she didn't. However, as her daughter was getting out of the car, Mom said, "Listen, I'm going to drive up this street for a block or so and find a place to park. I'll wait for a few minutes . . . just in case."

"Okay, Mom."

Mom didn't have long to wait. Less than 15 minutes had passed when she looked into the rearview mirror and saw her daughter walking up the street.

"I'm really glad you waited," she told her mother. "There was a lot of stuff going on there that I didn't like—and I'd rather be at home."

Now, any child who makes a good choice like that deserves to have his ego stroked.

Go ahead and tell him you're proud of him for making the right decision. Teenagers need to feel good about themselves, so when your teen has done something that makes you proud, don't be afraid to tell him so.

Be careful, of course, not to tie your encouragement to the level of accomplishment, but rather to the effort made.

What does that mean? It means that if Johnny gives school his best effort, it doesn't really matter if he comes home with straight As. The important thing is that you recognize the effort he's put into his schoolwork. Your teenager should know that it's not as important to get straight As as it is to be an A sort of person!

Remember the biblical story of the widow who put two mites into the temple treasury?[3] Now, two mites wasn't very much money, perhaps a couple of pennies or a nickel, and yet Jesus told his disciples that she had put more into the "offering plate" than anyone else. Why? Because she gave all she had.

Some kids never crack a book and still come home with all As, whereas others can spend hours studying and still struggle to achieve Bs or Cs. You can't judge someone's effort by the results he gets.

And always remember that you can go easier on a firstborn teenager because he's generally hard enough on himself!

Give him some guidance and help him make the best decision, sure, but don't be overbearing and push too hard.

Should your teenager find himself in some sort of trouble—whether he's depressed, or angry, or struggling with perfectionism—don't throw your hands up in the air and think you did something wrong. The firstborn teenager is going to struggle occasionally as he sheds the cocoon of his childhood.

In his book *Teen-Agers—When to Worry and What to Do* Douglas H. Powell gives six ways parents can create a more helping environment for their teenagers who may be having difficulty with their lives:[4]

Maintain (Loving) Contact. This means exactly what it sounds like—keeping the lines of communication open and reacting to your children in a loving fashion.

Foster the Ability to Enjoy Working, Loving, and Playing. In other words, teach your children good habits and try to see to it that they learn to enjoy those three areas of their lives: work, whether schoolwork or a part-time job after school; loving, involving his relationships with his siblings, his friends (and especially his friends of the opposite sex), and his God; and playing, whatever form it may take.

Promote High-Level Adaptation to Stress. The best way to show your teenager how to handle stress is to show him that you can handle it well yourself. Sure, you're under tremendous pressure sometimes, but it's not the end of the world, and your life doesn't fall apart.

Encourage the Development of Resources. This, basically, involves stressing the pluses in your teenager's life and adding to those pluses however and whenever you can.

Secure Sources of Support. Don't be hesitant to reach out to others when you need them.

Keep Trying New Approaches. If something doesn't work, try something else!

Leman's Laws
for Firstborn Teens

Let me add to these and give you a few quick laws of my own for dealing with firstborn teens.

1. GIVE YOUR TEEN LESS WORK TO DO INSTEAD OF MORE.

Some people think that you ought to give your firstborn more work to do as he grows older. I disagree. When your firstborn gets into high school, he'll have many activities bidding for his time, and his work load at home ought to be lessened so he can pursue them.

He may want to play in the band, be in the school play, go out for the football team, or be involved in a club. Then again, he may want to have a part-time job. Whatever it is, your teenager needs and deserves the freedom to begin involving himself more in these healthy activities. That's why, when your firstborn enters high school, it's time for the other children in the family to assume some of his responsibilities.

2. IT'S NOT ALWAYS THE FIRSTBORN'S FAULT.

"Mom, he's picking on me!"

"Harold, you stop that this instant. How many times have I told you to be nice to your little brother?!"

Does this sound familiar?

It should, because it's probably one of the most common dialogues in the English language. And admittedly there are plenty of occasions when the firstborn needs to hear something like that. But there are also plenty of times when he doesn't deserve it.

Just in case you've forgotten, Mom and Dad, let me remind you that little brothers and sisters often delight in getting the firstborn in trouble. They'll push and pull and tease and cajole, but when they finally get what they've been going after—when the firstborn shows the least inclination to strike back—it's "Hey, Mom, he's picking on me again!"

How does the firstborn handle the situation? He tries to present his point of view:

"But Mom, he was—"

"I don't care what *he* was doing! You're the oldest, and you should know better."

And while the firstborn is getting his lecture from Mom, what is the little brother doing? He's probably over in the corner, sticking his tongue out at his brother and making faces.

Do you wonder why I know so much about this? Don't forget, I'm a little brother myself! I learned all the tricks of the trade years ago!

Why does the firstborn always take the blame? Bill Cosby says it's because parents aren't interested in justice—they just want quiet![5] I think there's a great deal of truth in that, but I also think that parents just naturally take the side of the smaller, underdog sibling. And that isn't always fair.

One friend told me how he and his older brother loved to wrestle when they were kids. The older brother would always win, but my friend wouldn't give in. All he had to do was say "I give," and the match would be over, but he simply refused to do it.

And so his brother would have him in a hammerlock.

"Say give."

"No!"

"Say give!"

"You're hurting me!"

"Well, just say give and I'll stop!"

"Mom! Mom! He's hurting me! Owooooo-ow-ow!"

Mom would come in to see what all the hollering was about and quickly size up the situation. Big brother was being a bully, and he was going to be punished.

"You know," my friend said, "I was thirty years old before I ever apologized to him for all those times!"

Well, despite Bill Cosby's very funny line, I think that parents should be interested in justice, and they should also remember that it isn't always the firstborn who's being a bully!

3. KNOW YOUR FIRSTBORN'S STRENGTHS.

Every child has innate strengths and weaknesses, and it's the job of his parents to help him discover and develop those strengths.

What is your firstborn's area of strength? It may be any one of hundreds of things: art, music, sports, math, writing, mechanics, carpentry, fashion design, drama, public speaking, and on and on the list goes.

When you see your firstborn do something well, point it out to him.

Tell him, "You know, you really did a good job on this painting."

"Do you think so?"

"I really do! You have a lot of ability!"

Sometimes it's not easy for parents to be objective about their children's talents. If you're a math whiz, for instance, but your daughter is interested only in her music, don't try to turn her into a math whiz, too. Some parents try to live their lives over again through their children, and it just doesn't work. Look for and seek to develop the talents that your firstborn really has and not the ones you would like him to have.

Another thing to remember is that you can develop your child's talents without pushing too hard. For example, say your child is a good swimmer and likes to race against you. But he's only eight, so there's no way he can beat you.

Should you go ahead and beat his brains out every time, showing him that he has a long way to go? Or should you let him win every time in order to build up his confidence?

My answer is neither. If you beat him all the time, he might become discouraged and give up, and there's no reason to discourage him. On the other hand, if you let him win all the time, he will have false confidence in his natural abilities.

But it's okay to let your kid win once in a while.

I have always loved baseball, for instance, and I will never forget a game I was playing with a group of older kids—including my brother and sister—in the front yard of my house when I was four or five years old.

Somehow I hit the ball, which was kind of a miracle in itself, and then I began running around the bases. I was almost out at first but—whoops!—the first baseman dropped the ball. I headed for second, and he probably would have had me out by a mile, but he made a bad throw and the ball went on into center field! By the time someone had picked up the ball I had rounded third and was heading for home. Here came the throw—but it was way off line and got past the catcher.

Not satisfied with one run, I took off for another trip around the bases—and you know what? I made it! Not bad! Two runs on one base hit! And I was as proud as I could be.

Looking back on that long-ago scene, I know now what was going on. The bigger kids were giving the little guy a break. And that makes the memory mean even more to me.

I'll never forget how excited I was that day. And I'm sure I owe some of my love of the sport of baseball to that two-for-one home run.

4. BE FAIR TO YOUR DAUGHTER.

It has been my firsthand observation that the firstborn female often gets a raw deal. She gets all of the responsibilities of being a firstborn, but very few of the privileges.

People will look you in the eye and tell you they don't believe in the double standard, but the way they treat their firstborn daughter says otherwise.

She is expected to be mature, levelheaded, and wise, but she's also expected to keep her toe firmly glued to that line.

Meanwhile her younger brother may be footloose and fancy free, and he also may have more input into important family decisions. Her curfew may be earlier than his, she may be expected to do much more around the house than he is, and so on. (Most firstborns are expected to do more around the house, as we've talked about before, but even this can be exaggerated in the case of the firstborn female.)

Well, 'tain't fair, and you can be assured that this sort of treatment will take its toll. She's going to either rebel with a vengeance or grow up believing she can't measure up to others.

If you're not being fair to your firstborn girl, I have a good piece of advice for you:

"Cut it out!"

5. LEARN HOW TO SLIP
IN AN OCCASIONAL COMMERCIAL.

Suppose you have done a good job on point number three, and you are keenly aware of your firstborn's abilities. Your little Mary Margaret is blessed with tremendous musical talent, and you want her to attend music camp this summer. She's not so sure about it.

One approach would be to say, "Mary Margaret, there is a music camp this summer, and you're going, and that's all there is to it." It might be effective in the short term, but I doubt very seriously that that approach will instill into Mary Margaret the desire to develop her musical skills.

What I suggest is that you learn to slip in an occasional soft-sell commercial about the camp, such as:

"Maybe I'm biased, but I think you've really got a lot of talent, and I'd like to see you develop it. Again, this is just my opinion, and I'm not going to force you to go, but I really do wish you would think about it."

In other words, encourage the child, make it her decision, but help her to see that she will be doing herself a favor by attending the camp.

It could be that she'll think about it and say, "I still don't want to go."

But chances are better than 50-50 that she'll decide camp might be a pretty good idea after all.

Now, what if your child comes to you and asks for your opinion about something? First off, that's a pretty good sign. The child respects your opinion, or she wouldn't ask for it.

But even then it's time for a little soft-sell commercial.

"First of all, honey, remember that this is just my opinion . . . and I could be wrong. But I really think this music camp will be a very good opportunity for you."

What happens when you say something like "I could be wrong"? Does your child automatically think, "Gee, Mom's not too sure about this; I'd better ask someone else"? Not at all. Actually it makes your input more valuable. It shows that you're doing your best to see the situation from the child's point of view. You're not playing dictator and trying to run the child's life for her, and she will appreciate that. In addition to that, she will feel good about the fact that you are being open and vulnerable with her, admitting that you don't know all the answers.

This sort of honesty will raise, not lower, your stock in her eyes.

So if you want to guide your firstborn safely through the teen years, remember to stick to your guns and keep Leman's Laws in mind, and—believe it or not—both you and your firstborn will survive!

Oh, yes, one more suggestion: Be sure to tell your firstborn every day that you love 'em.

Remember: The average teenager has only two emotional outbursts per year. The problem is they last about six months each.

9

Meet Superfirstborn– The Lonely Only

Y ou know what they say about only children.

They're likely to be spoiled, selfish, lazy, perhaps a bit aloof.

After all, they've spent most of their lives being the center of attention, probably being waited on hand and foot, living in what amounts to the lap of luxury, even in the poorest of families. (They don't have to share their toys and other goodies like the rest of us, so even if they don't have as much, it just naturally seems like more.)

If that's the way only children are, what sort of adults would you expect them to make? Does the word *useless* sound right?

Well, let's take a look at a short list of some lonely onlys and see if they turned out to fit the stereotype:

Franklin D. Roosevelt, Leonardo da Vinci, Charles Lindbergh, Ted Koppel, Steve Allen, T. Boone Pickens, Carl Icahn, Dick Cavett, and Indira Gandhi.

Oh, yeah, I see that the critics of only children are 100 percent correct. What a bunch of no-accounts!

Well, I hope you know by now that I don't agree with the misconceived stereotype so many people do seem to believe about only children. Far from being people who are used to having things handed to them, and who insist on being waited on for the rest of their lives, only children are among the top achievers in every area of endeavor.

In fact the only child tends to take on all of the characteristics of the firstborn. Magnify that two or three times and you've got it.

Where the firstborn is organized, the only child is superorganized!

Where the firstborn tends to be a perfectionist, the only child is in the perfectionist hall of fame!

If you can trust a firstborn to do the job right, you can bet your last dollar on the only child, and he won't let you down.

You can expect a certain type of behavior from an only child, and then there are things he just wouldn't do.

You know, for instance, that I'm a lastborn. You probably also know that I live in Tucson and live and die with the fortunes of University of Arizona sports teams. I am one of those people who cheer for two teams: the Wildcats from the U of A and whoever is playing the Sun Devils from Arizona State University.

That's why it made perfect sense for me to spend $25 extra and get a personalized license plate that says, "Zap ASU."

I got it primarily because it gets a chuckle, especially when I'm driving around Tucson, and I like to see people laugh. When I'm sitting at a red light, I'll look into my rearview mirror and see someone in a car behind me pointing at the license plate and chuckling. I like that.

Most likely the only child would look at my license plate, or at least the fact that I paid $25 extra for it, and say, "What's the point?"

I'm not saying that only children don't have a sense of humor. It's just that their humor might be a bit more planned and sophisticated. They are not the sort of people to say, "Oh, what the heck, I think I'll do it, just for the fun of it."

If that kind of spontaneous behavior is what you're seeing, then I doubt very much that you're looking at an only child.

An Only-Child Honor Roll

A number of the people I most admire in this world are only children.

I think of James Dobson, the best-selling author, psychologist, and founder of Focus on the Family. I can't think of anyone who has done more to build up the family than Dr. Dobson. He's a man who's absolutely tireless in his efforts to improve family life. Look at any best-seller list, and you are likely to see at least two or three books by this fine man—books on parenting, disciplining children, dealing with marital relationships, etc. And his films are shown in churches all across America, cutting across every denominational line.

Now, you might look at James Dobson and think, "What would someone who grew up as an only child really know about the inner workings of the modern family?" Well, he knows a great deal. There are people throughout this country who have followed his advice and who can tell you that they're glad they did.

Dr. Dobson applied the special traits of his only-child nature to his field of study, and that's one of the reasons he has been so successful.

He's scholarly, organized, conscientious, and reliable. He wants to make sure that the advice he gives is the very best, because he knows that people are depending on him.

I treasure a bit of advice I received from him one day not too long ago when my wife, Sande, and I were having lunch with him.

"Jim," I asked, "if there was one bit of advice you could give to me, what would it be?"

Without hesitating, he looked over at Sande.

"Kevin . . . before you do anything, whatever it is, run it by Sande first."

That's good advice for any man who is married to an intelligent, perceptive woman, but it's doubly good advice for someone like me—a lastborn flake, who is married to a wise firstborn!

You'd expect that sort of advice from a no-nonsense only child such as James Dobson.

And there are many other only children who have my respect and admiration. Among them are television personality Steve Allen, ABC's Ted Koppel, and Dick Cavett.

(If you live outside of Arizona, you've probably never heard of Pat McMahon. But those of us who are residents of the Grand Canyon State know that he is one of the best radio/television personalities in the business. The man is a marvel. And he's an only child.)

One of my favorite newspaper columnists, Darrell Sifford, is an only child who has written an excellent book on the subject. His book, in fact, is called *The Only Child.*

So you see, all those criticisms of only children have been well off the mark.

Even Dr. Alfred Adler, whom I mentioned earlier, and who all but founded the school of psychology that stresses the importance of birth order, had some harsh words about only children.

Said Adler, "The Only Child has difficulties with every independent activity and sooner or later they become useless in life."[1]

I'm sorry, Alfie, but "it ain't necessarily so."

Onlys do have certain special problems, but they also have special strengths and abilities.

Special Problems of Onlys

We will talk later on about the special strengths and benefits derived from being an only child, but first let's get the bad stuff out of the way.

1. BEING THE SPECIAL JEWEL

Remember what W. C. Fields said about how anyone who hated dogs and children couldn't be *all* bad? Well, I never agreed with the funny man about that, but if there was ever anyone who could have changed my mind, it was little Ruth Ann.

The girl, at eight years of age, was an absolute terror who did not believe in the theory that our solar system revolves around the sun. As far as she was concerned, it revolved around her. The problem was, of course, that for too long her parents had made it seem that way.

They gave her everything she wanted, but she was a bottom-less pit who only wanted "more, more, more" and was never satisfied. They would spend the entire day giving in to her endless demands, but then their attempt to refuse her anything at all would be met with an incredible tantrum, seemingly worthy of entry in the *Guinness Book of World Records*.

"I'm sorry, Ruth Ann, but you can't have any more soda today. You've had too much already."

"Oh, you're so mean to me. You never let me have anything! I hate you!" And on and on she would go.

Ruth Ann was an only child, and it was easy for me to see why. If I had to live with a little monster like that, you can bet that I wouldn't be in a hurry to have any others just like her. The very thought is enough to give me goose pimples, even now!

But you see, Ruth Ann's parents had tried for 10 years to have a child before they were finally successful. Not only that, but her mother had suffered two miscarriages before giving birth to Ruth Ann. You can imagine how she felt, finally having her own, precious little baby after those two miscarriages. No wonder they spoiled their baby girl rotten from the time they got her home from the hospital. It was understandable, but not really excusable, because they had created a monster just as surely as if they had moved to Transylvania, hired a man named Dr. Frankenstein, and hooked up some electrodes to their daughter's temples. She was a mess!

When her parents brought her to me, it was obvious that they were hoping I would wave a magic wand or sprinkle some pixie dust on her and change her behavior overnight. But of course that wasn't possible. The only solution was for the parents to get tough, and they didn't seem to be the type.

We had a lot of work to do!

It didn't take the little "lady" long to see that I wasn't going to put up with the same type of behavior her parents tolerated. At first she was as snotty and rude as a child could be, but once she saw that I wasn't intimidated, she calmed down and became more cooperative.

Actually the primary need wasn't so much to change Ruth Ann's behavior as it was to change the behavior of her parents. Quite simply their job was to stop giving in. If their daughter threw a tantrum, so what? If they were in a public place, and she began screaming about something, I advised them to let her scream.

"But what will people think?"

"If anybody looks at you," I said, "just roll your eyes, shake your head, and say, 'Can you believe how some people's children behave?' Then at least they'll think you're taking care of her for someone else!"

It wasn't easy for Ruth Ann's parents to change their ways. They tried not to give in, but they kept doing it anyway.

Then, as time went by, they began to get tougher. They realized that if they really loved their daughter, the best thing they could do for her was learn how to say no to her. Then they had to remember that after they had told her no, it didn't matter how much she screamed or cried or stamped her foot; the answer was still no!

After eight years of being spoiled, Ruth Ann's behavior didn't change overnight, but she eventually began to come around. Today it's hard to believe the pleasant young lady used to be Lady Frankenstein!

In some instances, the parents of the "special jewel" do everything for him in an attempt to keep him closer to them. The message they send the child is "We're the only real friends you have, the only people you can trust."

They love their child so much they are afraid to share him with anyone else. What happens to this child as he grows up? Either he becomes a mama's boy, who will still be single and living at home when he's 40, or he rebels and cuts all ties with his parents. Either way, everyone involved in this situation winds up losing.

Darrell Sifford says:

> Parenting has been described as the only job in which the object is to put yourself out of business—by preparing your child to leave home, when the time is right, and live independently.
>
> If this is the heartbeat of good parenting, and I think it is, then it must be said that many parents are coming up short by encouraging their child to remain dependent on them, whether or not they realize it, long after it has ceased to be appropriate or healthy. The chances that this will happen are dramatically increased with an only child because parents seem to have a more difficult time turning him loose. The child is so very special, and he owes it to them to stay close, to maintain the integrity of the triangle. It is, unfortunately, a mindset that almost always backfires at some point and everybody loses. The child feels manipulated and angry, and the parents feel unappreciated and misunderstood.[2]

This is akin to what I call "smother love," where the parents want so much to protect the child and shelter him from anything bad or evil that they wind up creating an emotional dwarf.

Every child makes a mistake now and then. Every child takes a misstep. Every child gets his toe stubbed or his heart broken. As painful as that is in the short term for the child, and as hard as it is for the parents to stand aside and watch it happen, it is a necessary part of growing up.

2. THE RECEIVER

No, this is not a position on the University of Arizona football team. The "receiver" is a child who gets and gets and gets to the point where that's all he knows how to do. If you told him that the Bible says it is more blessed to give than to receive, he'd sit there and stare at you with a blank look on his face. He wouldn't know what you were talking about.

The "receiver" is kin to the "special jewel," with the primary difference being that the former is much more a "natural condition" of being an only child. You remember that we talked earlier about dethronement. This is when the firstborn child is knocked off his throne by a little brother or sister. His life is turned upside down for a while as he learns to share his parents' attention, his toys, and perhaps even his room.

Well, the only child is never knocked off the throne and as a result sometimes does not learn as easily about sharing.

He may go off to kindergarten and be traumatized by the fact that other kids want to play with the toys, too!

It is easy for parents who have only one child to fall into the habit of giving too much. At Christmas, on his birthday, and on any other special occasion you can think of, the kid is given everything he could possibly want. He has way too much of a good thing, to the point where he's jaded and unenthusiastic.

"Look, Tommy, a Retro-Blast Triple X Rocket Racer!"

"Yeah . . . [yawn] . . . thanks."

Most kids love birthday cake and ice cream, but you wouldn't

give it to them anytime they wanted it. You know that too much
of the stuff is bad for them. But many parents don't seem to
understand that kids can have too many things handed to them,
whether toys, records, books, or anything else.

First of all, children need to learn how to share. That's why
it's important for the only child to have friends his own age
. . . to teach him the give-and-take of interpersonal relationships. It's not healthy for the child to be with his parents all of
the time or to sit around watching TV—even if it's educational
TV.

You can talk to him all you want about the importance of
sharing or let him listen to Mr. Rogers talking about what it
means to share, but until he's come face to face with the reality
of "one red toy truck and two boys," he won't understand.

One mother had her son invite two other little boys over to
play with him. But then she noticed that he was hogging the
video game system for himself. He didn't want to share, but
when Mom insisted, he reluctantly let the other boys take turns.
It wasn't long before she heard all the boys whooping it up and
laughing, whereas they had been sitting in stony silence before.

What happened? Her son had learned the importance and the
fun of sharing. There was a new excitement in seeing what the
other boys could do and in competing with them rather than
just playing the game by himself.

Another thing such children must learn is that things worth
having often require work and sacrifice. A child who has everything handed to him comes to assume that it will always be that
way, and he is in for a very rude awakening!

"Dad, can I buy this pack of baseball cards?"

"Of course you may—if you have the money."

"Oh . . . but . . . see, it's a dollar, and I only have twenty-
five cents."

"But your allowance is three-fifty per week."

"I know, but I already spent that, and I really want these
cards. How about if you advance me the money, and I'll pay you
back out of my next allowance?"

"I'm sorry, son, but you're just going to have to wait until you get your next allowance. Then, if you still want the cards, you can come back to the store and get them."

Don't make any mistake about it—taking a stand like that is not going to win you any popularity awards, at least not right now. Your child will be thinking, even if he doesn't say it out loud, that you enjoy "being mean."

If only he knew how hard it is! And how necessary it is.

3. JEALOUS JOSHES
AND FRIEND-SNATCHERS

The child who never learns how to share his toys may have trouble with personal relationships as well. As a child he may jealously guard his relationships with "best" friends, making sure that no one else tries to move in on his territory. At the same time he may become what other children think of as a "friend-snatcher," someone who is always trying to take their friends away from them.

Seven-year-old Brian came into the house one day and announced to his mother that he "hated" Larry.

"But I thought Larry was your best friend."

"Not anymore!" Brian said, sticking out his lower lip defiantly to show he meant business.

"Why? What happened?"

"He wants to play with Justin now."

Mom figured that Brian had gone to Larry's house to play and that Larry had said he would rather play with Justin today. Naturally an incident like that would have hurt Brian's feelings. But a closer investigation showed her that that wasn't really the case at all. All Larry wanted to do was invite Justin into the boys' game of cops and robbers.

Brian, an only child who was something of a "receiver," had nothing against Justin, but he was not about to "share" Larry with anyone. When Larry wanted to be nice to Justin by letting him into the game, Brian saw this as betrayal, and now he "hated" Larry.

Fortunately Brian's mother saw what was really going on, and she was able to talk with her son about the importance of sharing. She also determined that she would provide him with more opportunities to share, as well as show him the importance of doing so through her own actions.

Now admittedly, there are all sorts of jealousies among small children, and I'm not suggesting that if your child is jealous and seems hesitant to share his best friend, he has a particular problem.

But if this type of jealousy is a recurring theme in your child's life, if he seems to have only one very close friend at a time, or if he is constantly dropping one "best friend" for another one, you may need to act to correct things, just as Brian's mother did.

Now, what do you do about a "friend-snatcher"? This child differs slightly from the receiver in that he is willing to share material possessions but only as a means of attracting friends.

Bonnie was 11, and her mother would overhear telephone conversations that went something like this:

"So what are you going to do today? Oh, really? Well, why don't you come over to my house instead? My mom just made a chocolate cake. And I'll let you borrow my new record. Sure! Her? Nah, we don't need her. Just you and me, okay?"

Bonnie was constantly trying to bribe other girls to be friends with her. That in itself would have been bad enough, but she was also using her bribes to steal friends away from other people.

She was never quite so open about it as to say "I'll give you ten dollars if you won't be Wanda's friend anymore," but she came awfully close. And she didn't seem capable of sharing her friends, even for a moment.

"You don't want to invite Jodi along, do you? Well, if she comes, I'm not!"

The problem with this sort of behavior was not only that it

was rude and selfish, but also that it backfired more often than it worked.

"Okay then," she was told. "If you don't want to come, you don't have to. Jodi and I will have fun without you."

It got to the point where she couldn't get enough of a bribe together to buy a friend, and she didn't know any other way to get one. She was increasingly isolated, lonely, and bitter.

Bonnie tearfully told her mother that "the other girls don't like me, and I don't know why."

She and her mother had a long talk in which Mom pointed out to her some of the mistakes she had been making and suggested ways she could change her behavior.

It wasn't easy for Bonnie to change, but she had to agree with her mother that she hadn't had very good results up until now. She wasn't impressing anyone, and friends weren't really friends if all they really wanted was a piece of chocolate cake and a chance to borrow the latest Cyndi Lauper record!

Bonnie agreed that she would try not to be so jealous and possessive, and even if she felt that way she'd do her best not to show it. Maybe she could try to be friends with more than one person at a time and allow other people the same freedom.

The other girls were suspicious of Bonnie at first, and nobody could blame them. They wondered what her motives really were. And as for Bonnie herself, it wasn't all that easy to change. It was a long, slow climb to the point where she could relax and allow herself to be part of the group.

She was helped by a mother who was especially patient. At the end of every day, in fact, they talked about what had happened. Thankfully they were able to communicate well. Bonnie wasn't afraid to share her innermost feelings with her mother, because she knew Mom would do her best to understand. She was also willing to consider any advice her mother offered, because she knew it was always intended to help. And so they went over Bonnie's failures and successes insofar as her relationships with the other girls were concerned—and after a while Bonnie reverted less and less frequently to her old ways.

The other girls began to accept her, and for the first time in her young life she had some real friends who didn't like her just for what they could get from her. Not only that, but her own attitude changed, too, as she discovered the truth of the old saying—that the only way to get a friend is to be one.

4. THE TARGET

The only child who believes that the universe revolves around him has another problem besides being self-centered. And that is that whenever anything bad happens he automatically assumes that it is aimed at him. This occurs for two reasons: (1) because he sees himself as the center of everything and (2) because he has been sheltered and kept from any kind of harsh reality in his earliest years.

Let's say the teacher keeps Ronnie's entire class in at recess. Ronnie knows that all of the kids are being punished, but he still feels that he is the one who is being hurt most of all. Why? Because he's the most important person in the class!

If his teacher gives him an F on his English composition, it's because she just doesn't like him and not because he didn't do a good job.

In other words he magnifies his importance in every situation and believes he is the one being singled out for unfair treatment. When life is unfair, as it often is, he can sink into deep depression and bitterness.

"Why is God doing this to me?"

"How could this happen to me?"

And so on.

I'm sure that almost all of us have asked questions like those at one time or another, but the "target" is prone to ask them much more often that most people.

The target needs to understand that life isn't always peaches and cream and that everyone hits a few bumpy spots in the road along the way.

In a recent popular movie, *Coming to America,* Eddie Murphy portrays a prince from a mythical African country. Everywhere he goes from the moment he gets out of bed in the morning, he is accompanied by girls who strew rose petals in his path. When he objects to this treatment, his father chastises him and tells him that as a prince it is only fitting that he should always walk in rose petals.

It's silly stuff, to be sure, but it reminds me that there are a lot of parents out there who do their best to see that their precious children are always "walking on roses." But that's not the way life is. Someday, for whatever reason, those feet will hit the pavement. And when they do, they'll find that it's hot from the sun beating down on it, or bumpy, or full of sharp stones.

Those who are well adjusted know from an early age that life is a mixture of good and bad. They understand that bad things simply happen once in a while—an ice cream cone melts before you can eat it, you get a paper cut on your finger, someone blames you for something you didn't do—and when they do, it doesn't mean that life (or anyone else) is out to get you.

More Help For Onlys

There are some other specific things parents of only children can do to see that their children grow up well adjusted and secure in their identities.

1. SET LIMITS.

Sounds simple enough. But it's not always as easy as it sounds.

"Timmy, it's nine o'clock, and that's time for you to get to bed!"

"Ah, Mom . . . can't I stay up another hour? I really want to watch this movie!"

"Well, son, I—"

"Dad, can I, please, please . . ."

About this time Mom and Dad look at each other. Mom

probably wants Dad to tell the kid no. Dad's not sure what Mom wants, so he's trying to get a clue from her face—and even after 15 years of marriage he still can't do it right.

So Dad says, "Well, I suppose maybe it's okay . . . just this once."

Did you hear the man say "Just this once"? What he probably means is "Just this once tonight. And then just another once tomorrow night, and so on."

You must set specific limits and then stick with them.

I'm not telling you to turn your home into a police state, where everything is done by the book. You should have the freedom to be flexible, but even that is something Mom and Dad should talk about on their own and in private.

Such as "Timmy's bed time is nine o'clock, but we may occasionally let him stay up later *if* he has an important reason. But never more than once a month."

Understand, though, that this discussion really isn't about the child's bedtime. He needs to know what limits you have set for him in every area of life and that you are serious about those limits.

2. KEEP YOUR PRIORITIES STRAIGHT.

Does your child come first in your life?

If you're married, your priorities are messed up!

Your mate should always come first in your life, and the child should be second. Does it hurt to hear me say that? Now, I didn't tell you to go off dancing and leave her at home alone in an unheated house! I simply said that your first priority has to be your husband or your wife. It's been said many times, and I really do believe it, that the best thing a man can do for his child is to love the child's mother. (And of course the reverse is true, too.)

In case you haven't noticed it, children will often try to manipulate their parents and in the process will turn them against one another.

Mom and Dad have to present a unified front, and I would go so far as to suggest getting together to discuss how to handle situations that might arise. Beyond that the child who knows that his parents really love each other will benefit from their love for each other and will be made to feel more secure because of it.

You need, Mom and Dad, to spend some time alone together once in a while, to make sure the romance isn't leaking out of your marriage. And that brings me to point number three.

3. GET A BABY-SITTER ONCE IN A WHILE.

Dan and Barbara were proud of the fact that they took little Angela with them everywhere they went. She had never once had a baby-sitter in all of her seven years.

They puffed up with pride when they told me that and couldn't understand when I suggested that this was appalling. Let's face it, having a baby-sitter every so often is a normal part of growing up. It doesn't make a child feel he's been deserted.

I wondered what friends of Dan and Barbara thought whenever they went with them to a restaurant and found that Angela was going along.

Please, for the sake of everyone concerned, get a baby-sitter occasionally!

4. PROVIDE CONTACT WITH OTHER CHILDREN THE SAME AGE.

Children need to be around other children. That is how they learn to share, develop socially, and learn how to handle interpersonal relationships.

It is sad to see an only child who has spent most of his childhood associating with adults. He is like one born out of time. He doesn't know how to join in games with the other children, and so he is ostracized and laughed at. And yet he doesn't fit into the adult world either.

How do you find these other children? I suggest that even before your child's first day of school you might want to enroll him in preschool or at least Sunday school. If there are no children his age in your neighborhood, give a party and invite some of the children from your church or synagogue.

I would go so far as to say that developing relationships with other children is almost as important as the education itself, especially in the early years.

5. DON'T OVERCOMPENSATE FOR A LACK OF SIBLINGS.

Bill and Joanna wanted to have more children, but the doctor said there could be no more after the birth of their son, Roger.

"Poor little Roger," they thought. "He'll always be alone."

And so, to make up for what they believed he was missing, they showered him with enough goodies to sink the *Queen Elizabeth II!* For his part, Roger didn't feel like he was missing out on anything. He was quite happy, thank you, and he wouldn't have traded any of his treasured goodies for a little brother or sister!

There is no need to pay any type of "compensation" to an only child. It's not a handicap, and in many ways it can be a very good deal. (Just ask poor little terribly spoiled Roger!)

The Strong Places

Now let's take a brief look at some of the most obvious strengths of only children. In general, they are:

1. Reliable. Only children are the kind of people you can count on. If they say they're going to do something for you, they'll do it. Their word is their bond, and that's something rare and wonderful in today's world.

2. Conscientious. If you want something done right, give it to a firstborn. If you want it to be flawless, give it to a superfirstborn —an only child!

3. Well Organized. I can't help it. As many times as my wife goes into it and straightens it out, my sock drawer is always a mess! I can dig in there for 20 minutes and still not come up with a matching pair. But it would be different if I had been an only child. A lot different. If I ever want to know where something is or how to get somewhere, I try to ask an only child. They'll give you the clearest, most concise directions you could hope for. And they're always right!

4. Scholarly. I've already mentioned that Albert Einstein was an only child; so was Jean-Paul Sartre. What more can I say?

5. Cautious. Youngest children tend to live by the proverb "He who hesitates is lost." We know from sad experience that it isn't always true. The only born knows and lives by another proverb: "Look before you leap." The only born's hesitation seems sort of silly to the rest of us at times—until we find out that he was right to be skeptical!

For some reason our society has long looked at only children as if they were to be pitied—as if being an only child were a handicap. It's not. Far from it. The life of an only child can be every bit as full, successful, and rewarding as anyone else's life.

Being an only child can be a special kind of adventure, especially if he has parents who will do everything they can to help him live that adventure to the fullest!

PART THREE

All in
the Family

10

The Firstborn and Alcoholism: Through a Glass Darkly

Diane is 29, the oldest of three children.

When she was little, she thought her father was the neatest guy in the entire world. He was always so happy and so generous. He laughed a lot, and he sometimes gave her money, even when she hadn't asked him for any.

She knew that he had trouble holding on to a job and that her family was poorer than most of the others she knew, but that wasn't her father's fault.

And then, too, her mother often seemed angry and nervous, but Diane didn't understand why she couldn't be more like her father. And why was Mom so mad anyway? It wasn't Dad's fault that he couldn't seem to find a good job.

And then one day when she was in the fourth grade, some of the other kids started teasing her about her father at recess.

"Diane's a punk—her daddy's a drunk!"

"Diane's a punk—her daddy's a drunk!"

"He is not!"

She put her hands over her ears, but the other kids wouldn't stop taunting her, shouting the rhyme one of the boys had made up.

When she couldn't get them to stop, Diane ran out of the schoolyard and kept running the entire mile and a half to her house. When she got there, she ran upstairs to her bedroom and locked the door, vowing not to come out until her mother got home from work or her father got home from wherever he was. She wasn't going to come out even if the principal came over and tried to make her come back to school.

It wasn't too long before she heard the creaking sound of the front door being opened. Her father was home, and she couldn't wait to run down and tell him what the other kids were saying about him.

But as she was hurrying to unlock her door, she heard a crash downstairs, as if someone or something had fallen.

Running down the stairs, Diane found her father crumpled in a heap on the kitchen floor. At first she thought he might be dead, but then he lifted his head, looked in her direction, and began laughing—"a crazy sort of laugh."

He seemed surprised to see his daughter home this early in the day, and when he tried to talk to her, his speech was slurred and almost unintelligible. She saw that his eyes seemed to be swimming in a sea of red, she smelled the whiskey on his breath, and she knew that he was drunk. She also knew, for the very first time, that it was true: her father was an alcoholic.

"It seems incredible that I hadn't know before—or maybe I did know, but my mind just wouldn't let me believe it."

Diane was immediately filled with horror and revulsion toward her father. How could he do this to her? The kids were right, and she felt sick to her stomach. She ran back upstairs, locked herself in her room, and didn't come out for the rest of the day.

"I hated my father, and I told myself that the last thing I'd ever do was be like him when I grew up."

That was the same promise children of alcoholics all over the world make every day. Unfortunately a great many of them don't keep that promise, and Diane is one of those who didn't.

As the years went by, she found herself drawn increasingly to the comfort that alcohol brought to her troubled mind.

"I'll never be like Dad," she'd tell herself, even as she was mixing her third or fourth drink of the day.

"Dad was an alcoholic, and I'm not. I can stop anytime I want to. It's just that right now I need something to steady my nerves—I've had such a rotten day!"

Two years ago Diane finally came to see reality. Just as she had denied for so long that there was anything wrong with her father, she was now denying the same thing about herself. The truth hurt, but she had to face up to the fact that she was an alcoholic.

Once she faced the truth of who and what she was, she took some important steps toward changing the situation, including joining Alcoholics Anonymous. Today she has been sober for six months, and she is well on her way to a total recovery.

But she wonders:

What if she is tempted at an especially weak moment and falls back into her old habits?

What about her daughter, Leslie? Will she become an alcoholic, too?

And that is a good question. Is Leslie, the firstborn child of an alcoholic, destined to follow in the footsteps of her mother, who was also the firstborn child of an alcoholic?

Is there any hope at all for the firstborn sons and daughters of alcoholics?

The answer, of course, is yes, but the sad fact is that children of alcoholics do often turn to the bottle themselves—and especially firstborns.

The firstborn child of an alcoholic is more likely than the other children in the family to become an alcoholic himself for two reasons:

First of all, he has been the one to serve as the shock absorber. He's been the one to try to shelter his younger brothers and sisters from Mom's or Dad's drinking, and he's been the one who's really had to deal with it. You might think that seeing what alcohol has done to a parent would give the child sufficient cause to stay away from the stuff. In theory that's true, but it rarely works that way. Remember the promise Diane made not to grow up to be like her father.

The second reason the firstborn has the most trouble dealing with alcoholic parents is that he is most often the one who will follow in his parents' footsteps. The firstborn either reaps the benefits of who and what his parents are or suffers the consequences. You will find a high proportion of firstborn sons and daughters of doctors, lawyers, ministers, teachers, etc., choosing to follow in their parents' footsteps, and that's the good side of it. You will also find firstborns following their parents into negative areas such as alcoholism. But it is not true in any way that the oldest children of alcoholics are destined to become alcoholics themselves. It is not an automatic occurrence, and it can be avoided.

The National Association of Children of Alcoholics says that such children have certain characteristics in common. Some of these are:

> We become isolated and afraid of people and authority figures.
>
> We become approval seekers and lose our own identity in the process.
>
> We are frightened by angry people and any personal criticism.
>
> We either become alcoholics, marry them—or both—or find another compulsive personality such as a workaholic to fulfill our sick need for abandonment.
>
> We live life from the viewpoint of helping and seeking victims, and we are attracted by that weakness in our love and friendship relationships.
>
> We have an overdeveloped sense of responsibility, and it is

easier for us to be concerned with others rather than for ourselves.

We get guilt feelings when we stand up for ourselves; instead, we give in to others.

We become addicted to excitement.

We confuse love with pity and tend to "love" people we can pity and rescue.

We have stuffed back our feelings from our traumatic childhoods and have lost the ability to feel or express our feelings.

We judge ourselves harshly and have a very low sense of self-esteem (sometimes compensated for by trying to appear superior).

We are dependent personalities who are terrified of abandonment. We will do anything to hold on to a relationship in order not to experience the pain of abandonment. We are conditioned to these types of relationships.

Alcoholism is a family disease, and we became para-alcoholic—we took on the characteristics of that disease even though we did not pick up the drink.

This list is followed with the important words "This is a description, not an indictment."

Neither is it a description that fits every firstborn offspring of an alcoholic perfectly. But the important thing, for those who do see themselves mirrored in this list of characteristics, is to realize that you can change things. And a major step toward changing a personality problem is merely to admit that the problem exists.

Just how common is it for children of alcoholics to wind up following in their parents' footsteps? According to the book *Dying for a Drink,* by Anderson Spickard, M.D., and Barbara R. Thompson, some 30 percent of the children of alcoholics marry alcoholics, and fully 50 percent become alcoholics themselves![1]

What are some of the problems faced by children of alcoholics?

Bill says, "I had to grow up too fast. When my parents should have been taking care of me and worrying about my welfare, I was having to take care of them."

Ron remembers, "I was always embarrassed and afraid. Embarrassed because I wondered what my friends thought about my father, and afraid because I never knew when he was going to beat the daylights out of me."

Rhonda's mother didn't become violent when she was drunk. Instead, Rhonda recalls, "The only time she ever told me she loved me was when she was plastered!"

For Lawrence, growing up with alcoholic parents was like living in a "Jekyll and Hyde" nightmare. "When my parents had been drinking, they'd be generous and happy, and they'd let me do just about anything I wanted to do.

"It would be 'Hey, Dad, can I have the car Friday night?' and he'd say, 'Sure, son, go ahead! Do you need any money?' And then, when Friday night rolled around and I wanted the car, he'd tell me I should know better than to ask him for anything while he was drunk. He'd accuse me of trying to take advantage of him, but the truth was I couldn't avoid asking him for things when he was drunk because he was drunk most of the time."

Dying for a Drink tells the story of a woman who was caught up in another problem common to children of alcoholics. She seemed unable to tell the truth.

Her problem started when, as a child, she was always compelled to lie in an attempt to cover up for her parents. But as she grew older, she continued to lie, often for no reason at all and about things that didn't matter.

" 'I found myself saying preposterous things, and then I was too embarrassed to retract them. Over the years, I lost many friends because they discovered I could not be trusted.

" 'The turning point came when I met a man who remained my friend even after he discovered that I did not always tell the truth. His acceptance and loving confrontation enabled me to face my problem honestly. I realized that just as my father was addicted to alcohol, I was addicted to lying. Through much prayer and hard work, I learned as an adult what most people learn as children—how to tell the truth.' "[2]

Marta is typical of a firstborn child of alcoholic parents in that she always played the role of the "hero."

She saw that her parents were not able to function in their proper role in the family, so she did her best to take it on her shoulders. From the time she was in the sixth grade she did most of the grocery shopping, planned meals, did the laundry, and kept the family budget to the best of her ability.

She would occasionally go through her parents' liquor supply and pour everything down the drain. She always hoped that if the liquor was gone, they simply wouldn't drink anymore. It never worked, of course, but it never got her into trouble either, because her parents always assumed they had drunk it all.

Because her home life was so unhappy, Marta poured herself into her schoolwork. She was an A-minus student, active in student council and on the debate team, and in high school she joined nearly every club there was. Flip through the pages of her high school yearbook, and you'll find her smiling out at you from almost every other page.

She was so busy at home and at school that she didn't have time to think about the unfair burden life had given her. Every night she fell into bed exhausted. And every morning she was the first one up so she could help get her younger brother and sisters off to school.

Somehow Marta made it through her high school years, went off to an excellent college, and became a schoolteacher. But long after she was out on her own she was still rushing around at 120 miles per hour 18 hours a day, doing everything she could to prove that she was a capable human being. She knew she was killing herself, but she didn't know what to do about it. She had never learned to relax or take time for herself. When she thought about trying to cut back on her work load and finding some time to "just take it easy," she felt guilty and wound up doing the opposite—taking on more responsibilities and larger challenges.

She was rushing through life, steamrolling over her friends, trying to take charge of their lives, and feeling personally responsible for nearly everyone she knew. And it wasn't all that hard to take responsibility for her friends, because most of them were easily manipulated. They didn't mind letting her make decisions for them. In that respect they were just like her parents. But she was afraid to develop relationships with people she could not control. She simply didn't trust them.

Marta is not one of those children of alcoholics who become alcoholics themselves, but she was scarred deeply by her parents' sickness just the same, and it took years of therapy before she was able to change her life and emerge from the shadow their alcoholism had cast over her.

Roy was a firstborn son of alcoholics who, for the most part, kept their drinking hidden from their friends and neighbors. His father controlled his drinking enough that he was able to hold down a position as sales manager for a local automobile dealership, and his mother was active in church and social organizations.

Roy's parents were actually respected and admired in the community, but nobody knew what really went on at home, behind the false front that was always presented to the world.

If Roy's parents weren't screaming at each other in a drunken rage, they were screaming at Roy and his three younger brothers. Although both parents cultivated a public image of competence and sophistication, at home they couldn't seem to do anything.

"During the day, I suppose both of them held their acts together pretty well—although I'm not sure how they did it. But as soon as they came through the door at the end of the day, they headed straight for the liquor cabinet. They drank themselves silly, and we were left to fend for ourselves."

Roy reacted in much the same way Marta did. He became the parent his brothers needed—helping them with homework, making sure they took their baths, and even disciplining them when they needed it.

His record at school was impeccable, and he wound up being nominated and accepted into the Air Force Academy.

It was during his first year there that he tasted liquor for the first time. And he liked it.

"I thought it was great. And I liked the way I felt when I was high. Not drunk, you know . . . just high enough to feel really good."

He also told himself that he was different from his parents.

"I felt like they couldn't handle it [booze] but I could. I was wrong."

It wasn't long before alcohol was the centerpiece of his life. To complicate matters, he also married a woman who was an alcoholic—a woman who had four young sons. It was as if he was trying to step back into his youth and change things. Perhaps those four boys reminded him of himself and his brothers, and he was going to see to it that they didn't suffer the way he and his brothers had done. Instead he was helping to perpetuate the nightmare.

At 30 years of age he found himself heavily into drugs and alcohol and staring at a mountain of debt that was nearly three times his annual salary. His life was totally out of control.

Like Marta, Roy found his way back. For him too the first step was the realization that he was an alcoholic.

He says there are two reasons he found his way back to a normal life:

1. God
2. Alcoholics Anonymous

A friend introduced him to Alcoholics Anonymous, and a man he met there introduced him to God.

"That, for me, was an unbeatable combination."

Now, I'm telling you all these things about Marta and Roy because they are people who managed to find their way back from the precipice. Are you an alcoholic who thinks he can never change? Roy did. Marta did. Are you the child of an alcoholic who is caught up in the same traps that entangled

Marta and Roy? Their stories can show you what you may be doing wrong and help you avoid making the mistakes they made.

Whether you are someone struggling with alcoholism who wants to make sure his children don't follow the same tragic path or an adult child of alcoholics who is still wrestling with the doubts and fears of his childhood, my message is that things can get better.

If you are the firstborn child of an alcoholic, remember that you and the other members of your family can "get well," even if the alcoholic himself refuses to change his ways. Remember, too, that even though alcoholism is a disease that affects the whole family, family members must proceed along the road to recovery at their own, individual paces. You shouldn't expect everyone in the family to achieve the same breakthrough at the same moment.

Keeping that in mind, I believe there are at least eight steps you can take to deal with alcoholism in your family.

1. RECOGNIZE THE PROBLEM FOR WHAT IT IS.

You can't do anything about the problem until you admit that the problem exists. The alcoholic will often make excuses for himself: "It's just that I'm under so much pressure at work and I need a few drinks to help me unwind." In that way he's finding a scapegoat instead of looking to the real problem, which is his addiction to alcohol.

Sometimes his family does the same thing: "Poor Dad. Well, he does work hard, so who can blame him for taking a few drinks?"

But two six-packs of beer every night is more than a few drinks.

Let me say something else about alcoholism. I like to inject as much humor as I can into what I write. I believe that anyone who has a good sense of humor is going to stay healthy mentally and probably physically too. But when it comes to talking about alcoholism, I can find very little to smile about and absolutely nothing that makes me want to yuck it up.

I've seen much too often what alcoholism can do to people. It's no laughing matter. It's deadly serious. And to me that's part of recognizing the problem for what it is!

2. LEARN ABOUT ALCOHOLISM.

If the doctor told you that you or a loved one had some strange disease or condition, wouldn't you want to find out more about it?

Well, that's the case with alcoholism. The more you know about it, the more you're ready to fight it. Don't sit on your hands and wait for a miracle. Start learning about the disease so you can know how to overcome it!

3. DON'T WORRY ABOUT THE PAST.

I've heard the quote dozens of times. "Those who forget history are condemned to relive it." It's variously attributed to various sources, but most often to George Santayana, and I know it's true. If we don't learn from mistakes, whether ours or anyone else's, we're going to keep goofing up in the same old ways.

But here's a little gem straight from Kevin Leman, and you can quote me on this: "Those who spend too much time thinking about the past won't have much of a future."

Whatever has happened to you in the past is over and done, and it's time to let it go.

Learn from your mistakes and failures, but don't let them hold you back, whether they were your failures or someone else's. The attitude "I trusted you once and you let me down, so I'm never going to trust you again" does not help anyone.

Putting the past behind you may not be easy. But whenever those hurtful incidents come to mind, try your best not to dwell on them. Make a conscious effort to be positive and forward-looking.

Now, I am not suggesting that you should let someone continue to "get away" with selfish behavior or hurtful actions. If you close your eyes and pretend nothing has really happened, you are not doing your loved one any favors. Instead you are becoming an "enabler," making excuses and allowing wrong behavior to go unchallenged and uncorrected. But you must learn to keep short accounts. Deal with the situation as it presently exists and avoid dredging up ancient history.

4. Don't Expect Too Much Too Soon.

Whereas you shouldn't dwell on the past, you shouldn't put it entirely out of your mind either. Experience should teach you that life with an alcoholic is going to have its ups and downs. You should know that his recovery may take quite a long while, and during that recovery period he may not be the most pleasant person in the world to live with.

"Boy! I liked him better when he was drinking! At least he was funny then. Now he's in a bad mood all the time!"

"I thought she was always complaining about things because she was drunk. But she's been sober now for a month, and she still complains about everything."

I've heard those lines or variations of them on several different occasions. I knew the people who said them didn't really want their recovering loved one to go back to the bottle, but I understood their frustration. They had expected that as soon as their loved one had been sober for a few days or weeks everything would be wonderful. When it didn't turn out that way, they were frustrated and angry.

The recovering alcoholic has many problems to work out besides the most important one of simply stopping drinking, so recovery may be a long, gradual process.

I have known of other incidents where relatives of recovering alcoholics have thrown up their hands in despair after discovering that their loved one has broken his vow to remain sober.

That's unfortunate, but it's not the end of the world. It happens quite often, and it can be a temporary setback rather than a permanent one.

5. LEARN TO TRUST OTHERS.

The child of an alcoholic often has a difficult time trusting anyone. He may even view God with a bit of suspicion, since a person's perception of the Creator is most often shaped by his relationship with his own father. If Dad is an unreliable alcoholic who is full of false promises and can't tell the difference between a bald-faced lie and the truth, it's going to be hard to think of God as a loving, trustworthy, truthful Father. You may know with your mind that God is trustworthy and loving and wants only the best for you, but it may be extremely difficult to come to an emotional acceptance of those truths. You know it's true, but you can't quite believe it anyway.

Now, it's wise to be cautious. You don't want to go around trusting everyone you meet. Nor do you want to put people on a pedestal and expect too much of them. But the child of the alcoholic desperately needs to learn how to be voluntarily vulnerable and to establish relationships based on trust.

You may want to begin with learning how to trust God. The best way to do this is to read the scriptures, particularly the psalms, and to become involved in an active church or synagogue—if you're not involved in one already.

In such a place you will find people who can say "I have walked with God for twenty years [or thirty or forty], and He has never let me down." If I come up to you and say, "God can always be trusted," you may nod and agree with me, at least in a theoretical sense. But if I add that I know firsthand that He can be trusted because I've seen continuous evidence of it in my life, and if I can even tell you of specific incidents where He proved Himself to me, that's going to have a much greater impact on you.

But how do you go about learning how to trust others? You

just do it, that's all. It won't be easy. I'm not suggesting you take your life savings out of the bank and ask someone you just met if he would mind watching your money for a while. But I am suggesting doing everything within your power to cultivate friendships that are based on mutual respect and, thus, trust.

Find friends you can trust with small things, and you will grow to trust them with the more important matters. Everyone needs a friend to lean on, confide in, and dream with, and if you don't have such a friend, you're missing one of life's greatest treasures.

Where can you find this friend? In church, at work, in a service club or social organization, at an AA meeting, at school. . . . There are good, trustworthy people everywhere you go if you make the effort to look for them.

6. OVERCOME SELF-HATRED.

Children of alcoholics often grow up being abused, verbally if not physically. The alcoholic may be angry and frustrated, so he lashes out at others, including his spouse and his children.

The children may come to believe they deserve the abuse their alcoholic parent dishes out. If your father tells you you're a no-good bum, it's hard not to believe him, even if you know that alcohol has distorted his thinking.

You may even think, "I'm probably the main reason he started drinking in the first place."

Wrong! You didn't have anything to do with it.

That's the first thing you need to know. Tell yourself that until it sinks in: "I didn't have anything to do with my father's drinking. I didn't have anything to do with my father's drinking." Keep saying it until you discover that you mean it and believe it.

And then there are a few other things to keep in mind:

• An alcoholic is angry and bitter with himself and his lot in life, so he often strikes out blindly at anyone within range. His anger really had nothing at all to do with you.

· Some people are always critical. They complain and criticize and say nasty things to everyone. You can't please a person like that, no matter what you do.

· You are under no obligation to believe what anyone tells you, even your parents—and especially your parents, if they are alcohol abusers.

· You are a unique individual, someone created in God's own image. No one else on this planet has your exact talents and skills. Consider that no two people have the same fingerprints. This is just one example of how special you are. Someone designed you and put you on this earth for a purpose. Have you ever seen the poster that says "I know I'm special because God doesn't make junk"? Well, it's true, and you'd better believe it, especially about yourself.

Remember, too, that there are a number of excellent organizations and support groups that can help relatives of alcoholics cope with the most difficult situations. The support and fellowship of others who know what you're going through because they've been there themselves is very important. You can find such a group in your area by looking in your telephone book under "Alcoholism."

7. DON'T FOCUS ON THE ALCOHOLISM.

In any family that is touched by alcoholism the disease can become the center of everyone's attention.

That's easy to understand, because it colors everything that happens within the family.

"I wonder if Mom's going to be drunk today when I get home from school."

"I hope we're going to get to go on the picnic like Dad said, but he'll probably get drunk and ruin everything again."

When there is an alcoholic in your life, you are forced to live moment by moment. You can't plan for tomorrow, because you don't know what tomorrow will bring. Life can be distorted in the same way a funhouse mirror distorts a person's reflection.

Dr. Anderson Spickard puts it this way: "Whether or not the alcoholic recovers, it is important that family members learn to remove him from the center of their thoughts and that they fill the vacuum with new interests and activities. For some, stepping out of the alcoholic's orbit takes an enormous amount of courage, and initially they will need a great deal of support from friends and other family members."[3]

Once again, remember that you're walking on a balance beam. Don't overdo it and become involved in a dozen different activities so you don't have to think about reality—the way Marta did, for instance. But developing some outside interests will keep alcoholism from consuming you.

8. WORK AT KEEPING LINES OF COMMUNICATION OPEN.

The family that has been invaded by alcoholism is generally a place where there is a great deal of what Shakespeare called "sound and fury signifying nothing." There are a lot of empty words filling the air, often delivered in the form of yelling and screaming, either on the part of the alcoholic or else directed at him . . . but very little real communication.

There may be a lot of talking but not much listening.

Keeping the lines of communication open means being able to confront the alcoholic about his behavior in a way that allows him to listen. If his behavior has disappointed you, tell him so, but as dispassionately and as fairly as possible, without raising your voice or seeking to humiliate him.

Realize, too, that communication has to be a two-way street. Take time to listen to the other members of your family, including the person who is an alcoholic.

There can be no progress without honest communication.

As long as honest dialogue is taking place, growth is occurring.

If you need help in opening up those lines of communication and in dealing with the hurts that have occurred in the family because of one member's alcoholism, I suggest family therapy.

But as always, it's important to find a therapist who understands the situation and whose goal is to help your family through trying times. If you become involved in therapy and don't like the way it's going, pull out and look for another therapist. There is no law that says you have to keep the therapist you start out with.

But finding a competent and caring therapist can be one of the best moves your family has ever made.

11

The Dreadful Secret

Karla had been happily married for 20 years to Barry, a high school English teacher who had the ability to instill within his students a passion for literature and writing.

One summer evening Karla had a headache that wouldn't go away, so she told her husband she was going to bed an hour earlier than usual. She left him watching television with their two daughters, aged 12 and 14.

She was asleep almost as soon as her head touched her pillow but woke up suddenly a couple of hours later. The house was silent, but Barry was not in bed beside her, and she decided to go looking for him.

No sign of him in the living room or the den. Where could he be? It wasn't like him to go for a walk late at night. She shrugged and decided to go back to bed.

Wherever he was, he'd be back shortly. On the way back to her bedroom she decided to peek in on her daughters and make sure they were both sleeping soundly.

The 12-year-old was sprawled across her bed, her deep breathing proving that she was sound asleep.

But as she opened the door to the 14-year-old's room, she knew immediately that something was wrong. Quickly she flicked on the light, and the sight that greeted her filled her with horror and revulsion.

Her beloved husband was in bed with their daughter, having sexual intercourse with her. She couldn't believe what she was seeing and had no idea what to say or do, so she just stood there looking at them, not doing anything. Finally she turned and ran out of the room.

Her husband ran after her, pulling on his pants at the same time he was asking her not to jump to conclusions and promising that he could explain everything.

"Explain?!" Karla shrieked at him. "How can you explain? I want you out of this house . . . right now!"

Barry put his hands on her shoulders. "Come on now, honey, it's not that big of a deal. You don't really want me to go. Let's sleep on this, and we'll talk about it in the morning."

She couldn't believe he was being so nonchalant about the whole thing. She wanted him to pack his things and go. She wasn't going to have him around where he could do any more harm to those girls.

So he went about the business of throwing some of his things in a suitcase, fuming all the while because he couldn't understand why she was "overreacting" like this.

When he was finally ready to go, he said sweetly, "Now, listen, hon . . . after you've had some time to cool off, give me a call, and then we'll sit down and talk about these things."

But Karla knew that time was never going to come. How could a supposedly loving and devoted father force himself on his daughter? Her rage intensified when the oldest girl admitted that her father had been having sex with her for the past four years.

"I hate him," she said with tears pouring down her cheeks. "You don't know how many times I've prayed that God would strike him dead. Every time he goes somewhere I pray that he just won't come home." She hadn't told her mother, she said, "because I knew how much you loved him."

As for the 12-year-old, she told her mother innocently, "I thought Daddys were supposed to hold you like that."

Karla said, "I felt, first of all, that I was a total failure as a mother. I mean, there must have been some signs that this was going on—there had to be—but I somehow managed to miss them . . . or maybe even chose to ignore them.

"I keep thinking of all those times when I lectured the girls because they spoke disrespectfully to their father or didn't seem to appreciate something he had done for them—and all the while he was raping and abusing them!"

We were talking earlier about alcoholism, and I have read statistics, and I believe them, that say that 55 percent of all family violence is connected to alcoholism.

Some of this violence takes the form of the alcoholic parent grabbing the nearest blunt instrument and attacking his wife or children. And that's terrible.

But some of this violence takes the form it took in Karla's house, with fathers raping their own daughters—and that is the far greater crime.

This is a terrible, terrible tragedy, and although alcoholism seems to increase the chances of its happening in a particular family, it is happening everywhere, all across this country, whether or not alcohol is involved.

Did you know that one of every four American girls is molested by someone in her family—father, uncle, brother, cousin, etc.? That may be hard to believe, but it's true—and it's also true that whenever anything like this happens in a family, the firstborn is most affected by it.

When I first heard that figure, I was not inclined to believe it either. But my years as a practicing psychologist have convinced me that if anything, the percentage is too low. I have come to the point where I ask my female clients, almost as a matter of routine, "When were you first molested?"

Usually there will be a shocked look, followed by a word or

two of protest and indignation. But then the floodgates open, and the tears and the story come tumbling out.

"I was eight years old, and my mother had gone to help her sister for a few days. . . ."

Whenever you think of a man who would molest his daughter, you probably get a definite picture in your mind. He's uneducated, dirty, somewhat of a slob, never held a decent job in his life, and probably looks like he just crawled out of a swamp. An interesting picture, but not an accurate one. The man who molests his daughter is a doctor, a lawyer, an engineer; he's respected in his community; he may be active in his church; he seems to be happily married. This is a problem that cuts across all layers of the social strata.

And just as the firstborn child of an alcoholic parent often suffers the most from his parent's addiction, it is usually the firstborn daughter who must deal with being raped and used by her own father. Because she is the oldest she is most often the one her father turns to.

Not only must she deal with what is happening to her, but she also generally becomes fiercely protective of any younger sisters. She worries about them constantly and tries to see to it that they are never alone with "dear old Daddy." She may think that it is too late to save herself but may feel that she has been thrust into the role of being everyone else's guardian angel.

What kind of trust does a little girl place in her father? Usually she will do just about anything he asks her to do. She believes in him and knows he wouldn't do anything to hurt her. He can take a three-year-old and set her up on a high wall and say, "Jump and Daddy will catch you," and most likely she'll do it. But as far as I'm concerned, the father who is molesting his daughter is standing aside and letting her hit the ground. She trusted him with her life, and he wasn't worthy of it.

Karla has made the long journey back to a normal life, and so have her daughters. But it wasn't easy. The older daughter, especially, was plagued with recurring nightmares in which her father forced his way into the house and raped her.

As for Barry, six years later now, he still has not come to terms with what he did.

"He still acts as if it was no big deal," Karla says. "He kept asking me to take him back, but he never once said anything to the girls about being sorry.

"He sent them things—cards with money in them, perfume, things like that—but he never for one minute showed any remorse or even understanding of what he had done to those girls."

Shortly after Karla discovered what her husband was doing to her daughters, the older girl, Holly, achieved an emotional breakthrough when one of her teachers took her aside and asked her what was wrong. The teacher knew that something was troubling the girl and was worried about her. Sensing the teacher's concern, and needing someone to talk to, Holly poured out the entire story.

Her teacher sat there listening with tears running down her face. When Holly finished her story, the teacher said that she too had been a victim of sexual abuse as a child. She had kept it to herself for more than 20 years, having never told a soul—not even her mother. But now, as she heard Holly's story, she felt the need to share her secret.

The two victims of abuse sat there and embraced one another, binding one another's deep wounds with love.

Was it a one-in-a-million coincidence that Holly's teacher just happened to be an incest victim, too? No. Sexual abuse is just that common.

Let me tell you that Karla was not a particularly strong woman, and there were times when her husband almost convinced her that she should take him back.

But in the end she remained firm, and I'm glad that she did.

Now, I'm not usually in favor of divorce, but I applaud Karla for acting responsibly in this instance. Those girls didn't need an abusive father in the house, and choosing their welfare over his desire to come back into the family was a wise choice.

She could have said, "Well . . . he is a good provider, and

he's my husband . . ." and so on, but she didn't. She summoned up her courage, removed her husband from the scene, and got her girls quickly into therapy.

If you have been or are currently a victim of sexual abuse, remember that it's not your fault. The very last thing you need is a heaping helping of guilt on top of everything else.

Don't sit and suffer quietly, either. It's time to do something about it. Let someone know what's going on or what went on all those years ago. Take control of your life, and please don't think you have to submit to anyone's abusive behavior!

I have counseled many women who were molested years ago, and ever since then they have been carrying around a 10-ton weight of anger and guilt. The typical victim is likely to be angry at her father, uncle, or whoever it was who molested her, and that is certainly understandable and justifiable. But when I start probing a little deeper, I discover that the person she resents the most is herself.

Deep down she feels that she was worthy of being abused or that she did something to cause it. Nonsense! It's not true!

The victim of such abuse needs to forgive herself, to understand that it wasn't her fault, and to change her life to see that it doesn't happen again!

When I talk to a woman who has been sexually molested, I often discover that I am the first one to hear about it. It may have happened 20 years ago, and she's never told another soul. She's been carrying this dreadful secret around all this time, wondering what people would think of her if they found out.

One sobbing client, a young woman I'll call Rosemary, told me how, when she was 15, she went so far as to pack her bags and make plans to move out of the house. Then she told her stepfather, who had been abusing her for several months, that she was going to tell her mother what had been happening.

When the man heard it, he got down on his knees and begged her for mercy.

With tears in his eyes he promised her that it wouldn't happen again. If she told her mother, they'd wind up getting a divorce, and that wouldn't be good for anyone. Wouldn't she please unpack her bags and agree to stay?

The girl finally gave in. After all, she didn't want to hurt her mother.

It was true that her stepfather never molested her again, but it wasn't because he never tried. Instead it was because she had put up with it long enough, and whenever he made advances toward her or sexual remarks to her, she told him that if he didn't leave her alone, she was going straight to her mother. She was fortunate in that he was intimidated by those threats.

Rosemary had two younger sisters, and she also threatened to turn her stepdad in if he took one false step toward them.

"I don't think he ever touched them, but you know, I'm really not sure. I worried about them all the time, but I never had the guts to talk to them about it. They don't even know what happened to me."

And so there was an uneasy truce in the family over the last three years of her high school career.

But after her high school graduation she moved to another city 500 miles away from her parents' home and has seen them only once a year in the 10 years since.

"I just can't stand being around Charlie after what he did to me," she says. "Mom doesn't understand why I act the way I do. She thinks I'm ungrateful and snooty, but I just can't help myself.

"When I'm around him, I feel nervous, sick to my stomach, and I just want to kick him. I'm not very good at hiding my feelings, so it's better for me if I just stay away."

Sexual abuse in itself is a terrible violation of a young girl's physical being. But what makes it even worse is that it most often involves someone she has been very close to—someone she has trusted implicitly.

I think of sexual abuse as being like taking the finest piece of cloth you can buy, ripping it in half, throwing the pieces in someone's lap, and saying, "Here, take this to a good seamstress, and you'll never know the difference."

I don't care how good you are at healing this one, the scar will remain and the pain will be felt. It doesn't go away.

I've had women tell me that they had done everything they could to put the incident behind them and thought they had succeeded. But then they go to a family reunion or some other gathering where they see the person who molested them, and all those old feelings come rushing back—the anger, the shame, the guilt, the intense hatred.

If you have been molested, you need to understand that there is a time and a place to let your feelings out. You have to give expression to the anger and hurt that was caused by your betrayal.

I suggest that you express your feelings as close to the source of the problem as you possibly can. It may not do a lot of good to go and tell your elderly father how you feel about something that happened many years ago—but on the other hand, it may be well worth the attempt. Perhaps you might want to do it in a letter, expressing your feelings as clearly and as concisely as possible.

If, for whatever reason, you can't talk to the person who molested you, find *someone* to talk to, whether it's your husband, pastor, rabbi, or a qualified therapist.

Don't go around suffering silently, carrying all that anger and shame within you. That is a heavy, heavy load to bear, and it's about time you let it go.

12

The Critical Parent
vs.
The Firstborn

Looking back at growing up firstborn in a home where Mom or Dad was an alcoholic is to look back on a childhood full of tears or pain.

The same is true of looking back and knowing that your innocence was stolen from you by a parent who was sexually abusive.

But abuse doesn't always take the form of an alcoholic mother or a sexually abusive father. The firstborn child is more often done damage by the person I call "the critical parent."

Just who is the critical parent, and what is he like?

Are we talking about someone who is patterned after Cinderella's evil stepmother, who has a sharp and wicked tongue and who never tires of heaping abuse on her poor, fair-haired child?

Could be.

But the critical parent could also be as smooth as honey and just as sweet. The critical mother could seem to be nothing but sweetness and light, full of concern for her child, but destroying the kid as surely as the "wicked stepmother" variety.

The critical parent very often doesn't know he's being abusive. He believes he has the child's best interest at heart, but either he's wrong about that, or else he doesn't know very much about what's in the best interest of children!

Most often it is the firstborn who locks horns with the critical parent. That's because more is expected of the firstborn, and also because the firstborn is the "experimental" child. By the time firstborn Betsy is in high school, her parents may realize they've been much too harsh with her, so they determine to do better from now on. That's really good news for 10-year-old Brenda and seven-year-old Buford, but it doesn't do Betsy any good at all. The mark of "discouraged perfectionist" has already been stamped on her personality in indelible ink!

I believe there are several ways parents can be overly critical, and in those ways they abuse their children.

Overt Verbal Abuse

I was in K mart the other day, waiting for the blue light special to start, when an obviously angry woman barged past me. She was pushing a shopping cart in which sat a little girl of perhaps 18 months and holding the hand of a little boy who looked to be about five. Her anger was obviously directed at the little boy.

"I don't know why I bring you with me! You never do anything but cause me trouble—"

"But Mom," he whined, trying to stop the barrage that was coming his way.

"I don't know how you could be so stupid! That's what you are, stupid! Don't you have any brains at all?"

The little boy hung his head. I didn't know what he had done, but my heart went out to him. Maybe he had knocked over a display or broken something. Maybe he had simply asked her for some candy or a toy after she had told him not to ask for anything. But whatever it was the little fellow had done, it wasn't worthy of the sort of abuse his mother was heaping on him.

A little later on I saw the same family heading across the parking lot toward their car. This time the little boy had let go of his mother's hand and stepped off the curb when a car was coming. Now, there wasn't any danger involved, really. The driver of the car didn't have to swerve to avoid him or slam on the brakes; it's just that the path wasn't completely clear.

Once again Mom began screaming. "For crying out loud, Billy, watch what you're doing!" And then, in a sarcastic voice, she said, "Yeah, that's it! Go ahead! Run in front of a car now and get yourself killed. I guess that would be the end of my troubles, wouldn't it?"

She kept up her tirade all the way to their station wagon. I couldn't hear what she was saying, but I could still hear the anger in her voice as she loaded her packages into the car, as she strapped her little girl into her car seat, and even as she backed the car out of its parking space, with her son sitting dejectedly beside her.

I felt like running after them and yelling "Stop! Stop! Don't you see what you're doing to your child?" But of course I didn't. I know what I would have heard. Things like "Who do you think you are?" and "It's none of your business anyway," and then things would have only been worse for the boy. I did send up a short prayer, though, and asked the Lord to help the woman see what she was doing and even have the grace to apologize to her son.

Now, if the boy did something deliberately wrong, he should be disciplined, but not in anger, not in that fashion. This sort of thing goes on all the time, and it seems to me that some parents stay angry all the time.

"You are so stupid." "You dummy!" "What a klutz!" "Can't you do anything right?" "You're just hopeless, do you know that? Hopeless!" "You're the messiest kid I ever saw!" "Don't be such a little jerk!" "I'll be glad when you're gone!"

Have your parents ever said these sorts of things to you? Have you ever said them to your children? Some parents don't realize how much their kids love and respect them. They believe what their parents say, and "if Mommy says I'm no good, it must be true." Life is not easy for the children of parents who are verbally abusive.

Overdoing "Constructive" Criticism

Let's listen in as Mrs. Throckmorton and her daughter, Henrietta, have lunch with Bernice Propper.

Mrs. Throckmorton is talking to her friend Mrs. Propper:

"You know of course that the Daileys have gone to Europe again—sit up straight, Henrietta. They won't be back for at least four weeks and—Henrietta, dear, please try not to slurp your soup—so they have asked me to look after their precious cat. Henrietta, sit up straight and get your elbow off the table! But as you know, I am allergic to cats and—no, Henrietta! No! You don't fold the napkin that way!"

What's going on here? Is Henrietta's mother being overly critical and abusive? If we ask her, she's going to say, "Are you joking? I'm just teaching my daughter some manners."

Well, I'm sorry, Mrs. Throckmorton, but there's a right way and a wrong way to go about this—there's a time and place for instruction, and this isn't it. Some children go through life hearing a steady barrage of such "constructive criticisms."

I'm sure we've all heard many of them: "Sit up straight." "Quit slouching." "Come on, you can tie your tie better than that!" "Did you even try to comb your hair this morning?" "Don't shuffle your feet!" Just fill in the blank with your favorite!

Is there anything wrong with any of these comments? Not really, especially if they're true. If you were running off to school without combing your hair, you needed someone to tell you to get back in that bathroom and comb it. If you were slouching and shuffling, it's good that someone was concerned about your posture. Where the problem occurs is when children don't hear anything but a steady stream of such criticism.

Some parents are very quick to point out what their children are doing wrong, but they never even open their mouths when they see their children doing something right. That is a mistake of major proportions!

Doing Everything for the Child

This is another dangerous trap many firstborns fall into, and I talked about it briefly back in Chapter Two.

Firstborn Brucie has a project due at school, and he wants to do the best job he can. His class is studying Eskimos and how they live, so he's made an igloo out of sugar cubes, cut a few whales out of construction paper, and fastened the whole thing to the inside of a shoe box. The problem is that the igloo looks like a prime property for urban renewal, and the whales look more like Thanksgiving turkeys than they do whales.

Bruce wants to show Mom his handiwork, and he stands there feeling as proud as the proverbial peacock as she looks at what he's done.

She resists the urge to say, "Brucie, what are those turkeys doing swimming in the Arctic Ocean?" Instead she tells him that he's done a terrific job and then sends him out to play. As soon as he's out the door, she starts pulling the entire thing apart and doing it over.

But Brucie is no dummy. He notices later on that substantial improvements have been made on his original effort.

He may be only eight, but he realizes what this means. His own effort wasn't good enough. That sends an unfortunate message to the child, and it may be a long time before he is able to take pride in anything he does.

Or picture little Melvina, sitting at the table with her family, trying to cut her meat for the very first time. Daddy is about to have a stroke watching her because she is so slow and so unsure of herself.

First of all, she holds the knife upside down.

"No, dear, it goes the other way."

"This way?"

"Yes, dear, that's fine, but, now, but . . ." Now she's put her knife in front of the fork, instead of behind it, with the result that the meat is jumping around on her plate as she tries to saw through it. No sooner does her father get that situation fixed than she makes a violent sawing motion and almost knocks over her milk. Dad's had enough, so he grabs her plate.

"Here, I'll cut it for you."

"But, Daddy, I want to do it!"

"I've been watching you, and you can't do it! At the rate you're going, you'll still be here next Thursday! No, I'll do it for you!"

It's too bad Melvina's father didn't have enough patience to let his daughter cut her meat for herself and that Brucie's mother didn't realize that it's her son's best effort that counts. Both of them, by their actions, sent a message saying "You're not good enough on your own. You're always going to need someone to bail you out."

Later on in life Melvina's father will probably be doing her school science project for her, and when Brucie gets a paper route, his mother will get up every morning to help him fold and deliver his papers.

If you told either one of the parents that this sort of behavior is actually "critical" of the child and harmful, I'm sure they'd think you had been munching on a magic mushroom or something. But the truth is that they are not allowing their children to grow, to become self-sufficient, and to feel good about themselves. Later on in life they'll know that everything they do is doomed to failure, and they'll always be looking for someone to bail them out.

Making Up the Child's Mind for Him

I told you earlier about a young woman I counseled who was full of anger toward her parents. She also suffered from a total lack of self-esteem. It was hard, at first, to figure out what had happened to cause her to be this way, because when she looked back on her childhood all she could remember were blue skies and sunny days.

She had had two years of piano lessons, become proficient in ballet and gymnastics, and gone to an exclusive camp every summer. The family lived in a pleasant neighborhood, and she had always had the best of everything. Her parents had even helped to see that she was accepted into one of the finest colleges in the country and, despite the fact that they were not wealthy by any means, had helped pay for her education there. She had always had everything she could need or want, so why was she so unsure of herself?

When we began looking at things a little more closely, an interesting pattern began to emerge.

"Did you really want to take those piano lessons?"

"No, but it was important to my mother that I learn to play the piano. When I finally convinced her, after two years, to let me stop taking the lessons, I know she was really disappointed."

"And the ballet?"

"Actually, I remember crying the first day of ballet class. I hated it . . . at least at first."

"But your mother . . ."

"Oh, yeah . . . she insisted."

It turned out that even the college she went to was her father's alma mater. As a matter of fact, Lorraine had always been interested in pursuing a degree from an art school, but her father wanted her to be a success in the business world. That's why she had a degree in business administration!

Lorraine's parents, you see, always wanted what was "best" for their daughter, and only they knew what that was!

Not only that, but whenever Lorraine didn't come through as they hoped she would, they were disappointed in her, and she knew it. Oh, they never walked up and told her they were disappointed, but they showed it in plenty of other little ways. When she quit taking piano lessons, her mother's sad expressions, sighs, and body language toward her daughter did as much damage as if she had just walked up to the girl and said, "I think you're a real dummy for not learning how to play the piano!"

Lorraine was getting the message that she had let her mother and father down, but they were really too nice to say anything about it.

Her subconscious was telling her, "Poor, long-suffering Mom and Dad! Trying to be so nice to me when I keep disappointing them!"

Lorraine eventually came to the realization that her parents had indeed been critical of her, even though they never yelled at her, called her names, or abused her verbally in any way. Now that she was grown, she was carrying on where they had left off —second-guessing her every step, questioning her abilities, putting herself down. She also had an extremely difficult time making up her mind about anything and always looked for someone else to choose for her!

Fortunately, once Lorraine realized that her self-doubts had grown out of the way her parents had always dealt with her, she was ready to make an attempt to be gentler with herself. She began to think about what she really wanted out of life and to realize that there was nothing wrong with her if what she wanted for herself didn't line up 100 percent with what her parents wanted for her.

Was Lorraine's case unusual? Not at all! I've known dozens of men and women just like her, people who never grew into poised, self-confident adults because their parents wouldn't let them.

Fighting Back

Damage inflicted by the critical parent can last a lifetime. You could be 90 years old and still react to the things that happen to you on the basis of the way your parents treated you when you were a child. Or you can be 55 and still have to put up with a critical, picky parent who won't ever recognize that you're grown up and don't need to be treated like a child!

But at the same time you can overcome the extra burdens imposed by the critical parent—and it's never too late to get yourself free.

How can you do it? The best thing you can do is to figure out why the parents were, or are, so hard on you in the first place.

1. CONSIDER THE MOMENT.

Almost every parent, at one time or another, has lost her cool and said something like "Don't you do anything around here but make messes?" or "All you do is cause me trouble."

That's because any parent is only human. She's made out of flesh and blood, and she'll get to the boiling point and say things she doesn't really mean.

If you ever poured a bottle of pancake syrup all over the carpet, your mom probably said quite a few of those things! It didn't mean that you really were the sloppiest kid in the world, or that she couldn't wait until you were grown up and gone, or any of those other things she probably said.

You may not have done anything. Your dad may have had a terribly stressful job that kept him jumpy and on edge, and this was reflected in the way he treated you. This too is a part of considering the moment.

You would think that children would learn to watch for the

right moment to ask their parents for things, but I know from watching my own kids that it just isn't so. It sometimes seems as if they pick the absolutely worst time to ask for something.

I can be crouched under the kitchen sink with a couple of wrenches fighting a leaky pipe, and someone will come up and ask me if I have time for a quick game of something or other. If I'm enjoying the rarity of a few days off and have some time to spare, nobody wants to do a thing.

That's the way kids seem to be. I remember that when I was a youngster my timing wasn't always the best. Kids aren't always tuned in to the mood and availability of Mom or Dad, and that can account for a great deal of "parental abuse."

2. IS THE PARENT JEALOUS?

What? My dad jealous of me? No way!

Are you sure?

Almost all parents will tell you that they want their children to have it better than they had it—and I suppose most of them think that's true. But deep down inside there may be some jealousy that erupts into a critical attitude.

Jimmy's father, for instance, is always saying how proud he will be when his son goes off to college. He'll be the first one in the family who's ever done that. But no matter how often he may say how proud he is, underneath it all he resents the fact that he had to drop out of school in the tenth grade. Because of this, he does his best to keep Jimmy in his place. He keeps up a steady barrage of belittling comments, overlooking the good and overemphasizing the bad.

Jimmy becomes frustrated and withdrawn, wondering why he can't do anything to please his father. He may grit his teeth and determine to try harder, and harder and harder; but no matter what he does, it's never good enough—for his father or, eventually, for himself.

And then there's Judi's mother, who says that she's proud of her daughter's beauty and popularity.

And yet she can't find a decent thing to say about a single one of the boys her daughter has dated. She also finds things to tease Judi about.

"You know, you'd really be pretty if it weren't for that double chin."

"Double chin?"

"Well, yeah . . . but don't worry about it. It's not really that bad. Of course, if we could do something about your hair, that would help, too."

Poor Judi may begin to withdraw or to be discouraged about her appearance. It never even occurs to her that her mother is jealous.

This isn't as rare as you might think. I see it on a regular basis. If your parents were supercritical of you, take another look at the situation. It could be that they were simply jealous.

3. IS THE PARENT ALWAYS CRITICAL?

Charlotte couldn't understand why her mother was always picking on her.

"I can't seem to do anything right. Nothing is ever good enough, and I suppose I'm just a real disappointment to her."

"Now, wait a minute, Charlotte," her friend Rita told her. "I know your mother, and she's never been anything but critical about anything."

"What do you mean?"

"Oh, come on now! I don't mean to be disrespectful, but have you ever heard your mother say an encouraging word to anyone?"

"Well, I . . ."

"I asked her once how she was feeling, and she gave me a ten-minute lecture on everything that was wrong with her, including her fallen arches, her bursitis, and her bladder problem!"

Charlotte had a problem, but the problem wasn't with herself. It was her mother's approach to life, pure and simple.

What I am saying is that some people are impossible to please, and there's nothing you can do about it.

What can you do if your parents are some of those "impossible-to-please" people? Not much for them. But for yourself you can realize that their treatment of you has nothing at all to do with your abilities and accomplishments. It may not be easy to learn to grin and bear it, but if you're stuck with a parent or parents like that, it's the only sane thing you can do!

4. IS THE PARENT DISAPPOINTED IN HIMSELF OR HIS SPOUSE?

We talked before about the firstborn as a scapegoat. I've seen this happen many times. It's not always easy to spot, but it's wise to remember that the parent who is a chronic fault-finder may be picking at himself or his spouse rather than you.

Dad thinks, "Here I am, forty years old and still in the same old job. I told myself I'd be a millionaire by the time I was forty, and instead I haven't done anything with my life!"

He comes home from work angry and frustrated and starts yelling at his son.

Who is he really mad at? Himself. But he can't pick at himself, so he finds a convenient substitute.

Or Mom is angry because she's had a fight with her husband. Her firstborn son does something, anything, that reminds her of her husband, and she goes on the attack. The son is left wondering "What did I do?" And the fact is that he hasn't done anything at all except to get caught in the cross fire!

I'll say it again: It's not always easy, or even possible, to figure out why some parents become supercritical fault-finders. But one thing every child of such parents needs to keep in mind is that there are a variety of causes of and explanations for such behavior, and almost all of them have to do with the parents.

Are you the product of critical parents? If you are, let me ask you another question. Are your children going to be the product of critical parents? Are you continuing the cycle of rejection, failure, and discouragement?

If you realize that you are passing along this painful legacy to your children, take steps to change things.

First of all, sit down with your children and apologize to them. You can tell them that you are truly sorry for your wrong attitudes and actions of the past and that you're going to do your best to change things.

Admit to them that you know you might slip up every so often, but you're going to do your best not to be so critical.

When you admit your shortcomings to your children, you are encouraging them by letting them know that you love and care for them enough to be vulnerable to them. You are also helping them feel better about their own mistakes.

Another thing you need to do, if you are the product of critical parents, is to make an effort to forgive them.

It could be that they are the ones who got you started on a long journey of self-doubt and rejection. But it will not help you to hold on to anger and resentment.

So learn how to forgive yourself when and if you fall short of the mark. And then turn around and forgive your parents. Resolve that you will no longer let their attitudes hold you back.

Once and for all, put aside those chains your critical parents fastened on you!

PART FOUR

Not Such a
Bad Deal
After All

13

Firstborn and Friends: Developing Relationships

Iț's funny how some memories stay with you all your life. I'm not talking about those big events you'd be expected to remember, like graduating from high school or your wedding day. I'm referring to those ordinary afternoons from so many years ago that somehow stick in the mind and seem to be so near.

Many of those memories in my own life have to do with my older sister, Sally, whom I've mentioned several times before. Those memories are clear and sharp, as if the events happened yesterday.

I have many memories of parties we threw out in the backyard. She and I were usually the only guests. She'd give me a quarter, and I'd walk the half mile or so to the store, where I'd buy two bottles of pop and a bag of pretzels. (Yes, that was a long time ago!)

When I got back, we'd set up our table and get our teacups and celebrate nothing in particular—just being together, I suppose. I remember those times so well because Sally was, is, and always will be an extremely important person in my life. That's the way it is with firstborns—they are often of supreme importance in the lives of their younger siblings. The effect they have on their brothers and sisters can be tremendous.

The firstborn may not realize how much his siblings think of him. They may be jealous at times. They may resent the fact that he gets to stay up later and gets a bigger allowance. They may do anything they can to annoy and pester him. I remember waking Sally up by dangling a big, juicy night crawler in front of her nose one fine morning, for instance. But underneath all of that, there will be affection, respect, and emulation.

Looking back on those parties with Sally, I still am not sure why she was so willing to spend the time with me or why she talked to me the way she did. But she never treated me like a little kid or a pesky little brother. She took me into her confidence, gave me some straight talk when I needed it, and helped to make sure that I was headed in the right direction.

I remember one of our early conversations, for instance, which went something like this:

"Do you like girls?"

"No way! Yuck, why would I like girls?" I was busy making a scooter, and I didn't even look up. I couldn't figure out why she was bothering me at a time like this. Yes, sir, these old apple crates were going to be perfect for the body, but where was I going to find the right wheels? Hmmm . . . I wondered if Sally's old pair of roller skates might work.

"Do you like me?"

This seemed like the best time in the world to like her *very* much, especially when I thought about those skates.

"Of course I do!"

"But I'm a girl."

"Well, that's different. You're my sister. And you're not like any of the other girls I know. By the way, Sis, you remember those old skates . . ."

"Well, I want to tell you a few things about girls."

Maybe I didn't really want to hear it, but Sally was going to tell me anyway, and so she did. She told me what girls were like, how they ought to be treated, and how you could go about getting a particular girl to like you.

I'm sure I thought at the time that this conversation was ridiculous. Why in the world would I care what girls liked? I was sure, as most six- or seven-year-old boys are, that I would grow up to be a confirmed bachelor—just a man and his dog against the world.

But five or six years later, when I suddenly discovered that girls weren't quite the blot on society that I had always figured them to be, I remembered those talks with my sister, and I found the information to be extremely beneficial.

But it wasn't just in the area of girls that sister Sally helped me. She gave me the benefit of her wisdom and advice in a number of areas, and I know that she helped to shape me into the person I am today.

Even when I was in kindergarten I remember Sally allowing me to sit on the seat of her bike, while she walked me all the way to school, which had to have been more than a mile from the house. I always felt calm and assured when Sally was around, whatever the situation might have been.

I often think that it's no wonder I married a firstborn, when I got the sort of treatment I received from my firstborn sister!

Friends and Lovers

My point is not to tell you all about my childhood or just to say how important my sister is to me. The relationship I have with her is special, yes, but there are millions of men and women all over the world who look up to their oldest sibling in the same type of way. As I said earlier, the firstborn may not know that his siblings feel about him the way they do, but his relationship with his brothers and sisters is a very special thing.

But what about the other relationships in a firstborn's life?

Whom does he choose for his closest friends? Whom does he choose for a mate?

For one thing, firstborns generally tend to get along better with people who are either older or younger than they are. This is largely because of the special relationship they have with their parents and then, later on, with their younger brothers and sisters.

Sometimes a firstborn will have several friends who are older than he is, several who are younger, but not very many who are the same age. The age difference may be 10 or 15 years, or it may be two or three.

I recently talked to a firstborn acquaintance of mine who had returned to town after traveling across the country to attend his twentieth high school reunion. Rob hadn't been able to get away for the tenth, and I knew how much he had been looking forward to catching up on all those old friendships after 20 years.

When I asked him how he had enjoyed the reunion, he shrugged, smiled, and said, "It was . . . it was . . . okay."

He wasn't very convincing.

"Well, what happened?" I teased. "Did it upset you to see a bunch of wrinkled and graying people who told you they were your age?"

"No," he said, laughing. "It wasn't that."

"Well, then, what was it?"

"It's just that I didn't get to see as many of my old friends as I thought I would.

"Oh, it was good to see everyone from my graduating class, but I didn't really realize until the night of the banquet that none of my really good friends were in that class. I had two or three really good friends who were seniors when I was a sophomore, and then I had another couple of good friends who were in the sophomore class when I was a senior. I really wish they had been at the reunion. But of course it was only for the class of '68."

Another firstborn, Eric, remembering his high school days,

recalls that his very best friend was an older gentleman who ran a fix-it shop in their small town.

"I thought he was pretty old," he remembers, "but he was probably in his forties.

"I had a job in a department store every day after school. I had a half hour or so between the time school got out and the time I had to be at work, and I'd always stop in and talk to Tom. I had friends my own age, but there was nobody I could talk to like I could talk to him."

Eric remembers, "We always had a lot to talk about, and it seemed more interesting than the stuff the other guys wanted to talk about. I don't know why—it just seemed that we were on the same wavelength."

Rob and Eric are both fairly typical firstborns in that they seem to feel more comfortable with people a bit older or younger than themselves. Is there anything wrong with this? Of course not. By having friends who are older than we are, we benefit from the wisdom they've gained through their experiences. And having friends who are younger than we are helps to keep us young and up to date.

If you feel comfortable around someone and can trust him with your innermost feelings, that person is a true friend, no matter what his age might be. If you feel uncomfortable and on guard around someone, for whatever reason, he may be an acquaintance, but he can hardly be a friend. And it is generally true that firstborns are more comfortable around those who are older or younger than they are.

Am I suggesting, then, that firstborns should seek out those who are different ages from themselves? The answer is yes . . . and no!

I am certainly not telling you that there's no possibility of having a lasting, strong, true friendship with someone who is your own age. Don't cross someone off your list of potential friends because of his age or add him to your list because of his age.

But if you have trouble making friends, it could be because you don't relate all that well to people your own age.

If you feel uncomfortable around people in general, it may be that you are actually uncomfortable only around those of your own age, and you would do better to involve yourself in a group of people who are older or younger.

Deanna was a 22-year-old firstborn who had recently moved to town and was attending the same church as Don and Vicki, a couple in their late thirties. Deanna hit it off immediately with both Don and Vicki, but she couldn't seem to make a dent in her own age group. Week after week she sat in her young-adult Sunday school class feeling like an alien. One or two people said hi to her every Sunday, but that was about it. She was discouraged and lonely, and finally told Vicki that she was going to start looking for another church.

"I hope we'll still be friends," she said, "but I just don't think I belong here."

Vicki didn't want her to leave the church, and neither did Don. They asked her to give it one more try, and she agreed. What's more, Don suggested that she start attending their Sunday school class, if she didn't mind "being surrounded by people who think having a good time consists of a rocking chair and a bottle of Geritol."

"You're not *that* old—well, at least Vicki isn't," Deanna teased. Then she agreed she'd give it another try.

Three weeks later Deanna was amazed.

"The people in your class are so friendly," she told Vicki. "I can't believe it's the same church." She decided she was going to keep attending the church, because she was beginning to feel more at home among the people there. But she told Don and Vicki that she still didn't understand why the people in her own age group had been so unfriendly.

The truth undoubtedly was that Deanna felt uncomfortable around people her own age. She didn't know how to relax and make friends with them. She was an attractive and personable young woman, but her uneasiness had been noticed by the others in her age group. They didn't know exactly what it was, but they all felt that Deanna was sending out a message to "keep your distance," so they did.

In the class with the older group she felt more relaxed and easy. She related better to their gentle humor, appreciated their more serious approach to their classwork, and was free to be herself.

In this way Deanna was a fairly typical firstborn, one who improved her life by becoming involved with a group of people who were older than she was.

I want to remind you again that what I'm saying isn't written in stone. There is no ironclad law that says that the firstborn will get along better with those who are older or younger. But if you are a firstborn, there's a pretty good chance that this will be the case.

Quality Counts

Another thing to keep in mind regarding firstborns and their friends is that firstborns are not likely to have a great many of them. That doesn't really matter, though, because quality is more important than quantity, and if you have one or two really good friends, you are blessed.

I have counseled firstborns who were jealous of their middleborn brothers or sisters because they seemed to have so many friends.

"If it's not the phone ringing, it's the doorbell, and it's always for her," one such firstborn told me, referring to his younger sister. The truth is that middleborns generally find it quite easy to make friends. From being in the middle they learn to be good negotiators, masters of compromise, and the sort of people who can get along with almost anybody.

The problem for them, though, is that they are sometimes the sort of people who can change friends the way most of us change our underwear. I know of one young girl who had dozens of friends, but it seemed to be an ever-changing roster, including three "very best friends" in six months' time. The firstborn who wonders why he doesn't have more friends should remember that one lasting friendship is more than worth a dozen relationships that come and go!

Choosing a Mate

I find that people often wind up in bad marriages because they refuse to make proper choices where their romantic lives are concerned.

"I couldn't help falling in love with him. I was just swept along, deeper and deeper."

Excuse me, but I must disagree. You may have enjoyed the feeling, you may have wanted to be in love, but you went into the situation with your eyes wide open. Perhaps you chose not to look closely at the person you were falling for or to analyze the situation too closely, but the choice was yours to make.

I have been a guest several times on *Oprah Winfrey,* and even though I admire Oprah very much and think she has a terrific show, this is one area where I am in total disagreement with her.

Her advice is to follow your feelings, to go with the flow. But your feelings can and often do mislead you. Use your common sense and be thoughtful, even in areas of the heart.

Now, in my marriage counseling sessions I always ask the battling couples about their birth orders. And I've come to the conclusion that the worst thing one firstborn can do is to marry another one.

No, it's not true that every married couple in trouble consists of two firstborns, but a great many of them do. Certainly a disproportionate number of those who come to me are both firstborns. And if two firstborns is bad, you ought to see what happens when two only children get together. The result can be pure disaster.

I can hear the question already. "Are you saying that two only children or two firstborns should never marry each other?" No, I'm not saying that, because it is true that love can conquer all. But if you're a firstborn or an only child who's planning to marry another firstborn or only child, you'd better make sure you have a tremendous amount of love in your heart!

Firstborns tend to be strong-willed and sure of themselves and to have strong points of view. Put two of them together in a marriage relationship, and you're likely to find out what happens when an immovable object tangles with an unstoppable force; namely, there's a lot of heat, noise, and confusion.

I counseled one couple of firstborns who couldn't even stop fighting long enough to talk to me. I finally came to the end of my patience and threw them out of the office.

"Come back when you're ready to make a real try at marriage," I told them.

I didn't hear from them for about a month, so I figured their marriage was all but over and was blaming myself for acting so rashly.

And then one day I got a call from the husband, asking if they could come in and talk to me and promising that they would not fight—at least in my presence.

Their decision to continue their counseling and to remove the boxing gloves, at least temporarily, was a major step in the healing of their marriage.

The major problem for firstborn couples is that both of them may tend toward perfectionism, and each has a different idea of what is perfect. It's not the big things that drive such a couple into the divorce court. More often it's a combination of little things, like her squeezing the toothpaste tube from the top and his leaving his wet towels on the bathroom floor.

One couple was on the verge of a split because his realm of perfectionist behavior was the office, while hers was the home. The wife could not understand how her husband could be so meticulous and tidy regarding his workplace but leave his books, papers, and everything else scattered throughout the house.

Another couple stopped being civil to each other because they fought over how best to water the lawn. They had two hoses with sprinklers attached, and the wife always started both of them in the back and worked around to the front of the house. The husband put one sprinkler in front and one in back and then moved around the house. Both of them thought their methods were faster, saved water, and basically did the job better. It sounds crazy, I know, but neither of them was willing to give an inch—or a drop.

Now again, I'm not saying that two firstborns cannot be happily married to each other. I know it can be done, because I've seen it. My sister, Sally, and her firstborn husband, Wes, have a very good marriage.

But it's not going to happen without compromise, without admitting your perfectionist tendencies and agreeing to yield to one another. A marriage where two people are always butting heads and running each other down is no marriage at all.

I would not base any marriage solely on birth order, but I do think it's one of the considerations that ought to enter into the decision to marry.

Generally a marriage involving two people from the same birth order, whatever that birth order may be, is not good. That's because one is weak where the other is weak, and the two of them will drag each other down in that area.

I hate to think what it would be like if I were married to another fun-loving and financially irresponsible lastborn! I'd probably have checks bouncing from here to Timbuktu, and that would be the least of my worries.

So who is the ideal marriage partner for a firstborn? It has to be the lastborn, and I'm not just saying that because my own marriage is so good. The first-and-last combination works so well because the strengths and weaknesses of the husband and wife in this situation tend to complement each other.

The fun-loving lastborn can teach the firstborn to relax and take things a little less seriously. On the other hand, the firstborn can keep the lastborn anchored, so to speak, and see that he doesn't go floating off into space. The lastborn can temper his mate's tendencies toward perfectionism, whereas the firstborn can help the lastborn to understand that there are times when life must be taken very seriously.

I believe that the combination of firstborn female and lastborn male potentially makes the best possible marriage combination, and this is borne out by years of firsthand observation and research.

The marriage of a firstborn female who has younger brothers to a lastborn male with older sisters has a great chance to be especially happy and harmonious. That's because the principals involved have learned how to relate well to members of the opposite sex. The younger brother has learned that women are human beings to be treated with dignity and respect, and the older sister has learned how to give the care and comfort that her lastborn husband will sometimes need.

Looking back over the firstborn and his relationships with other people, we can see three important things to keep in mind:

1. Firstborns tend to feel more comfortable around people who are younger or older than they are.
2. Having one or two good friends is better than having an army of acquaintances.
3. If there is any such thing as a marriage made in heaven, it's probably between a firstborn and a lastborn!

14

Making the Most of Being a Firstborn

It was right around Christmastime of 1986. Sande called me at the office and told me she was taking me out to dinner.

I'll have to admit, I was rather surprised when she picked one of the more inexpensive fast-food steak places in the city of Tucson—which is a nice way to put it—but I figured I wouldn't squawk about it. After all, she was paying for it!

At one point during our dinner she reached into her purse and pulled out a greeting card she had made for me. I thought it was really sweet, but it wasn't all that unusual, because she's a thoughtful, creative person.

The card said:

"Are you ready to change your summer plans?"

"Are you ready to work late?"

"Are you ready to change your work schedule?"

What in the world was she getting at? I flipped it over, and there was a picture of Santa Claus holding a little baby with a toothless grin. All it said was "Merry Christmas!"

I looked at her for a minute, wondering if this meant what I thought it meant. When she nodded her head yes, I let an excited whoop escape my lips. A few of the other people in the restaurant turned and looked at me, wondering what I was yelling about—but it didn't bother me. I was excited, and I didn't care if the whole world knew it!

Little Hannah Elizabeth was on her way! We were going to have a baby!

I'll tell you something else too. I couldn't wait to share the news with the other kids, and I knew exactly how they would take it. The girls, of course, would be ecstatic. Kevin might not take it too well—after all, he was the baby, and it might not be easy on him to give up his privileged position in the family to this usurper. This could mean he wouldn't be Mom's favorite anymore!

Boy, was I wrong on all counts!

When we told firstborn Holly that she was going to have a baby brother or sister, she sat there staring at us in shocked silence.

"Come on, Holly," I said. "Say something!" But she didn't say anything at all—for four days! She was so upset she wouldn't even talk to us.

Oh, she came to the table for her meals, but she ate in stony silence. And every question directed her way was either ignored or answered in the simplest possible terms. Eventually we just quit trying!

Krissy? She wasn't much better. She clapped her hands over her ears and started crying.

"I don't want to hear this! I don't want to hear this!"

The girls were both acting as if Sande's pregnancy were some sort of betrayal!

Oh, boy! Something I had been looking forward to had turned into a nightmare. If the older ones were reacting this way, just imagine the scene when we broke the news to Kevin.

My initial thought was "Maybe we don't have to tell him. Maybe we can do it later—like when the baby's three years old."

Sande didn't think that was a very good idea, so with fear and trepidation we sat down with him.

"Uh, Kevy . . . your mother and I have something to tell you."

"What is it, Dad?"

"Well . . . uh . . ." I said, wondering how a psychologist would handle this situation.

"I am going to have a baby," said Sande, who has always favored the direct approach.

"You are?" said Kevin.

"Here it comes," I thought.

"Hey . . . that's baaaaad!"

"Baaaaad?" I echoed.

"You know, Dad . . . that means 'gooooood.' "

"Oh."

"That's really great!" He leaned over and gave his mother a hug. "Hey, Dad!"

"Yeah?"

"Can we go to the store and buy some Pampers?"

We had to explain that the baby wouldn't be arriving for more than six months and there'd be plenty of time for "Pamper-shopping" later on. He seemed disappointed about that, but he wasn't at all upset that he was no longer going to be the youngest member of the family.

Now, don't worry about little Hannah, because it was only a matter of days before her sisters came around. By the time she was born, they couldn't wait to get her home from the hospital, and it would be impossible for them to love her any more than they do.

So why did they react the way they did when they first found out she was on her way? I'm still not sure I totally understand. Primarily, I suppose, because they were secure and comfortable with our family the way it was and knew that there were going to be some changes in their routines, as well as Mom's and Dad's, when the baby arrived.

What is my point in telling you all this? Simply that there is nothing about being a firstborn that predestines you to any set type of behavior. There are general rules, yes, and more often than not I can pinpoint exactly where someone fits into his family just by observing him for a while and asking a few questions.

It is true that every birth order has its own unique strengths and weaknesses. If you are a firstborn, you will, more than likely, be predisposed to the strengths and weaknesses we are discussing in this book, but you are not controlled by them.

Part of the reason I have spent so much of my career focusing on birth order is that I have discovered that it's a powerful way to help people understand their strengths, so they can take advantage of them, and their weaknesses, so they can strive for improvement in those areas.

We've talked about the person I call the "discouraged perfectionist," and you may be prone to thinking along these lines, but once you know that you can take steps to change your behavior, you can begin to improve.

We've talked about the person who has always been a role model and who, because of that, lives as if he were wearing a straitjacket, never doing what he wants to do. If you come to see that you are living this kind of life and destroying yourself in the process, you can take steps to improve.

When it comes to turning your weaknesses into strengths, I like what Dr. Harold H. Bloomfield says in his book *The Achilles Syndrome:*

"An Achilles Heel refers to the part of ourselves that is both our greatest handicap and our greatest challenge. If we can accept and learn from our Achilles Heel, it can be a source of power, a stimulus to our growth, an essential part of our humanity. Yet, too often, we are like Achilles, resisting our vulnerabilities and forgetting our strengths."[1]

Understanding your weaknesses can help you tremendously, as long as you realize you can change and make yourself strong in those weak areas. Understanding your strengths will help you to utilize them more.

Now, Holly, Krissy, and Kevin were free to act any way they

chose to act when they heard the news that we were going to be a family of six instead of five. They weren't robots who were forced to act a certain way because of their birth orders into the family!

It's the same with you. You are free to become whoever and whatever you want to be, and learning about the strengths and weaknesses common to firstborns is one of the keys that will help you unlock your potential.

You know, because I've written several books, because I often appear on talk shows or speak at seminars, and because I have a successful private practice, people sometimes assume that I've always been the sort of person who has worked hard and sought to achieve. Nothing could be further from the truth.

Do you know what it's like at the bottom of the barrel? I do, because I used to live there. When I was in high school, I was very near the bottom of my class. You didn't find my name on any honor roll lists, and you can bet that all the best colleges were not beating a path to my door. I was lost in a fog of underachievement, and my future looked like a dead-end street.

But one day one of my teachers helped me to see that I'd been playing a game with life, rolling along content to be, as she put it, "the best at being the worst."

Her words stung me, primarily because I knew she was telling me the truth. I was down, but I didn't have to stay there. I knew I had the ability to change, and I resolved that I would change!

It could be that you feel that you are near the bottom of the barrel in some aspect of your life. Please believe me when I tell you that you have what it takes to change things.

Every firstborn has special strengths that he should be using to achieve his maximum potential.

Flexing Those
Firstborn Muscles

Let's take a quick inventory of the birthright of the firstborn.

1. THE NATURAL LEADER

The firstborn is a natural leader. As a firstborn you are the sort of person people look to for guidance and direction. Leadership goes with the territory. When you're a child, your younger siblings tend to look to you to be their leader, and once you've assumed the mantle of leadership, it's not easy to take it off.

If I were the president of a corporation, I would be happy if all of my top lieutenants were firstborns. That's because I know the leadership qualities that firstborns possess.

In my own family I've seen firstborn Holly demonstrate those leadership abilities again and again.

When she was a ninth-grader, she ran for the office of president of her class. When the votes were finally counted, she had been defeated by four votes.

Now, I don't care how gracious we try to be, defeat is never easy to take, and especially when it comes by such a razor-thin margin. But I didn't hear one sour word from her.

She accepted defeat with the grace and dignity characteristic of a firstborn.

And then another year went by.

We were sitting at the table having dinner one night when she announced, "Oh, guess what? I'm the president of the sophomore class."

Well, you should have seen the buttons popping on old Dad's shirt. I was so proud of her! No, not because she was elected president of her class, but because she didn't let defeat grind her down or hold her back.

Having leadership ability doesn't mean you win every time. If you've suffered a few setbacks along the way, that doesn't mean you're destined to be in the background all your life. The world needs people who have the courage and the willingness to lead. Give yourself a chance, and your leadership abilities will be seen by others.

Firstborn George was the sort of fellow who sat in staff meetings at work and kept his mouth shut because he was afraid that his suggestions wouldn't be appreciated.

His coworkers would be grappling with a particular problem, going around and around without coming any closer to solving it.

George would sit there thinking that he knew what to do. Or at least he thought he could see what to do. But if he told them about it, they'd probably say he was nuts.

One day, though, after the meeting had gone on for what seemed like hours, and he was feeling tired and bored, he finally decided to speak up.

"I think what we could do is . . ." and then he presented a solution to the problem. Everyone was shocked, first of all because he had finally said something and second of all because his idea was just what they were looking for.

Afterward his boss took him aside.

"George, that was great! How did you think of that?"

Encouraged by his success, George began to speak up more often. He came up with ways for his company to do things more efficiently, to save money, to increase sales.

Everyone had figured old George was kind of dull and unimaginative. But that wasn't true at all. He was a natural-born leader, but he was also troubled by low self-esteem, and for that reason he had been hiding his light under a bushel all these years. It makes one wonder how many other Georges there are in this world and how much is being lost because of their silence.

2. THE GREAT ANALYZER

Firstborns are noted for asking a great many questions and for wanting to know all the details. Sometimes they can drive us less-patient types to the point of tears.

But you shouldn't apologize for your questioning nature. There is nothing wrong with wanting to know all the details so you can have a firm handle on the situation. You know that once you understand the situation you can sit down and figure out a step-by-step procedure for doing what must be done. If it weren't for such meticulous firstborns, some of the rest of us might go on running around in circles forever!

Do you remember those Rubik's Cubes that were so popular a few years ago? I had no patience at all with those things. I'd give it a few minutes and then, when I couldn't get the solution, I was through with it. It's my "baby-of-the-family" nature to be impatient and a bit impulsive.

On the other hand, I've seen some people spend huge amounts of time with one of those cubes—studying it, analyzing it, working on it with amazing patience. I would be willing to wager that most of those who worked so hard at solving that puzzle were firstborns.

Did someone say, "Well, so what? Firstborns are good at solving puzzles. That and fifty cents will get you a cup of coffee."

That's not true. Taking an analytical, thought-out approach can serve you well.

Learn to apply your natural thought processes to everyday life. Don't let the rest of us—the impatient, impulsive ones standing in line behind you—push you to a hasty and poorly thought-out decision.

As a firstborn you can generally trust yourself in matters that require carefully made choices.

Now, I'm not talking about procrastinating, analyzing things to death simply because you're really afraid to make a decision. But if a firstborn is faced with a major choice—say taking another job in a different city or staying in his current position—he is the sort who will get out a piece of paper and write down all the pros and cons. The positive aspects of the new job will go on one side of the paper, and the negatives will go on the other. After he's written down everything he can think of and had a chance to really scrutinize the situation, he'll decide what to do.

The lastborn will probably be off to the side snickering and saying "Man, this guy just can't make up his mind." But remember, nobody ever messed up his life by thinking too carefully about a decision!

3. THE SCHOLAR

Firstborns read more books than any other birth order, and this gives them a head start on the rest of the world.

The reason for this love of books is primarily that parents tend to spend more time reading to their firstborn children.

When Buford comes along, Mom and Dad buy him tons of everything, including books, and then they read to him at bedtime every night:

The Little Engine That Could, Tuffy the Tugboat, Babar Comes to America, and *Green Eggs and Ham* are read over and over and over! And Buford, who has developed a love for his books and an appreciation for reading, is often heard to say, "Read it again, Mommy."

And then Bradford is born. For a while Mom and Dad may keep up the bedtime reading, but then two boys are such a handful that this daily routine may be scrapped. How can Mom and Dad find time to read when they both fall into bed exhausted at the end of every long day? And as for books, well, Bradford can read all of Buford's old ones, so why should they buy him any more?

Bradford, for these reasons, never develops into quite the reader—and thus the scholar—that his older brother will probably always be.

By the time the firstborn is old enough for school, chances are he's been reading a few simple books on his own for some time. He's anxious and ready to get started in school, and he's got a jump on his education as well as on the other children in the classroom.

No wonder so many firstborns are teachers, professors, and scientists and are involved in other professions that require serious scholarship.

Now a word to those of you who may have rebelled over the years against your natural abilities in the realm of "brainpower." This is not as uncommon as you might think, and problems do arise when firstborns tend to downplay their natural intelligence and abilities.

One firstborn friend remembers how, when he was in elementary school, he would purposely miss words in the spelling bee so the other boys wouldn't think he was too smart.

He remembers, "They went easier on me about all my As, just as long as I messed up every now and then to show I was one of the guys."

Sometimes you start out playing those games, and then you get stuck in a trap. This may be especially true of firstborn women who've come to believe the lie that a man doesn't want a wife who's smarter than he is. It may be true that some men feel that way, but only the ones who aren't worth having as husbands anyway! Any really intelligent man would want a wife who was at least of comparable intelligence, so she could stimulate and challenge his intellectual capabilities.

After you've played the "Oh, I'm not really so smart" game for a while, you can come to believe it. You can get so accustomed to playing dumb that you begin to make bad choices in your life. If you've been playing that game, for whatever reason, stop it! There's nothing wrong with being a scholar, and it can take you far in life!

4. THE MASTER
OF ORGANIZATION

When the firstborn was a small child, he must have heard his mother saying "A place for everything and everything in its place." She must have said it quite often, in fact, because he believes it with a passion.

When I think of the organized firstborn, my beloved Aunt Evie comes to mind. Evie has handled my books and always done a masterful job. That's no easy task, either. If you think it would be a snap, then let me assure you that you've never seen the way I keep records.

(Remember, Sande had to get me a checkbook with carbon copies in it because I kept forgetting to keep a record of the checks I'd written.)

More than once Evie has called me to ask if I can tell her where a certain receipt came from.

"It's just thrown in here with all these other papers, and I don't know what it's for."

Sometimes at first I don't have a clue either. With Evie's persistent prodding I'm always able to get everything in order. But without her help—look out!

One time a few years back I was audited by the Internal Revenue Service because of my charitable donations and contributions. The feeling was that Sande and I couldn't be giving as much as we said we were, so we were called in for a chat.

Help! Once again it was time to ask firstborn Aunt Evie to come to the rescue. And that's exactly what she did.

She came with me to the IRS office and brought along a shoe box full of neatly organized checks and receipts.

My session with the IRS lasted about five minutes.

The auditor flipped through the checks, saw that they matched the numbers on my income tax return, and said, "Gee, I'm really sorry we bothered you."

I walked out of there breathing a prayer of thanks for "organized" firstborns.

Some of the rest of us might poke fun at the organized firstborn from time to time, calling him a neatnik or saying that he's a fanatic about being organized, but that's only because we're jealous of you. Some of us spend hours every week hunting for something we know we put "right here, and now it's gone." Later on, of course, we'll find it somewhere else, and then it comes back to us that this is where we really left it!

The organized firstborn doesn't do that. Oh, I'm not saying that firstborns aren't prone to occasional memory lapses, but their track record overall is much better than that of middleborns and lastborns.

Being organized is not a curse, but a blessing.

In general the firstborn is the one who should handle the family finances. He'll be better at it.

When it comes to planning the itinerary for the family vacation, again the firstborn is going to do a better job of covering all the bases and making sure all the pieces of the trip fit together.

If I were planning a banquet, I'd want a firstborn to make all the arrangements, because then I could be confident that things would be done right.

Because of their organizational skills, firstborns make wonderful attorneys, journalists, accountants, and librarians. And, of course, if you're looking for a secretary, someone to run an office and keep things flowing smoothly, you couldn't do better than picking a firstborn for the job.

Firstborns also do well in the world of motion pictures, where they can combine their organizational and creative skills.

Producing a major motion picture would seem to be glamorous, exciting work, and I'm sure it is. But it also must be painstaking and tedious—making sure that all of the scenes fit together, waiting hours for just the right shot, shooting the scene over and over to get it just right, etc.

It seems to be a job tailor-made for the firstborn, and no

wonder firstborns like Steven Spielberg and George Lucas have been so successful in the business!

You may remember my conversation with Skeptical Steve back in the first chapter. He thought I was off base regarding birth order because he was a firstborn who didn't consider himself to be well organized. His desk, in fact, seemed to be a mess. But beneath it all, he knew where everything was.

That may be the way you are. Don't let surface appearances fool you. Organization and neatness are not necessarily the same things. Don't get down on yourself because you may be messy on the surface. Underneath it all, Mr. or Mrs. Firstborn, you're a marvel of organization.

And you don't ever need to apologize for being that way. As a firstborn you need your life to be structured, and you need your lists of things to do.

The problem comes in when you allow your life to be run by your schedule and your determination to stay on top of things.

Overall your tendency to be organized is something that can benefit you tremendously. If you are able to share your skills in this area with others, you'll also be doing them a big favor. The world is full of people who, as the old saying goes, would lose their heads if they weren't fastened to their necks.

5. THE SELF-STARTER

Another exemplary quality of firstborns is their tendency to be one step ahead of the game. They have the ability to see what needs to be done and to get started on it.

In an office situation firstborns generally require less supervision because they are self-motivated and self-reliant. This is due in large part to the fact that their parents always expected more of them. As a result they've come to expect more of themselves.

That's why firstborns are so good in management positions. And yet there is a downside to this business of being self-reliant, and that is that the firstborn tends to want to do everything by himself. It is not always easy for him to delegate authority and responsibility, and this is something he has to learn. You may remember when Jimmy Carter was president, one of the criticisms he always faced was that he tried to do everything by himself. The result was not only that he worked himself into exhaustion, but that he wasn't able to accomplish as much as he might have if he had delegated more of the responsibilities.

I'm not saying that this criticism of Mr. Carter is valid, but it would not surprise me if it was, because this is the sort of behavior one might expect from a firstborn.

Part of the firstborn's problem may be that he knows those others won't do the job as well as he would. And that could be true. That doesn't matter so much, though, because no human being can be everywhere at once, not even the superfirstborn, so you simply must learn to delegate.

Still, I would say that the firstborn's ability to be a self-starter and to be self-reliant outweighs any problems that may arise because of his inability to delegate—which is something that can be overcome.

Every firstborn has to remember that he can't do it all. Not only must he learn to delegate, but he must also work on his ability to say no. You can't handle everything, and you can't do everything anyone asks you to do. You must know your limits! I am fond of telling firstborns to take smaller bites of life. They are noted for getting involved in so many projects that they don't have any time left for themselves or their families. That's a very good way to destroy your marriage, your health, and finally yourself.

Sure, you're the one they're all depending on, but you're not Atlas. You can't go around carrying the world on your shoulders!

The firstborn has many other qualities that serve him well in both his personal and professional life, and most of these are variations of the qualities we've discussed.

The firstborn tends to be exacting, precise, and yet creative at the same time. He is often confident of his own abilities—unless he has fallen into the trap of discouraged perfectionism, and we've already discussed how he can be set free from that particular malady.

We've already discussed a few of the occupations that seem custom-made for the firstborn. The list would include:

Accountant
Airline pilot
Architect
Attorney
Bank manager
Business executive
City planner
College professor
Computer scientist
Editor
Engineer
Film director or producer
Journalist
Librarian
Musician
Pastor
Physician
Politician
Research scientist
Secretary
Surgeon
Teacher

This is only a partial listing, but it begins to give you some idea of the many professions in which firstborns do exceptionally well.

It is true that being a firstborn has its drawbacks. But many of these drawbacks—such as always being expected to be the best, having to do more than your share around the house, being called on to set a good example for others, etc. —can turn out to be blessings and benefits in the long run.

If you are a firstborn, chances are that life has bruised you and battered you a little. You've been picked at, put down, and told to grow up. Sometimes, even as a kid, you may have felt as if you were in boot camp. It wasn't always easy, but you have become a stronger, more capable person because of all you've gone through.

Every firstborn has a choice to make. He can either let the pressures of his birth position make him angry and bitter, or he can turn them to his advantage!

If he does turn them to advantage, look out, world! Here comes someone who's going to have an impact!

Being a firstborn truly is a wonderful gift. It's up to you to use it.

NOTES

CHAPTER ONE

1. "What Scholars, Strippers and Congressmen Share"—Study by Richard Zweigenhaft, reported by Jack Horn, *Psychology Today,* May 1976, 34.
2. Ibid.
3. Dr. Alfred Adler, *The Practice of Individual Psychology* (London: Routledge and Kegan Paul, Ltd., 1923), 3.
4. Jane Goodsell, *Not a Good Word About Anybody* (New York: Ballantine Books, 1988), 50.
5. Adler, *What Life Should Mean to You* (New York: Capricorn Books, G. P. Putnam's Sons, 1958), 154–155.
6. Karl Konig, *Brothers and Sisters* (Blauvelt, NY: St. George Books, 1963), 21.

CHAPTER THREE

1. Luke 15:11–31.

CHAPTER FOUR

1. Genesis 4:9.

CHAPTER FIVE

1. Dr. Kevin Leman, *The Birth Order Book* (Old Tappan, NJ: Fleming H. Revell Co., 1985), 60.
2. Dr. Miriam Adderholdt-Elliott, *Perfectionism—What's Bad About Being Too Good?* (Minneapolis, MN: Free Spirit Publishing, 1987), 18–20.
3. Ibid., 16.
4. Goodsell, *Not a Good Word About Anybody,* 21, 26, 42, 44, 51.
5. Bruce Bohle, *The Home Book of American Quotations* (New York: Dodd, Mead and Co., 1967), 386.
6. Carole Hyatt and Linda Gottlieb, *When Smart People Fail* (New York: Simon and Schuster, 1987), 232–236.
7. Dr. Kevin Leman, *Measuring Up* (Old Tappan, NJ: Fleming H. Revell Co., 1988), 173.
8. Hyatt and Gottlieb, *When Smart People Fail,* 38.
9. Billy Joel, "You're Only Human (Second Wind)," copyright 1985 by Joel Songs.
10. Nathaniel Branden, *How to Raise Your Self-Esteem* (New York: Bantam Books, 1987), 22–23.
11. Ibid., 40.

CHAPTER SIX

1. Dr. Harold H. Bloomfield, *The Achilles Syndrome* (New York: Random House, 1985), 130.
2. Ibid., 135.
3. Ibid., 136.

CHAPTER SEVEN

1. Dr. Kevin Leman, *Making Children Mind Without Losing Yours* (Old Tappan, NJ: Fleming H. Revell Co., 1984), ch. 1, 4.
2. Judges 16:4–22.
3. Leman, *The Birth Order Book,* 237–238.

CHAPTER EIGHT

1. Dr. Kevin Leman, *Sex Begins in the Kitchen* (Ventura, CA: Regal Books, 1983).
2. Leman, *Making Children Mind Without Losing Yours,* 11.
3. Mark 12:42–44.
4. Douglas H. Powell, *Teenagers—When to Worry and What to Do* (Garden City, NY: Doubleday, 1986), 49–72.
5. Bill Cosby, *Bill Cosby Himself,* CBS/Fox, 1984.

CHAPTER NINE

1. Alfred Adler, *Understanding Human Nature* (New York: Fawcett World Library, 1969), 127.
2. Darrell Sifford, *The Only Child* (New York: G. P. Putnam's Sons, 1988), 294.

CHAPTER TEN

1. Dr. Anderson Spickard and Barbara R. Thompson, *Dying for a Drink* (Waco, TX: Word Books, 1985), 94.
2. Ibid., 83.
3. Ibid., 168.

CHAPTER FOURTEEN

1. Bloomfield, *The Achilles Syndrome,* 4.

For information regarding speaking engagements or seminars, write or call:

Dr. Kevin Leman
1325 N. Wilmot Rd.
Suite 320
Tucson, Arizona 85712
602-886-9925

INDEX